Social Planning and Human Service Delivery in the Voluntary Sector

Social Planning and Human Service Delivery in the Voluntary Sector

EDITED BY
Gary A. Tobin

with a foreword by David Horton Smith

Studies in Social Welfare Policies and Programs, Number 1

Greenwood Press
Westport, Connecticut • London, England

Library of Congress Cataloging in Publication Data

Main entry under title:

Social planning and human service delivery in the
  voluntary sector.

  (Studies in social welfare policies and programs,
ISSN 8755-5360 ; no. 1)
  Bibliogaphy: p.
  Includes index.
    1. Voluntarism—United States.   2. Social service—
United States.   3. United States—Social policy.
I. Tobin, Gary A.   II. Series.
HN90.V64S66   1985   361.3 '7   84-25307
ISBN 0-313-23892-8 (lib. bdg.)

Library of Congress Catalog Card Number: 84-25307
ISBN: 0-313-23892-8
ISSN: 8755-5360

First published in 1985

Greenwood Press
A division of Congressional Information Service, Inc.
88 Post Road West, Westport, Connecticut 06881

Printed in the United States of America

The paper used in this book complies with the
Permanent Paper Standard issued by the National
Information Standards Organization (Z39.48-1984).

10 9 8 7 6 5 4 3 2 1

To Arnold and Babe, of course

Contents

Illustrations ix

Foreword
DAVID HORTON SMITH xi

Preface xix

Introduction
GARY A. TOBIN xxi

PART I: The Structure of the Voluntary Sector

1. The Historical Role of the Voluntary Sector in Human
   Service Delivery in Urban America
   CLARKE A. CHAMBERS 3

2. The Urban Voluntary Sector: An Exploration of
   Basic Issues
   JENNIFER R. WOLCH 29

3. Religious Groups and Institutions
   ORVAL WESTBY 47

4. Serving the Needs of Children: Child Care in the
   Voluntary Sector
   FRANCES L. HOFFMANN 75

5. The Politics of the Voluntary Sector
   E. TERRENCE JONES   93

6. The Domain of Private Social Welfare: Comparisons
   between the Public Sector and the Voluntary Sector
   MICHAEL SOSIN   105

7. The Role of City Government
   WILLIAM DONALD SCHAEFER   131

PART II: Planning in the Voluntary Sector

8. Ethics in Planning in the Voluntary Sector
   GARY A. TOBIN   141

9. Defining Needs Identification for the Voluntary Sector
   RUSSY D. SUMARIWALLA   159

10. Strategic Planning in the Voluntary Sector
    GEORGE W. WILKINSON   189

11. The Planning Structure of Voluntary Organizations:
    The Relationship of Professional Staff to Lay Leaders
    JOHN FORESTER   209

12. Volunteerism: Attracting Volunteers and Staffing
    Shrinking Programs
    DAVID HORTON SMITH   225

Notes   253

Bibliography   261

Index   277

About the Contributors   287

Illustrations

FIGURES

2-1	The Flow of Voluntary Resources	31
10-1	The Strategic Process	191
10-2	Life Cycle of a Strategic Issue	198
10-3	Implications Wheel Exercise	199
10-4	Exploring Issues Exercises	201
10-5	Issues Priority Matrix	202

TABLES

3-1	Income Sources Reported	55
6-1	Comparison of Problems Covered in Voluntary and Public Social Welfare Agencies—by Rank and Frequency	110
6-2	Comparison of Services Rendered in Voluntary and Public Social Welfare Agencies—by Rank and Frequency	111
6-3	Comparison of Populations Served in Voluntary and Public Social Welfare Agencies	118

6-4 Frequencies and *t*-Tests Concerning the Domain of Voluntary Agencies; Public Funding and No Public Funding 122

Foreword

DAVID HORTON SMITH

In this foreword I should like to deal with three matters that I hope will make the rest of the book more intelligible and meaningful. The first concerns the definition of terms, always a matter of contention in discussing voluntarism and volunteerism and the voluntary sector. The definition presented here is not necessarily the one used by each chapter author of this volume, but this definition can be seen generally as underlying other implicit and explicit definitions.

The second matter taken up is the scope of volunteer work and volunteer activity in the United States of America. The entire book that follows takes on greater significance when the true magnitude of the voluntary sector is seen clearly and not underestimated. And the third matter taken up is the specific context in which social service volunteer work, the focus of this volume, takes place. Of crucial importance here is the distinction between voluntary associations, agencies, or programs that are isolated (unrelated to other organizations by formal affiliations) and those integrated with other organizations.

VOLUNTEER SERVICE DELIVERY

Although the concept seems simple, the term "volunteer" has proved to be somewhat elusive to define with precision (see, for instance, Part I of Smith et al., 1972), and scholars continue to disagree somewhat regarding the breadth with which volunteerism should be defined. Having given the matter much thought over the years and built on the work of others, I stand by my own recent effort at a definition, published elsewhere (Smith, 1982, p. 25):

Essentially, I define a volunteer as an individual engaging in behavior that is not bio-socially determined (e.g., eating, sleeping), nor economically necessitated (e.g., paid work, housework, home repair), nor socio-politically compelled (e.g., paying one's taxes, clothing oneself before appearing in public), but rather that is essentially (primarily) motivated by the expectation of psychic benefits of some kind as a result of activities that have a market value greater than any remuneration received for such activities. This definition makes being a volunteer a matter of *degree*, for the market value of one's activities can vary greatly, as can the remuneration (if any) received for such activities. . . . "Pure" volunteers, in the sense of people fitting the ideal type construct best, would be individuals receiving no remuneration whatsoever while performing very valuable services.

Within the broad category of volunteers, we are interested in this book particularly in *formal* volunteers as contrasted with informal ones. "Formal volunteers" may be simply defined as volunteers who engage in activities ("volunteer work") under the auspices of some organization or formal group, such as a human service agency (see Smith, 1972, for a definition of "formal group" or "organization"). Formal volunteer work is thought to be only a modest proportion of total volunteer work, with informal volunteer work, such as helping friends or neighbors, being more common in terms of time spent (Szalai et al., 1972).

Our special interest in this volume is with formal volunteers who provide their work (activities with market value that is not remunerated, or at least not fully remunerated) to human service agencies, whether these be private or public. Let us call these people "human service volunteers," for short. They may be sharply distinguished from other important types of formal volunteers, such as those working for recreational, political/advocacy, artistic/cultural, religious, work-related/economic, and other non-profit agencies and associations (see the typology of non-profits I present elsewhere, Smith, 1980). However, the distinction is not quite so clear for several types of volunteer work, such as those dealing with health, education, general fund raising, community improvement, and justice. For our present purposes, we shall use "human services" in its broadest sense and include other-helping (vs. self-help) volunteer activities.

Volunteerism in the broadest sense, and still more broadly the voluntary sector or non-profit sector, is a large and growing part of our society, as well as of other societies. This can be illustrated by the following: (1) Based on national sample surveys, an estimated 70 million Americans were active volunteers in 1974 (Smith and Baldwin, 1974, p. 279), and in 1980 an estimated 84 million were active volunteers (Independent Sector, 1982, p. 33). (2) About 8.4 billion hours per year, worth an estimated $64.5 billion, were contributed by volunteers in 1980 (Independent Sector, 1982, p. 33). (3) The total income of voluntary organizations in 1980 was about $192 billion, including an imputed value for the volunteer time just noted (Independent Sector, 1982, p. 33). (4) There were about 13,000 national voluntary organizations in this country circa 1975 (Smith et al., 1980), most of them relatively young (an average age of about 34 years). (5) Counting each separate local group, chapter, branch, agency, or other unit, there were an estimated 6 million voluntary associations in 1970 (Smith and Baldwin, 1974, p. 282), and by extrapolation, about 7 million in 1980 (based on the research-derived estimate of about 30 associations per 1,000 population). (6) Research on other nations shows volunteers and some form of voluntary organization in every nation so far studied (including the U.S.S.R. and China), with the suggestion of even higher participation rates than in the United States in such countries as Sweden and Norway, and generally comparable rates in industrialized nations around the world (Smith, 1973, Part I; Smith, 1974; Smith, 1975, p. 250; Smith and Elkin, 1981; Smith et al., 1983).

Moreover, current levels of volunteerism tap only part of the potential for volunteer activity. This is shown most clearly by the results of a Gallup Poll taken a few years ago. As George Gallup, Jr., reported at the 1980 National Conference on Citizen Involvement (Gallup, 1980, p. 26), America's urban residents, who constitute the large majority of our total population, "state that they would be willing to donate an average of nine hours per month to their city and their neighborhoods." Extrapolating to the total non-rural U.S. population provides an estimate of *one billion hours per month* of volunteer time that could be utilized for the particular purpose investigated. Even larger estimates of available, untapped volunteer time would probably result if a similar inquiry were made in regard to other widely perceived community or societal needs and problems. A striking 69 percent of the urban Americans polled stated specifically that "they would be willing to engage in . . . neighboorhood activities, including assisting in the performance of some neighborhood social services" (Gallup, 1980, p. 27). This brings home the fact that there is great potential for more volunteer human service work in America—and probably elsewhere as well.

VOLUNTEER SERVICE WORK SETTINGS

Proper understanding of the settings in which human service volunteers work is essential to understanding human service delivery by volunteers. This is because volunteer work settings place important constraints as well as confer special advantages with regard to human service delivery by volunteers. Such work settings differ in terms of special purposes within the broad category of human service, as suggested earlier. But we have in mind here more "structural" distinctions in work settings. One of the most important of such structural distinctions is whether or not the voluntary organization work setting is formally related to some other, usually larger, group or organization. There are two different types of relationship here, which I term "vertical integration" and "horizontal integration." A voluntary organization may or may not be vertically integrated, in the sense of being a smaller, lower-level part of some larger organization that covers more territory (as a local Red Cross chapter is part of the larger American National Red Cross). Similarly, it may or may not be horizontally integrated, in the sense of being part of some larger organization at the *same* territorial level (as a hospital volunteer program is part of the hospital in a given town). Some voluntary organizations stand alone, with neither type of relationship.

Horizontal and vertical integration of a volunteer work setting has a powerful effect on recruitment of volunteers and on other processes. In general, the greater the integration, the greater the direct and indirect facilitation of volunteer recruitment. Thus, a voluntary organization that has both types of integration (which is infrequent) is better off than an organization that has one or the other type of integration. Of the two types of integration, there is no firm evidence regarding whether one or the other type is better on the whole. Vertical integration (e.g., to a state or national organization) usually provides significant "name recognition" and the effects of higher-level (state or national) publicity. This gives the local unit a base of "good will," usually, on which to build its recruitment program. The local unit, whether new or old, is viewed by potential volunteers as more of a known quantity than a local volunteer work setting without vertical integration. Of course, if the state or national organization itself is relatively new or little known, this advantage is not present. Where such is the case, increasing public awareness should be a high priority for the state or national organization if it seeks volunteers to local units as a long-term goal.

Horizontal integration (e.g., to a local hospital, school, prison, or welfare agency) of a volunteer work setting may give the same sort of "name recognition" as vertical integration, though there are often significant differences. Specifically, horizontal integration has positive effects on volunteer recruitment only to the extent that the larger local organization in which the work setting is embedded has a positive local image. Where this may be true for a school or hospital, it may not be true for a prison or welfare agency. In the latter instances, image problems of the volunteer work setting may be a hindrance to recruitment of volunteers. Where this is the case, the problem should be met head-on by focusing on the large-scale service to the community rendered by the organization in which the work setting is embedded. Public misunderstanding of the organization's value may need to be dealt with by this organization if recruitment of volunteers to the work setting is to be accomplished adequately.

Volunteerism in America (and in certain other nations—Great Britain, Belgium, France, and a few others) has developed a special procedure and special resource organizations for assisting horizontally integrated human service volunteer work settings in recruiting volunteers, partly in order to meet the kind of problem just noted. Volunteer Bureaus, and more recently Voluntary Action Centers, at a local level serve specifically the recruitment needs of horizontally integrated human service volunteer work settings. They have grown up not just because of the image problems that local non-profit agencies have (whether weak image or negative image), but also because these agencies are often not known to the local community as human service volunteer work settings. Instead, the agencies are perceived by the local public generally in terms of agency primary service delivery goals—medical personnel engaged in health service delivery, prison personnel engaged in full-time custody of criminals, and so on. Volunteer Bureaus and Voluntary Action Centers, along with certain other similar resource organizations, develop a prominent local image, insofar as they are able, as a place where potential volunteers can go to find suitable positions (i.e., be recruited) in volunteer service work settings of which they were previously unaware.

It should be clear that those volunteer work settings lacking either type of integration—those voluntary organizations that stand alone—are usually in the least advantageous position regarding volunteer recruitment and often other processes too. Such groups are often the smallest, least known, shortest lived, poorest (financially), and correspondingly most in need of volunteers. They are also often the most innovative and responsive to local community needs. At some time, now well-established voluntary organizations were usually in a similar situation; but while they survived other groups did not, in part because of inadequate recruitment and placement of volunteers, in part because of other problems.

The obvious conclusion is that human service volunteer work settings should seek either vertical or horizontal integration in order to increase their relative advantage in the general "volunteer marketplace." This seeking of integration with another organization should be done, ideally, without giving up either relative autonomy or original purpose. Where the price of vertical or horizontal integration is too high in terms of these or other crucial matters, recruitment and other functions can still be accomplished by "stand-alone" or, as I term them, "monomorphic" voluntary organizations ("monomorphic" meaning "having one and only one form"; roughly, "unique"). Such recruitment will generally be more difficult than that for integrated volunteer work settings, but techniques mentioned later on will help in overcoming these difficulties to a significant degree without entirely eliminating them.

There are many other structural distinctions that can be made among volunteer work settings, although none seems to be as important for recruitment as the one just discussed. Some of these other structural distinctions are ratio of paid staff to volunteers, number of "analytical members"—roughly speaking, paid staff and volunteers (see Smith, 1967, 1972)—geographic scope, locus of control (centralization-decentralization), and cyclicality and periodicity of activities. (See Smith et al., 1973, for a fuller listing and discussion.) Other things equal, volunteer work settings with higher prestige, power, wealth, perceived effectiveness, and positive public image tend to attract more volunteers, but such generalizations should be fairly obvious. What is perhaps less obvious is the special importance of *perceived effectiveness* of the work setting among these. Volunteers are especially attracted to work settings where they think they can make a real contribution, and this in turn means that the work setting itself must be perceived as effective in its social service delivery of whatever type.

When the perspective of other organizational processes is taken (e.g., fund raising, leadership), the monomorphic vs. polymorphic distinction remains important. However, for certain purposes, other structural distinctions of the sort just indicated may be more important (e.g., organizational power and prestige as characteristics for understanding the functioning of power processes).

The focus in this volume is on the formal, social service delivery volunteer, not on *all* volunteers and voluntary groups. The scope of U.S. volunteering is very large by a variety of measures, making this book all the more important. Voluntarism is a tremendous resource; hence, it needs to be well and thoughtfully used. Voluntary groups have a wide variety of structural characteristics that affect how they operate. For example, vertical and horizontal integration are especially important for recruitment. Groups vary by structure, purpose, and relationships.

Preface

I would like to extend my thanks to the individuals who helped in the completion of the volume. All of the authors were prompt in delivering all drafts of their essays, and they were responsive to editorial requests. It is difficult to imagine a more cooperative group of scholars with whom to work. Leonard Duhl first awakened my interest in these areas. Barry Giller is responsible for much of my involvement in the voluntary sector over the past few years. Charles Leven has encouraged my work for over ten years. Other colleagues have helped me much as I have worked in this field, including Les Levin, John Geist, Nancy Boguslaw, Al Chenkin, Chaim Lauer, and Evan Bayer. Vicki Ibera prepared the manuscript and kept my life organized at Washington University. I give my gratitude and appreciation for her skill and good spirit. I have had many long and wonderful conversations with Jack Dyckman about the issues discussed in this volume, and he remains my most treasured colleague, teacher, and friend.

Introduction: Planning and the Voluntary Sector

GARY A. TOBIN

The voluntary sector has many names. It is also called the non-profit sector, the independent sector, the quasi-private sector, and, of course, the quasi-public sector. It is also called the third sector, one of the supporting legs of the American system, along with the public and private sectors. Each of these names attempts to describe the nature of the set of agencies, organizations, and institutions that fall between the profit-making private sector and the governing public sector. But each name connotes only one aspect of the system. It is deemed to be independent of the public sector and has a rationale other than profit. The term *voluntary sector* indicates that the effort comes from volunteers—time, money, or materials. No single name is entirely satisfactory, because no name captures the complexity of these systems. Furthermore, the intricate relationship among the three sectors is difficult to recognize if one assumes that the "other" sector is somehow outside or removed from the public sector. The third sector can be more properly described as another dimension, coexisting with other aspects of the structure—with them but separate, inextricably intertwined but sometimes autonomous. Yet the term *voluntary sector* most aptly describes the spirit of these organizations and institutions, and will be used in this volume.

The voluntary sector is a complex creature for three reasons. First, there are relationships between the public and private sectors that include vastly varied roles, purposes, and efficiency. Second, the voluntary sector includes multi-billion dollar umbrella agencies, as well as storefront churches. The differences in terms of scale alone are staggering. Third, the voluntary sector is multi-functional, including fund raising, education, political lobbying, and service delivery. Varied in size, function, and degrees of interdependence and relationship between aspects of the system, the voluntary sector is in many ways undefined or misdefined, and little understood in terms of its role in the delivery of human services.

Despite definition and identity problems, a huge non-governmental network, or set of networks, does indeed function in the delivery of human services. United Ways, Catholic Charities, Jewish Federations, Salvation Armies, the Red Cross, and thousands of other organizations provide food, shelter, day care, and hundreds of other human services. Some are part of national networks; some are single organizations in a specific city. Some cooperate with local, state, or federal government, receiving financial support. Some have no ties to government at all. Some organizations are crisis-oriented and have very short lives, while some have their roots one hundred years or more in the past. For example, hundreds of organizations are listed in *Social Service Organizations* (Romanofsky, ed., Greenwood Press, 1978), yet even this comprehensive list does not capture the immensity of the voluntary sector network.

The following essays are concerned with the planning and human service delivery aspect of the voluntary sector, both at the micro level and at the macro level. Other functions are of interest in this volume and are discussed only as they inform us about the human service delivery system and the planning process.

The first section of this volume discusses the structure of the voluntary sector. "The Historical Role of the Voluntary Sector in Human Service Delivery in Urban America," by Clarke Chambers, describes the historical development of the modern system. Jennifer Wolch explores the ways in which the voluntary sector adds to or detracts from an urban economy. Orval Westby, in "Religious Groups and Institutions," gives a detailed description of the religious groups and institutions that constitute a major portion of the non-profit world.

Frances Hoffmann takes a specific service, child care and day care, and shows how the entire system must be restructured for the delivery of this service to be substantially changed. The way the voluntary sector fits into the political system is discussed by E.

Terrence Jones. Differences between the public and private systems are discussed by Michael Sosin, "The Domain of Private Social Welfare: Comparisons Between the Public Sector and the Voluntary Sector." Mayor William D. Schaefer discusses the relationship of the voluntary sector to local governments, using Baltimore as a case study.

The second section of the volume discusses planning in the voluntary sector, which varies a great deal in terms of sophistication and experience. But it is less understood and less formalized than planning in the public and private sectors, although some organizations, such as United Way, have elaborate planning systems. Two essays in this volume, "Needs Identification: Needs Assessment in the Voluntary Sector," by Russy Sumariwalla, and "Strategic Planning in the Voluntary Sector," by George Wilkinson, discuss needs identification and strategic planning as specific techniques for more efficient delivery of services in the voluntary sector.

The complex nature of the planning process as it relates to the interaction of clients, lay leaders, committees, volunteers, and professional staff is discussed by John Forester, "The Planning Structure of Voluntary Organizations: The Relationship of Professional Staff to Lay Leaders," and David Smith, "Volunteerism: Attracting Volunteers and Staffing Shrinking Programs." The particular ethical concerns of planners in the voluntary sector are discussed by Gary Tobin in "Ethics in Planning in the Voluntary Sector."

A number of themes emerge in these essays concerning planning itself. Planning is a purposive set of actions that are designed, executed, and evaluated to reach a desired set of goals. Whether in small community groups, church boards of directors, or through elaborate planning systems such as the United Way network, planning takes place. The focus of this planning may be more efficient or broader net fund raising, designing new programs, evaluating existing delivery systems, and other activities that are routinely part of the voluntary sector. Levels of sophistication, resource commitment, and available state-of-the-art technologies and processes differ a great deal among types of organizations, but most organizations do plan to some degree.

Planning in the voluntary sector involves a complex set of actors who meet in the service delivery system. These include professional staff of organizations and agencies, financial contributors, and lay committees, all of whom constitute planning and decision-making bodies. They also include volunteer workers who supplement professional staff (or vice versa). There are the foundations, corporations, and trusts that are major sources of funding for voluntary organizations. In addition, public sector agencies and departments funnel public dollars through voluntary organizations. And finally there are the clients or recipients of voluntary sector services.

Planning in the public sector also involves funders, consultants, advisors, bureaucrats, and a host of interest groups and decision makers. Yet the processes and relationships are more studied and better understood than those in the voluntary sector. As resources become more scarce, planning within the non-profit sector becomes more essential. Careful assessment of programs, needs, sources of revenue, and efficient delivery of services are of great importance. Lay leaders and professionals are demanding more prudent expenditures, and planning techniques and skills are required.

A second set of themes revolves around the differences among the sectors. There are fundamental differences between the ideal public and the non-profit sectors in their pre-Great Society form. First, the public sector has at its base the notion of defining and serving the public good. Interest group politics notwithstanding, the system is constitutionally blind to race, sex, and age, and promises equal protection, justice, and opportunity, if not benefits. The voluntary sector is not so bound. While many organizations have universalistic goals in terms of reducing hunger or providing day care, most voluntary organizations are much more particularistic, whether for Jews, Catholics, the visually handicapped, or the victims of a particular disease. While most voluntary organizations are not exclusionary, their raison d'étre is quite often focussed upon a particular clientele that may be defined by race, religion, or other factors. In many ways, the voluntary sector reflects certain groups' organized efforts to take care of their own. Of course, certain organizations, especially larger national networks, exist to take care of anybody, or everybody, but they are rare. Even within these organizations, varying functions and purposes may focus the organization on particular sets of clients. In terms of overall purposes and rationales, the voluntary sector cannot substitute for the public sector in providing for the general welfare.

The second difference between the voluntary and public sectors is the ability to generate revenue. The public sector has taxing ability to raise the needed revenues, but the voluntary sector has only pleading and persuading ability. Ultimately, of course, elected officials who make taxing decisions are responsible to their constituencies. Politicians and the bureaucrats who serve them reflect the changing values and opinions of the body politic. Nevertheless, these public officials often have more latitude than do voluntary sector actors. The bulk of the moneys that are received by the voluntary sector comes from corporations, foundations, and individual philanthropists. A small number of individuals can and do influence policy: they hold the purse strings. Small but powerful oligarchies can control expenditures.

This leads to the third major difference: the lack of countervailing influences, unless they are between powerful individuals or organizations. In some sense, interest group politics is reduced to this most basic denominator: single individuals or coalitions with their own agendas, goals, and values. Many boards of directors of these organizations have "life members," those who make large gifts and thereby gain permanent enfranchisement in the decision-making process. Furthermore, influence is often determined by the size of the gift. The public sector has outlawed such practice, of course, feeling that elections ought not be bought. In the voluntary sector, such processes flourish.

Many of the differences have disappeared from the contemporary scene, where the blending of the two systems has often made the public and private sectors indistinguishable. Two significant changes have contributed to the relationship between the public and private sectors. First, "purchase-of-service" contracts have increased the public sector's use of private agencies' services. Second, service-oriented, profit-making organizations, partly or fully funded by the public sector, are appearing throughout the private sector. The consequence of these changes is the formation of a fragmented but complex public/private service network which makes accountability of either sector difficult to obtain. (See Gilbert, *Capitalism and the Welfare State*, 1983.)

A third set of themes is concerned with myths about the cultural aspects of the voluntary sector. A well-accepted and admired mythology about the non-profit sector has developed as an integral part of American culture. A vast set of permanent and ad hoc organizations, religious institutions, and large and small fund raisers, constitutes a segment of American life that is not driven by profit or capital accumulation. The maintenance of order and the administration of law are left primarily to the public sector. The voluntary sector is supposed to help individuals and groups by providing a vast array of services. Often steeped in religious tradition, the voluntary sector maintains an aura of moral superiority to both the public and private sectors. The moral structure of its organizations and institutions is at the core of the myths and mystique of the voluntary sector.

These myths are powerful reflectors of the American view of government itself. The first part of the cultural mythology is the belief that the non-profit sector is more humane, personal, and closer to the people it serves than the public sector. Government is often viewed as an intruder and usurper, a threat to our collective private lives. The voluntary sector, on the other hand, is viewed as a supplementer and nurturer. Welfare has a terrible connotation in contemporary society, while philanthropy is seen as positive. Reaganomics is steeped in this philosophy, consistently denigrating the ability or role of government to deal with essentially "voluntary" problems. (See Palmer and Sawhill, *The Reagan Experiment*, 1982.)

The second part of the myth concerns the clients or recipients themselves. The public sector is seen to be obligated to serve the unworthy, often cheaters and malingerers. The voluntary sector, however, seeks out the worthy poor—it chooses whom it will serve and how much. It is often selective in terms of religious group, for example, so an effective screening takes place before services are delivered. Often standards are imposed in terms of income for service delivery. But these standards are believed to be more flexible yet more efficient than those of the public sector.

The third part of the cultural myth rests in the notion that both the private sector and voluntary sector are more efficient in the delivery of services than the public sector. The public sector is seen to be detached and removed, a lumbering bureaucracy that cannot effectually deal with the clients. The voluntary sector is seen to be more organized, closely watched by smaller boards and committees, and monitored more because people are involved.

The fourth part of the mythology concerns the imagined infinite ability of the voluntary sector to raise funds, attract volunteer time, and deliver services. The public sector is seen as an unnecessary, inefficient, and inhumane layer of administrative bureaucracy. The populace, so the myth goes, will respond as needed to the wants of the people, and if called upon will provide the labor and contributors necessary in the voluntary sector. This part of the mythology assumes that no real need will be left unattended.

The fifth part of the myth is that ordinary folks can do many of the tasks that trained staffs or professionals can do, thereby eliminating the need for large expenditures for labor. It is argued that a full-time counselor, for example, can be replaced by part-time counselors who are trained in their field and will volunteer their time. In some cases it is argued that professional tasks do not require professionals at all.

The sixth part of the myth is that the voluntary sector is truly independent of the public and private sectors. It is thought to be less subject to political manipulation or public whim because it is independently financed and labor is provided by volunteers. The moral character of those involved in the voluntary sector is entwined in this myth. Politicians, who have replaced the "public servant," are seen as self-serving, tied to special interests, and more likely to act in their own interest than in the public interest. Voluntary sector participants are acting out of a sense of moral commitment to help the needy.

It is the concept of the needy that is at the core of these myths concerning the voluntary sector. Programs and services are designed to meet crises, supplement public efforts, and fill gaps. Income redistribution, maintenance, and support are not at the core of the voluntary sector's functions. The voluntary sector has long served the middle class as well as the indigent, with Boy Scouts, family and children services, and so on. The public sector assumed increased responsibility for low-income groups during the New Deal. As Social Security, unemployment, and other benefits developed in the public sector, need was redefined beyond sustenance to include public subsidy of the delivery of human and social services.

We are now in the position of reexamining the myths and the partnership. The Reagan election and the subsequent assault upon the New Deal and Great Society programs, coupled with deep recession and structural changes in the economy, has forced public attention on the role of the voluntary sector. What are its proper roles? What can it do and what can it not do? What is the relationship between the voluntary sector and the public and private sectors?

Each of the myths has its counter-side as well. The voluntary sector is not always more humane than the public sector. Historically, the voluntary sector has distinguished between "worthy" and "unworthy" poor. Traditionally, many religious groups have attached a stigma to poverty. Others have mandated the acculturation of a particular set of values or group norms as a precondition or unstated agenda for giving or receiving aid. Furthermore, the particularistic nature of the voluntary sector can allow for exclusion or even discrimination. While public dollars sometimes require voluntary organizations to be ecumenical or non-discriminatory, these rules are sometimes subverted, while other voluntary organizations would choose not to take any public assistance. Because of this selectiveness, the voluntary sector is perceived to be less vulnerable to cheaters than the public sector, but organizationally it is not necessarily better equipped to separate the truly needy from the freeloader. Indeed, the only way this separation is possible is through the closer surveillance and monitoring that comes from more intimate contact and knowledge, the very practice that is most feared from big government.

Little empirical evidence shows that the voluntary sector is really more efficient than the public sector. What is to be compared clouds the analysis, such as local government to large umbrella organizations, or a single client to the Department of Human Services. The matter of efficiency is a critical one and needs to be examined in assessing the proper balance between public and voluntary sector efforts to provide human services. The ability of the voluntary sector to substitute for government efforts is also discussed in the essays.

The voluntary sector has its limits. The role of the public sector cannot be eliminated, and indeed, grew out of the failure of the voluntary sector to handle the crises of industrialized urban life. The rhetoric calling for a greater role for the voluntary sector is far removed from the reality of service need if it assumes that the gaps left by the public sector retreat will be filled by the voluntary sector. Voluntary fund raising has its theoretical limits, of course; this is why governments are empowered to tax. The voluntary sector cannot compensate for the ability of government to tax and redistribute income.

In the same way, individuals cannot compensate for the loss of trained, competent staff. Commitment must be shown not only through a desire to help, but through career incentives. Volunteerism can supplement; it cannot replace.

The non-profit sector and the government are inextricably linked and intertwined. The independent sector is linked to the public sector, to the corporate sector, and to individuals by income tax laws, property tax laws, grants, research agendas, and in many other ways. Governments at all levels support the voluntary sector, and its health relies a great deal on government commitment and financing. Direct subsidies are a result, for example, of citizen Jane being able to reduce her income taxes by contributing to her church or United Way.

Clearly, the more the government does, the more the voluntary sector will do. The converse is also true. The public retreat will lessen the ability of the voluntary sector to fulfill its goals. Recent studies by the Urban Institute demonstrate the serious negative effect government cutbacks have on voluntary sector programs. Increased food drives, emergency shelters, and emergency heating aid by the voluntary sector may result as recession deepens or the number of permanently unemployed increases. Certain organizations will be more visible, and many will be busier. Many organizations may be forced to allocate a greater proportion of their resources to the temporarily or permanently destitute. But the quality and quantity of services will be seriously hampered by the federal government's retreat from both the poor and the middle class, which many voluntary organizations serve. The more the federal government reduces its direct efforts, the more the voluntary sector will be hampered.

Other options are open. The federal government can retreat from client service delivery and more broadly subsidize the voluntary sector through increased grants, more tax incentives, and other such programs. The wisdom of this agenda is yet to be tested. In a pluralistic society, the diverse character of the voluntary sector can be both its attractiveness and fundamental flaw. Diversity may encourage greater efficiency, humaneness, and quality. On the other hand, it may also foster exclusion or discrimination, with certain racial or other groups not receiving an equitable portion of the service goods. The public good, regardless of the moral goals of individual voluntary sector groups, must be assumed at the public level. The public sector can nurture voluntary sector efforts and encourage their individual moral and ethical purposes. But the broadest agenda is a national one. A partnership is desirable, as long as the public sector provides the bounds.

Rhetoric about the volunteerism of Americans and about the non-profit sector's ability to pick up the slack of government retreat is useless. Which services are properly the role of which sector, where they can be most efficiently delivered, which services ought to be provided, and the moral and social obligations of each sector —this is the proper language in which to discuss these issues. Careful analysis and planning are required, or we are left with a population that is less well sheltered, fed, and educated, and less medically fit and productive than it might be. Obviously, the voluntary sector will continue to operate, and the public sector is not going to abandon all social welfare support systems. But a good fit between the sectors may be lost. This is not to say, of course, that the fit has ever been attained. But hope for an American human service delivery system resting primarily on its volunteers is a dim hope indeed.

PART I

The Structure of the Voluntary Sector

1

The Historical Role of the Voluntary Sector in Human Service Delivery in Urban America

CLARKE A. CHAMBERS

Politicians, editors, ministers, and civic leaders—spokespersons (often self-appointed) for the republic—have been inclined, over the generations, to make rhetorical pronouncements proclaiming a tradition of voluntary giving to less fortunate members of society. In fund-raising campaigns of the United Way, conducted annually in hundreds of communities throughout the nation, appeals are made to the American way of health and welfare: the solicitation of moneys from citizens and businesses to underwrite human services in the private, non-profit sector. Conservative public figures —Herbert Hoover and Ronald Reagan spring to mind as powerful illustrative figures in the twentieth century—assert the moral superiority of the voluntary sector in providing assistance to people and families in need. The act of giving, it is declared, strengthens the character of those who provide (even if it be only the biblical widow's mite), and thus advances the republican virtue of self-reliance; a personal bond is established between provider and recipient (although it is deemed always more blessed to give than to receive); services provided by voluntary agencies are seen to be inherently more humane and more efficient than comparable assistance provided by governmental bureaucracies, always assumed to be cold, impersonal, inefficient, and vulnerable to corruption. Those who celebrate this tradition are apt to call upon the testimony of history—the generosity of the nation's colonial forebears and the charitable impulse that moved nineteenth-century Americans to great acts of philanthropy until the emergence of the welfare state, with its presumed rigid, formal, and extravagant programs financed through compulsory levies on overburdened taxpayers, subverted these arrangements and values.

These perceptions have proved to constitute a myth, often benign, that continues to carry great authority in American life. It is the purpose of this chapter to examine the course of social services in the voluntary sector over generations of experience; to assess intent, motive, and consequences; to set forth factors of ideology, social class, altruism and self-interest; and to trace the changing shapes and forms that welfare strategies assumed with the passing of time.

FORMS OF CHARITY IN COLONIAL
AND EARLY NATIONAL ERAS

According to the Elizabethan Poor Laws, which were applied everywhere in the British North American colonies, families had the primary responsibility to care for their own, whatever the source or character of need might be; if family resources proved insufficient, if orphans or widows were left bereft of family support, then local government, using public funds, was obliged to provide assistance, most often to persons in their own homes. Because other pressing projects had first claim on tax moneys—public buildings, roads and bridges, for example—and because economic levels in most communities remained relatively low well into the eighteenth century, funds for public assistance, often provided in kind (food, clothing, or fuel), were tightly controlled.[1]

By the same token, and because the pressures for the private accumulation and investment of capital were intense, colonial citizens had limited financial resources for the exercise of private acts of charity. Ministers of the gospel, Puritan and Anglican, raised modest sums for the supplementary relief of widows, orphans, the handicapped, and the aged through annual charity sermons, but these occasions probably proved more significant in the long run for the elaboration of a rationale of Christian stewardship than for the proximate relief of need within the parish. Colonials, whatever their religious denomination, accepted without question the premises and structures of a hierarchically ordered society, and they were subject to strict rules of power and deference. The poor were not blamed for their plight—as they were in the nineteenth century—but they were expected to know their place and to honor the authority of superior classes. The more fortunate, in their turn, assumed responsibilities with their privileges and earned social approbation, and presumably divine pleasure, by manifesting a spirit of Christian charity. Until 1750 or so, however, the sums so raised and spent were modest indeed; chief responsibility for care remained with the family or with the parish, the town, or the county.[2]

Increased wealth and the rise of great family fortunes, especially in the port cities of Boston, Philadelphia, and New York, together with the emergence of national consciousness and social confidence, characteristics associated with the success of the American Revolution and with the triumph of rationalism, provided opportunities for more extensive and more scientific philanthropical efforts on the part of wealthy merchants and financiers, of private church societies, and of associations created to ameliorate the conditions of needy members of particular ethnic groups—Scots, Irish, and Germans, for example. The motives of the benefactors were, in every instance, mixed. Some wealthy individuals gained social prestige through funding hospitals or charitable agencies; churchmen played out obligations of stewardship. Loyalty to fellow nationals, especially to recent immigrants who were ineligible for public assistance owing to rules of settlement and residency, undoubtedly underlay some work. Others were undoubtedly provoked to the doing of good works by humanitarian impulses or by a desire to render more orderly the potentially chaotic lives of a social underclass.[3]

PRIVATE BENEVOLENCES, c. 1820–1860

The true breakaway and proliferation of voluntary benevolent societies came, however, at an accelerating pace beginning in the 1820s, especially in the burgeoning cities of the Northeast. Indeed, it was in response to the rapid growth of urban centers, with all the problems attendant upon that growth, that benevolent societies were born. New York City, for example, which had tripled in population between 1790 and 1820, going from 50,000 to 150,000, numbered over 300,000 in 1840 and 725,000 by the Civil War. The growth of population registered in Philadelphia, Boston, and Baltimore was not quite as spectacular, but all such metropolitan centers had truly become cities in these years and were plagued by social problems for which that generation had no resolution—crowded and squalid slums, primitive or non-existent sanitation systems, and woefully inadequate provision for public health, safety, and education. Tens of thousands of Irish and German immigrants, together with American- and rural-born citizens, crowded into pestiferous neighborhoods where they played out their precarious and marginal lives—vulnerable to sickness, accident, and sudden death, and victims of irregular employment and of insufficient and insecure income.

In the face of such disorder, prospering middle-class citizens and local elites grew anxious. Informal systems of assistance and surveillance, which had sufficed in village America, ceased to function when persons in authority no longer knew their neighbors. Working-class families, many of them of immigrant origin, confronted conditions of deep insecurity; forced to move from one dwelling to another, from one neighborhood to another, broken by sickness, death, and recurring unemployment, they often became unable to sustain those networks of care and mutual assistance that had been a source of their survival.[4]

Part of the response to social disorder in urban America, as David Rothman sets forth in *The Discovery of the Asylum* (1971), was the creation of public institutions within which the lives of the unruly could be ordered. By the removal of the dependent poor, the insane, delinquent youths, and criminal adults to the sanctuaries of the poorhouse, the insane asylum, the house of refuge, and penitentiary, the social contagions of pauperism and deviance could presumably be rooted out.[5] At least so ran the hopes of the founders of these institutions. The creation of benevolent societies inaugurated parallel strategies for amelioration, salvation, and control.

Religious concerns informed many of their programs, and for several decades a majority of them maintained close connections to particular parish churches and religious denominations. Some, the more conservative, continued to be moved by motives of Christian stewardship. Others partook of the religious enthusiasm that had fired the Second Great Awakening of Protestant evangelism in the early generations of the nineteenth century. Central to this fervor was the notion that all persons, if they would but open themselves to divine grace and accept Jesus as their Saviour, could be redeemed and reborn, their immortal souls saved for eternity, and their lives reordered in this earthly vale of tears and temptations. All souls, however fallen, were open to conversion; all persons, however corrupted and despised, could be returned to useful and virtuous citizenship, their lives transformed through faith by grace. At least it was the fervent hope of those who founded diverse benevolent societies that redemption could be the beginning of a process through which the unchurched masses could be inculcated with the values of a Christian (and, as it turned out, a bourgeois) society—industry, thrift, temperance, frugality, prudence, and self-reliance, perhaps even cleanliness which stood next to godliness. Was it too much to hope that the "dangerous classes" (the designation was applied throughout the entire Atlantic community of nations in these years) could be rendered into responsible citizens, led to be obedient, sober, and disciplined workers? Regenerated Americans, moreover, could be gotten off the relief rolls and out of the poorhouses; burdens on the taxpayers would be lifted; the very heavens would rejoice.

In such a spirit—a practical attention to the social sorrows that accompanied urban life in a nascent industrial economy, a conviction of the efficacy of religious conversion, a longing for social stability, and an implied expectation that money could be saved —these benevolent societies went about their righteous business. Many, at first, devoted their energies primarily to the distribution of religious tracts and to the establishment of Sunday schools for the children of the urban poor, schools that instructed their charges not only in biblical piety and moral axioms but also in the rudiments of reading and writing. Such city missions often moved, in time, from moral exhortation to the inauguration of simple acts of charitable assistance—the giving of groceries, clothing, and fuel to families deemed to be deserving and responsive. Some societies provided services to specialized constituencies—widows with young children; orphans and half-orphans; abandoned, neglected, abused, and unruly children; handicapped persons—the blind, crippled, retarded, and mentally ill (the latter unless so disordered in mind as to warrant safe confinement in an asylum); "fallen" women, prostitutes, and unwed mothers; seamen stranded in port without money or family; infirm men and women without children to care for them in their old age.[6] The names the founders chose for these societies reveal both their spirit and program: any number of Bible and Tract Societies and Magdalen Societies, the Society for the Relief of Poor Widows with Small Children, the Society for the Care of Respectable Widows, the Association for the Relief of Respectable, Aged, Indigent Females, the Society for the Information and Assistance of Persons Emigrating from Foreign Countries, the Society for the Promotion of Industry, the Association for Improving the Condition of the Poor, the Children's Aid Society, the Home for Little Wanderers, the John Howard Society (named for an English prison reformer), and the like. Some of these societies built and maintained shelters for their clients, homes for unwed mothers, orphanages, hospitals, and clinics. Others provided economic assistance (always in moderate sums and most often in kind), moral homilies, or advice on child-rearing and house management to persons in their own homes. Neglected, orphaned, dependent, and incorrigible children might be relegated to an orphanage or, as came increasingly to be the case, placed out or apprenticed to other families (farm families in the countryside were favored hosts).

It is understandable that Catholic churches—most often serving Irish or German parishes—instituted their own societies in order to resist the intrusion of Protestant influence, as Jay P. Dolan has traced in *The Immigrant Church: New York's Irish and German Catholics, 1815-1865* (1975).[7] Special religious orders were created to comfort the sick, bury the dead, provide food and clothing and shelter for unfortunate parishioners, and to educate their young; thus did the Sisters of Charity, the Sisters of the Poor, the Sisters of Mercy, and the Sisters of the Good Shepherd go about their tasks. Just as Protestant women, the wives and daughters of respectable business and professional men, initiated good works, so did Catholic ladies' societies of charity distribute clothing to the poor, while laymen exercised charity in urban parishes through chapters of the Society of St. Vincent de Paul. Catholic societies also maintained orphanages and, like their Protestant counterparts, labored to place their unhappy wards in good Catholic families.

To keep the work of these varied societies in perspective it is necessary to remember that public assistance, in these antebellum decades, remained the primary source of financial assistance, especially in rural areas and in villages and towns.[8] There had been a rush to build public institutions everywhere in the nation, although the South lagged in this regard as it did in so many other areas (in the creation of a public school system, for example); but although indoor relief became the ideological preference, provision of outdoor assistance continued to characterize the policies of most communities. Orphanages, both private and public, became popular places to provide refuge for children—not only true orphans, but children whose families, for whatever reasons, could not care for them. Many young children lived with their needy mothers in public almshouses. Nevertheless, institutions of all kinds followed strategies designed to place children with what a later generation would label foster families.

The New York Children's Aid Society, directed with energy and imagination by Charles Loring Brace during the middle decades of the nineteenth century, placed tens of thousands of "street Arabs" with farm and small town families in frontier communities in the Ohio and Mississippi valleys.[9] A good Jeffersonian, Brace railed against modern cities as sinkholes of disease, misery, vice, crime, and moral degeneration. The urban poor, he asserted, lacked initiative, self-control, and habits of industry and thrift; they exhibited, in his words, "the appetite for liquor and of the sexual passion, and sometimes of the peculiar weakness, dependence and laziness which makes confirmed paupers."[10] Brace worked in alliance with clerical and lay leaders of Protestant churches, but he had no time for "distributing tracts, and holding prayer meetings, and scattering Bibles. The neglected and ruffian classes . . . are in no way affected directly by such influences as these."[11] Skeptical of city missions, he cried anathema against "the chilling formalism of the ignorant Roman Catholic" church, which, in his view, had no appreciation of "our spiritual life of free love towards God, true repentance and trust in a Divine Redeemer."[12] Declaring in the first sentence of his classic work *The Dangerous Classes of New York* (1872) that the "central figure in the world's charity is Christ," he proposed that the way to forestall the rising up of the dangerous classes or the pulling down of society by their contagion was to remove the children of bad families, corrupted by an evil environment, and place them on farms, for "the best of all Asylums for the outcast child is the farmer's home."[13]

Historians have no way of accurately judging the relative influences of welfare programs—public or private, church-based or interdenominational or secular, indoor or outdoor. Welfare in Victorian America was a mixed and complex system. Orphans or children judged to be abandoned, neglected, abused, dependent, or delinquent might find their ways, more by chance than by rational design, to residence in a poorhouse with their mother, to a religious or state orphanage, or to a house of refuge or a reformatory; they might, by the same chance, be placed by parents with an older sister or brother, or with an uncle or aunt or neighbor; or, lacking parental initiative, they might be apprenticed or placed out in other families by local magistrates, by superintendents of almshouses and orphanages, or by agents of children's aid societies. It is difficult to untangle the lines of authority and responsibility in such matters; the law was casual, if not capricious; records were not well kept and many, of course, were not preserved. Welfare was an intensely localized concern, whether in public or private spheres, and an accounting of sums spent by the voluntary and public sectors is quite beyond our scholarly competence. The investment of time by private citizens doing volunteer work through benevolent societies must have been enormous. To evaluate the consequences of all this effort is an enterprise fraught with hazard, although it might just be the case, as far as the impact of welfare progams as social control devices is concerned, that Victorian ideology did less to alter the behavior of client families than it did to reassure the host and patron classes that the evangelical and bourgeois values by which they lived were morally valid.

Benevolent societies—and there were thousands of them by 1860—were founded, financed, and managed by prospering middle-class and professional men. Society executives tended to be drawn from ministerial ranks or from persons trained for the cloth. Much of the volunteer work, especially with mothers and children, was taken over by lady volunteers, although it was often also the case that societies whose clientele was exclusively female (such as those working with prostitutes and aged widows) were directed by female board members and paid agents—this in the belief that women far more than men possessed qualities of instinct, intuition, and demeanor that made them inherently more apt at softening the hearts of the poor and at leading those who had strayed from the path of virtue back to the way of righteousness. Many such volunteers, learning through their work how human affairs were structured and managed in worlds beyond their own comfortable homes, turned, in time, to reform causes—temperance, education, women's rights, and abolitionism—moving thus from nurturing to the reforming roles of agitation and management. Working with prostitutes and deserted wives, some leaders were compelled to perceive women who had fallen into misfortune as victims of a patriarchal system that exploited all women, regardless of class and circumstance. Not all benevolent ladies were so moved, of course, and traditional feminine virtues of nurturance and domesticity survived, perhaps as a predominant strain, alongside more assertive forms of feminism.[14]

VOLUNTARY WELFARE WORK DURING THE CIVIL WAR

The Civil War provoked responses in systems of health and welfare far beyond the modest and largely uncoordinated efforts that had characterized the antebellum scene. It was the nation's first modern war and demanded a comprehensive mobilization of economic and human resources, both in the Union and in the Confederacy. Although the North resorted to conscription to muster manpower for its armies, no such authority of government was employed to sustain life and morale on the home front. In both the North and the South, the divided nation relied rather on the voluntary efforts of the citizenry.[15]

Families, as always in the American past, constituted the first line of response to the problems of mothers left at home with small children when their husbands marched off to war. As casualties mounted, many children lost their fathers, and when mothers could not cope by themselves, even with the modest assistance they were sometimes able to claim through public outdoor relief, the children had to be placed with relatives or friends. Orphanages, public and private, had to pick up the slack; lacking sufficient facilities, communities sometimes had to place orphaned or stranded children in houses of refuge or reformatories. General assistance to soldiers and to their families demanded more heroic measures.

The response in the North came primarily through the work of the United States Sanitary Commission, a nationally coordinated voluntary association modeled after the British Sanitary Commission, whose work during the Crimean War was well known in elite American circles. Authorized by the Congress, the commission was funded and administered entirely in the private sector. It set a high priority on programs designed to improve health and sanitation in military camps and army hospitals. Its staff counseled soldiers in applying for bounties and dependency allowances. It created communications networks among wounded and sick soldiers and their families. It collected and distributed food, clothing, bandages, and other supplies that soldiers might need. On the home front it raised and distributed funds to tide over mothers and children left dependent by the absence or death of husbands and fathers. Working with a small paid staff of around five hundred people whose responsibility was essentially the coordination of scattered local committees, the commission fulfilled its varied missions primarily through the efforts of thousands of volunteers working in hundreds of communities throughout the nation. Local committees gathered and distributed relief in kind for families made destitute by the absence of their chief provider; they also acted as contact points to maintain liaison with army personnel during a war in which communications between the battlefront and the home front were difficult at best.[16]

The South did not create any such coordinated program, but southern white women, working most often through their local churches, played many of these same roles. Anne Firor Scott, whose study *The Southern Lady* (1970) details such efforts, estimates that soldiers' aid societies numbered nearly a thousand, and concludes that although male clergymen often provided nominal leadership, "the groups were the result of women's initiatives and ran on women's energies."[17] Southern women also labored through hospital aid societies, as nurses and administrators, to care for the sick and wounded. Casualties were heavy, North and South, and tens of thousands of women had to seek ways to survive the psychological and economic trauma of widowhood while devising strategies for survival for themselves and their children.

Long-term consequences flowed from these events. The Sanitary Commission established models for coordination upon which the charity organization movement soon would draw; it laid down forms, moreover, that anticipated the structures of the Red Cross and of war chests during the First and Second World Wars. Of equal importance, myriad women gained experience in the administration of health and welfare services. They performed traditional nurturing duties, but they also learned to raise and administer funds and to manage complex operations in the local community, in the region, and at the national level. Diverse charitable enterprises would draw on these experienced and committed women in the generation to follow.

THE MOVEMENT TO ORGANIZE CHARITY

Everywhere in the Atlantic community of nations during the last third of the nineteenth century, the processes of industrialization and urbanization greatly accelerated, nowhere more dramatically than in the United States. What had started modestly and even tentatively a generation earlier became, in these decades, a rush toward the triumph of industrial and finance capitalism. The processes themselves were highly speculative, erratic, and irrational; wide-open competition and unregulated market forces combined to propel the economy forward in great lurching movements. Production, prices, profits, and employment all exhibited great swings from season to season and from year to year; financial panics beginning in 1873 and 1893 plunged the nation into times of prolonged depression.

The labor market was rendered more chaotic by the coming of vast numbers of immigrants from southern and eastern Europe. These "new" immigrants—as they came to be labeled because they differed in place of exodus, in religion, in folk culture, and in political and work experience from those immigrants who had come from northern and western Europe in earlier years—provided a reservoir of cheap, unskilled labor. They crowded into teeming industrial centers, lived in ramshackle slum tenements, and sold their labor in irregular markets. Attracted to America by wages and opportunities relatively more generous than they had known in Italy, Greece, and the national provinces of the Austro-Hungarian and Russian empires, they faced in the new world irregularity of employment, uncertain family income, and conditions of labor and life marked by high rates of accidents in factory and mine and high rates of environmental illness, such as tuberculosis, in squalid slums. Structural weaknesses in the economy rendered them vulnerable to the vagaries of an exploitive system. Families of the working class and immigrant classes found themselves thrown into sudden and severe crises by the closing of a plant, by the death of a chief wage earner, by sickness that carried away infants and mothers. They suffered not so much from endemic poverty as from uncertainty of income, which arose through no fault of their own.

The speculative nature of the economy had a bearing on the lives of millions of Americans who lived above the margin of existence as well. Even great entrepreneurs had to confront the chance of failure along with the opportunity for great material success. A longing for social order was everywhere manifest. Great industrialists and financiers sought ways by which society couild be brought under regular control: efficiency, rationalization, coordination became the orders of the day.

In such an era, it is understandable that agents of welfare in the voluntary sector sought to order the chaos about them by the scientific organization of charity.[18] Leaders in the field began to sense in the 1870s that the proliferation of private welfare societies, each going its own way with no reference to the programs of other societies and with but little reference to the true needs of client populations, compounded the problem of providing effective assistance and services. These conditions compelled them toward coordination and organization. First in Buffalo, in 1877, and then in all the great cities of the nation, charity leaders came together to create Charity Organization Societies (COS), composed of diverse member agencies which would agree to coordinate their services through this central society.

Applicants for assistance were referred to the COS of a given city, where centralized files were generated and maintained. The COS then sent out paid agents to investigate the existence, extent, and cause of need—if the need were judged to be authentic and the applicant "worthy," the society referred the case to an appropriate member agency, although in some instances the central bureau itself might offer aid. By such centralization COS leaders intended to discourage "mendicants," as they were labeled, from shopping around from one agency to another until they found an easy mark. The COS thus placed a high priority on rooting out beggars and fraudulent claimants so that the truly needy and worthy could be served efficiently, economically, and scientifically. Many such charity societies established employment bureaus, perceiving work rather than the dole as a true response to poverty. By the operation of workshops—typically wood yards for men, laundries and sewing rooms for women—a COS could enforce a works test on potential clients: those who would not work became ineligible for assistance. Relief, when awarded, was provided according to the same rule of less eligibility that characterized public assistance—that is, at levels lower than the lowest wages prevailing in a given community.[19]

Charities in most cities (New York was a major exception) gathered cadres of voluntary "friendly visitors" whose task was to visit the poor in their homes and offer them prudent advice on managing household budgets, on nutrition, on keeping the tenement clean; they also meant to uplift the spirits of downhearted mothers, to set them a moral example, and thereby to encourage sobriety, modesty, thrift, and industry. By friendly visiting, its proponents declared, the chaos of social class would dissolve in the warmth of human affection.

Faith in the efficacy of friendly visiting reflected the sentimental and romantic side of Victorian society. Contrary reflections prevailed. The precepts of social Darwinism came easily to charity leaders, for the world they knew was indeed moved by competition, struggle, and endeavor; to offer generous assistance to the poor was to encourage the survival of those they deemed to be "unfit" and to consume the capital substance of those, like themselves, who were numbered among the naturally "fit." The vehemence with which charity leaders fought public outdoor assistance was a token of their distrust of all government welfare progams, which they held to be inherently and invariably inefficient, corrupt, and pauperizing; charitable assistance that derived from the private sector would be administered by the objective criteria of a needs test and a works test, and society could thus be assured that only the "worthy" and the potentially "fit" would be lent a hand-up rather than be given a handout. "Not alms—but a friend" was the motto of many a charity organization society. It comes as no surprise that many charity leaders were also eugenicists and tended to attribute the squalor of the poor not only to their immoral behavior but to their bad genetic background as well.

The contradiction is central to an appreciation of the movement
to organized charity—on the one hand, an inclination to believe in
progress through humane measures, in the capacity of the dispos-
sessed to shape up and lift themselves to higher standards by individual acts of will, and in the efficacy of personal acts of friendship
across lines of class and circumstance; on the other hand, a cynical
and abiding fear that the great body of those who lived in poverty
lay quite beyond the power of redemption. To elite groups in the
host society, those who were in need seemed so very different from
themselves, in material standards, cultural values and behavioral
norms, in race, nationality, and class. This fundamental
contradiction did much to render private charity crabbed and
niggardly and to retard the development of public policies leading
to a welfare state.

THE SETTLEMENT HOUSE MOVEMENT

Settlement houses and community centers constituted a second
major response to all those human troubles that arose from industrial capitalism, urbanization, and immigration.[20] Just as American
charities took as their model the London Charity Organization
Society (1869), American settlements consciously emulated
London's Toynbee Hall (1884). By the turn of the century some
two hundred settlements were dotted about in immigrant, working-
class neighborhoods, including some settlements whose accomplishments would bring high visibility in progressive America: Jane
Addams' Hull House, Chicago (1889), Robert A. Woods' South
End House in Boston (1891), and Lillian Wald's Henry Street Settlement on the Lower East Side, New York (1893). By 1911, with
the founding of the National Federation of Settlements, they numbered nearly six hundred.

Founders of these settlements, in their initial stages, had little
idea of program; they sought, rather, simply to bear witness to their
human concern for demoralized neighborhoods and for their dis-
possessed neighbors. The gesture of going to live in an urban slum
partook, in some measure, of a Victorian romantic notion of the
inherent goodness of all human beings, the vitality of folk cultures,
and of a nostalgia for coherent, organic communities. Perhaps by
establishing personal relations across the chasms of class, religion,

nationality, and culture, some kind of reconciliation would come to pass. Settlement leaders, like charity leaders, had been made anxious by the consequences that flowed from the transformation of American society in the latter decades of the nineteenth century, but those who took up neighborhood work, more often as a mission than as a career, tended to be younger than the charity workers, better educated, of good family background (though rarely of great wealth), and in temperament altogether more open, hopeful, and democratic. Their leaders numbered hundreds of college-educated women who chose neighborhood work both as a way of life and as a means of accomplishing significant professional work in all those public spheres that lay beyond the confined homes of nuclear, middle-class families.

Their vision of society tended to be pluralistic rather than unitary. They instituted informal opportunities for their immigrant neighbors to learn the English language and to pick up American habits and customs on their way to naturalized citizenship, but they sought as well to preserve and extend that wide array of old-world customs that their neighbors expressed through music, art, dance, folk festivals, and family structures and styles. Most charity leaders, like most "progressive" Americans in that generation, feared and opposed the movement to organize labor; settlement leaders, on the other hand, saw unionization, especially the organization of young working women, as one means to introduce a bit of balance into the labor market through collective bargaining, and a way, thereby, to advance self-determination of economic groups and promote social justice. Rather than visiting the poor, settlement residents proposed to share the same neighborhood space with their immigrant neighbors. They exalted fraternalism over paternalism and, as the motto of one settlement house summed it up, they wished not to be their brothers' keeper, but their brothers' brother.[21]

In the writings of settlement leaders of that pioneer generation —and they were an articulate lot with both the written and the spoken word—recurred concepts and phrases that made manifest their ideological system: fellowship, spontaneity, involvement, social democracy, a shared life, self-governance, order without authority, spiritual awakening, ethical culture, and the like. Their philosophical ideas were derived from nineteenth-century English and European social critics and reformers: Christian socialism from Kingsley and Maurice, from Mazzini a belief in the culturally liberating force of nationalism that would reach out to embrace all of humanity (as presumably did Lincoln's common-man republicanism), from Ruskin's sense of the dignity of labor and the mystique of craft, and from Tolstoy's conviction of the sacredness of labor, the dignity of common people, and the moral necessity of peace among classes and nations.[22]

Reality often departed from rhetoric, of course. A commitment to cultural pluralism and social democracy could never fully wash out a lingering patronizing air toward lower-class and immigrant orders. It proved awkward to establish true sorority between settlement women and young women working in the textile and garment industries. Many of the immigrant neighbors—especially the menfolk—remained suspicious of settlement house programs, which they saw as intrusive and manipulative. On the other hand, settlement house leaders played prominent roles in initiating such organizations as the Urban League, the National Association for the Advancement of Colored People, and the Women's Trade Union League. Later, in the war years, 1914-1918, they were prime movers in various peace societies—the Women's International League for Peace and Freedom most notably—and in the American Civil Liberties Union.

The settlements became "Spearheads for Reform" in that generation, to employ the designation assigned by their chief historian, Allen F. Davis. At the municipal level they agitated for progressive school systems and compulsory school attendance ordinances, for public sanitation for poor neighborhoods as for affluent residential districts, and for the creation of parks and playgrounds. They joined with other reform groups to seek from state government effective regulation of factory conditions, the severe regulation or prohibition of child labor, minimum wage and maximum hour rules especially for women workers, the creation of juvenile courts, workmen's compensation for industrial accidents, and public assistance for widows with dependent children. In the cresting years of social justice agitation just before the First World War, they crusaded at the national level for comprehensive social insurance, for the inauguration of a Children's Bureau, for the federal prohibition of child labor, and for the legal right of workers to organize through unions of their own choosing. Some settlement leaders came down on the conservative side of these social issues, but the most prominent and influential among them formed coalitions with like-minded reformers and succeeded in achieving these goals.

In the meantime, they went about their daily routine of neighborhood activities. Because working mothers had no place to leave their children, many settlements established day-care centers and kindergartens. They engaged in club activities for boys and girls and, in the evenings, for their mothers, and in the summer they escorted their young charges to settlement camps in the great out-of-doors. They sponsored open forums on pressing social issues, where all sides of a public controversy had a chance to be heard. They initiated programs of after-school sports, music, drama, arts, and crafts. They housed medical clinics and launched educational programs to raise standards of nutrition and health. Sometimes they provided office space to charity societies so they could work closer to their clients. From their ranks came playground supervisors, visiting nurses, officers of juvenile courts, and visiting teachers (forerunners of school social workers). From all this busyness evolved the methods of group work and community organization.

Crucial to the settlement strategy in the first generation was the principle of residency: that the staff and volunteers live in the neighborhood. College students, young women and men, often took up residence while attending classes, doing their neighborhood work in the evenings, weekends, and summers in return for room, board, and the experience of living on the cutting edge of social change. Living in the neighborhood, settlement residents knew firsthand the concrete, anecdotal realities of urban life, and they were more likely than other reformers to be stirred to social action because they knew firsthand and close-up what others knew secondhand at a safe social distance. In the interwar era residency gave way slowly to the forces of professionalization, and settlement work came to be directed by people who came to neighborhood houses from their homes in other sections of the city. By the end of the Second World War residency had all but disappeared, and neighborhood centers became social agencies, much like others in the voluntary sector, tucked securely under community chest umbrellas and focused on providing group activities for young people.

THE DIVERSITY OF WELFARE SYSTEMS
IN TWENTIETH-CENTURY AMERICA

In addition to charities and settlements, a great number of institutions and agencies sprang up in these years to attend, with specialized services and diverse structures, to social needs. These institutions and agencies were so many and so varied that no simple descriptive summary can begin to capture their range and complexity.[23]

Religious agencies continued to proliferate in the twentieth century. Catholic charities, for example, were coordinated at diocesan and national levels to serve the Catholic community better.[24] Institutions included orphanages, hospitals, and homes for the aged. Of larger significance were the efforts of non-custodial agencies to provide services for handicapped children and youths, prisoners and people on probation or parole, families caught up in intergenerational troubles, and the chemically dependent. Such organizations offered day care for children of working mothers, temporary shelters for troubled children and unwed mothers, foster placement, sports and recreation programs, summer camping, retreats for youths and adults, and the training of volunteers who were then assigned such services as reading to the blind and escorting children to museums or to sports and artistic events. Parishes sponsored big brother and big sister programs, scout troops, and diverse protective and character-building programs through the Catholic Youth Organization. During the Great Depression of the 1930s, Catholic agencies provided assistance to unemployed families and homeless transient men; during the 1960s they organized Head Start programs, inaugurated centers for disturbed children unable to attend daily school, initiated treatment programs for delinquent and drug-prone youth, and set up vocational services and neighborhood youth corps. Overseas relief services to refugees and other victims of war became part of their world outreach. The National Conference of Catholic Charities, founded in 1910, provided leadership and inspiration at the national level, published the *Catholic Charities Review*, sponsored national and regional conferences and workshops, and agitated for such measures as social insurance, housing and health legislation, and prison reform—crusades in which Monsignor John Ryan, for many years chief of the Social Action Department of the National Catholic Welfare Conference, was a prime mover.

The Jewish community expended similar energy and devotion in the same range of human services and social issues.[25] The Young Men's and Young Women's Hebrew Associations engaged in recreational and cultural enrichment programs along many of the same lines as the Young Men's and Young Women's Christian Associations. Jewish charities and benevolent societies coordinated their activities through a variety of institutional arrangements, in the twentieth century most notably through Jewish Family Service, whose member agencies dealt with immigrant settlements in the New World, employment, financial and medical assistance, vocational training, and child protection. Jewish community centers, which offered the kinds of programs that settlement houses had pioneered, coordinated their services through the National Jewish Welfare Board. Groups such as the Hebrew Sheltering and Immigrant Aid Society met the special needs of immigrants, and later of refugees, for legal and financial aid, housing, employment, and education.

Protestant churches, denominations, and ecumenical associations poured forth money and human energy in like causes and services. Like their Catholic and Jewish counterparts, Protestant efforts came to promote professional standards in human services and to coordinate their activities through diocesan, denominational, and national umbrella associations. Like the other religious communities they added social action and social reform to their agendas of social service. At the local level they were compelled regularly to shift their focus of activities to meet new challenges and opportunities and to adapt to changes in the economic, social, and legal environment.

Let one example suffice to show the flexibility that marked the programs of so many agencies in the voluntary sector. In 1882 the Episcopal Diocese of Minnesota founded in Minneapolis a Sheltering Arms home for orphaned and dependent children. Like many such shelters it provided temporary care rather than a permanent home for its young charges, returning children to their families just as soon as an emergency had passed. With changes in state child welfare codes, and with the inauguration in 1935 of Aid to Dependent Children, Sheltering Arms shifted its focus to care for child victims of polio, cooperating in that program with St. Barnabas Hospital and employing therapies of Sister Kenny's. When development of the Salk vaccine eliminated the need for such medical treatment, Sheltering Arms became, in 1955, a day school and research program for mentally retarded children. The public school system's drive in recent years to "mainstream" such children—in response to a Congressional Act of 1975 which required that all handicapped children be provided an appropriate public school education—led in turn to a decision by the board of Sheltering Arms to transform it into a foundation to help finance child care projects in the community. Such stories reflect the remarkable flexibility of agencies in the voluntary sector in adapting to new circumstances.[26]

Volunteers of America, Goodwill Industries, and the Salvation Army represent initiatives of evangelical Protestantism to perform good works while engaged in religious missions. Volunteers of America, founded in 1896 by the son and daughter-in-law of General William Booth of England's Salvation Army, turned at once to welfare work as a coordinate part of proselytizing. It launched work with prisoners, developed day nurseries, founded food and shelter depots and lodges for homeless men. It pursued such traditional lines of service as managing orphanages and maternity homes for unwed mothers and distributing gifts to the needy in the Christmas season, but it also sponsored summer camps for slum children, initiated vocational rehabilitation programs for transient single men, and was an effective force in gaining relaxation of rigid prison discipline and in inaugurating networks of support for people on parole. More recently, tapping federal government funds, it established housing complexes for elderly, low-income, and one-parent families; these included facilities for health, education, recreation, and counseling. This latter development represents a major trend of the most recent generation: agencies in the voluntary sector have carried on their work not only with the solicitation of funds through religious and community chest channels but have won grants or contracts from the government to accomplish their missions.

Goodwill Industries, originally Methodist in religious and social mission, began its work with down-and-out immigrants, hiring marginal workers to renovate clothing and household items that were then distributed to needy families. From such activities it quickly branched out into rescue missions, children's settlements, fresh air farms, and day nurseries; by the 1930s it had added services to the physically and mentally handicapped and formed a partnership with federal-state programs for vocational and social rehabilitation.

The Salvation Army, popularly known for its mission work with single men presumed by society to be alcoholic and "derelict," did creative work in places other than skid row. They did human salvage work (to employ their term), but also worked effectively with other constituencies as well. They worked with servicemen during two world wars, created an emergency relief program during the depression, worked at high professional levels with families above the poverty line, and worked with out-of-school unemployed youths in the 1960s.

Many agencies took on broad and miscellaneous assignments; others assumed more limited charges. Work with youth, for example, took on a special urgency in the early decades of the twentieth century, and hundreds of movements responded to the challenge. The YMCA and YWCA had been around for some years and they expanded their services. Boy Scouts, Girl Scouts, and Campfire Girls specialized in summer camping programs but staged "character-building" activities in all seasons. The 4-H movement, linked to agricultural extension programs, elaborated enrichment and leadership programs for rural youths. Churches and settlement houses and related agencies did group work with young people in a variety of settings. Big Brothers and Big Sisters brought adult volunteers into a surrogate family relationship with young boys and girls, providing role models and informal support, affection, and guidance for youngsters lacking such adult figures in their own families. Charities were transformed into family and children's agencies and applied casework and psychiatric social work methods to troubled families.

Often ignored by historians of welfare are the myriad societies indigenous to immigrant neighborhoods that provided self-help and social cohesion for particular ethnic groups. Every immigrant group founded mutual aid fraternal associations through which its members insured themselves against sickness, accident, and death. Benefits (and dues) were modest—as befits low-income, working-class conditions—but at least they offered a modicum of security, and at the last a decent burial. Around these mutual benefit societies gathered other social and cultural programs designed to solidify these ethnic communities. Each national group, in its turn, also created community centers—or "national homes" as they were often called—where immigrants did for themselves what settlement houses presumed to do for them. They probably found comfort and support first in their own religious and ethnic communities and turned for assistance to the institutions of the host society only as a last resort.

As for black families in the South or in the urban North, they too had to rely primarily on arrangements of their own making, for they were excluded from most mainline social supports, public and private. The functionally extended black family and the black church were the chief sources of mutual assistance within black communities. In addition, the black middle class and professional urban elite established for their own people a range of services modeled on what they observed in white society: orphanages, homes for respectable aged citizens, youth programs, and all the rest.

Later, beginning in the 1930s, another kind of self-help movement got underway. Alcoholics Anonymous set the tone and pioneered the strategies.[27] Bill Wilson, hospitalized for acute alcoholism for which he was told there was no hope, underwent a religious experience and emerged determined to establish a fellowship of afflicted people whose strength would emerge from self-help and self-support. Resisting formal organization, turning aside outside contributions, and rejecting the guidance of professional experts, members of local AA groups depended solely on each other. Never part of any welfare system or network, AA remained autonomous and strong. Its success is best marked, perhaps, by the proliferation of self-help groups that have modeled themselves on AA philosophy and strategy: groups of people dependent on chemicals other than alcohol, self-support groups composed of the recently divorced, single parents, paroled prisoners, battered women, battering men, victims of cancer or heart disease, and other groups of troubled people who share an affliction and are dedicated to helping themselves by standing together and supporting each other.

EFFORTS TO COORDINATE HUMAN SERVICES
IN THE VOLUNTARY SECTOR

Given the number and variety of social agencies and their diversity in funding, structure, target clientele, management, philosophical and religious ideology, and therapeutic strategies, no wonder efforts to coordinate their activities have been a persisting and important part of welfare in the private sector.

One initiative, meant both to rationalize services and to raise levels of professional education and practice, came with the creation of national umbrella associations in different specialized fields.[28] The National Conference of Charities and Correction, founded in the mid-1870s to provide an annual forum where up-to-date programs and methods could be shared among providers of social services from all fields, continued to play that informational role. In 1917, reflecting the trend toward professionalism, it changed its name to the National Conference of Social Work, and again in 1956 to the National Conference on Social Welfare, the latter to reflect the commitment of the private welfare sector to issues of public policy. In 1911 social workers active in family service created an Association for Organizing Social Work which became, in the 1930s, the Family Welfare Association of America, and in 1946 the Family Service Association. Under whatever name, the national office assisted local agencies through its field service, through research and publication, and through conferences and workshops; with its affiliates it worked to promote the expansion of local departments of public welfare, the development of local community councils, and the enactment of social insurance and related welfare legislation. Building on this precedent, leaders in children's services created the Child Welfare League of America in 1920.

And so it went in other fields—the National Council on Crime and Delinquency (1907), the National Committee for Mental Hygiene (1909), the National Federation of Settlements (1911), the National Urban League (1911), Travelers Aid Association of America (1917), the American Foundation for the Blind (1921), the American Child Health Association (1923), and the American

Ortho-psychiatric Association (1924), to cite only a few out of hundreds of such national federations. The National Social Work Council (1923), now the National Assembly of National Voluntary Health and Social Welfare Organizations, was a holding company of such umbrella associations as those listed above; it encouraged cooperation among diverse agencies at the community level and urged its member societies to engage in social action and legislative lobbying. An accurate and comprehensive census of such coordinating leagues has never been compiled, but surely their number in any given year between 1920, let us say, and the present would be in excess of 150. In addition, there were a number of philanthropic foundations that sponsored basic research and its practical application in welfare fields—the Russell Sage Foundation (influential in the development of scientific social casework), the Foundation for Child Development, the Bureau of Jewish Social Research, the Rockefeller and Ford Foundations, and hundreds of others.

In communities throughout the nation the community chest movement (known today as the United Way) led the coordination of local services in the private sector. The impulse sprang initially from efforts, launched in Cleveland in 1913 and in some 25 other cities by 1917, at joint fund raising and budget planning. The emergencies of war encouraged the rapid expansion of "war chests," whose funds were expended on overseas servicemen, in military encampments, and on the home front. In the years that followed, representatives of participating agencies created community councils, parallel to the chests, to provide professional advice on the allotment of funds and the monitoring of projects. Leaders of business interests hoped that by coordinated fund raising and allotment the base of philanthropic giving would be enlarged and that they themselves would be spared the harassment of special appeals made by hundreds of local agencies. The executive directors and boards of social agencies hoped, for their part, to achieve more reliable financial bases for their own operations and hoped as well to be able to raise the provision of services to higher levels of efficiency and effectiveness. In large measure these expectations were fulfilled; however, purely budgetary considerations often played the primary role in shaping community priorities. Budgeting tended to be incremental, just a bit more total funding from year to year (or decremental in bad years); this meant that when new and authentic social needs were identified, local chests found it difficult to respond until new sources and higher levels of funding were achieved. This system dictated a natural prudence in the allocation process: established agencies using traditional methods and pursuing conservative goals were favored, while projects that threatened to rock the boat were treated with skepticism if not downright hostility. Settlement houses and neighborhood centers that fell under community chest influence tended to moderate their social action and to concentrate on club work, recreation, arts, and sports. During the tumultuous years of the 1960s, heroic efforts had to be exerted to persuade chests and councils to attend to the special needs of minorities.

Coordination of services was one major theme; another, closely related, was the urge toward professionalism and the transformation thereby of the role of volunteers. The founding of professional schools of social work constituted an important phase in this process—by 1980 75 professional schools offered graduate degrees, and over 100 offered undergraduate certification programs. The establishment of national professional associations began in 1917 with the founding of the American Association of Social Workers; there quickly followed special professional societies for people certified for service in hospital, medical, psychiatric, school, group work, and community organization settings. All of these associations merged into one National Association of Social Work in 1955.

Diversity has clearly been the chief mark of social services in the voluntary sector; it is a complexity of form, structure, motive, and consequence that this chapter has been able to survey only briefly. Given the vast increase in public assistance and in formal government programs that has taken place since the depression and New Deal, the persisting significance of the voluntary sector in shaping human services is a wonder. There is no definitive accounting of all this activity, but conservative estimates are that non-profit agencies and institutions in health and welfare fields spend about $40 billion of their own funds every year, and another $60 billion through government grants and contracts or through fee-for-service activities.[29] These enterprises involve the labors of hundreds of thousands of professional persons and volunteers, full- and part-time.

Experimentation in styles and modes of human service delivery systems probably derives chiefly from diverse efforts in the private sector, where structural arrangements tend to be less rigid and less bureaucratic than they are under public control, although clearly the major responsibility for financial assistance rests with complex transfer programs subsidized and managed by local, state, and federal government. As other chapters in this book will show, myriad private agencies—religious, sectarian, and secular— continue to perform significant functions. Added to the healing, ameliorative, preventive, and advocacy work of traditional agencies has been the rapid proliferation of self-help groups and the persisting authority of informal, often spontaneous, helping networks.[30]

The American dedication to welfare in the private sector is in some part mythic and legendary, but in large part real and vital to the well-being of contemporary society.

2

The Urban Voluntary Sector:
An Exploration of Basic Issues[1]

JENNIFER R. WOLCH

Although the voluntary sector is an important component of a city's vitality, it remains poorly understood and is seldom studied by social scientists. Past studies of voluntary organizations and their role in economic and social life have focussed on the nation as a whole, whereas the direct impact of voluntary sector activity is manifest at the urban level. Our ignorance about urban voluntarism poses an increasingly critical problem due to the economic events of the late 1970s and early 1980s. Public spending cutbacks, prompted by recession and political ideology, have hurt many cities, creating severe problems in urban service provision. The burden of providing such collective goods has been shifted to other institutional sectors, including voluntary organizations, many of which are themselves struck by resource scarcity. Their ability to bear additional responsibilities is only now beginning to be evaluated.

The process of evaluation has raised a number of basic issues concerning the nature of the urban voluntary sector, issues that have been the subject of a recent research program (Wolch and Geiger, 1983; Reiner and Wolpert, 1981). This chapter will explore several questions. What types of organizations are engaged in voluntary activity, and how much of the nation's resources do they control? How is voluntary activity related to other facets of the urban economy? In what ways does the voluntary sector contribute to urban population welfare, social patterning, and economic development? And with an eye to public policy, can the voluntary sector act as a "shadow state," substituting for the government in certain functions? Or are calls for a heightened reliance on voluntary effort only political ploys—to mitigate the contraction of public sector activity in American life?

These are fundamental questions, hard to answer because the evidence is so scarce. On the basis of information that is available, I argue that the voluntary sector is basic to the economic prospects of cities and to the well-being of urban residents. It can also be argued that the sector is troubled by contradictory imperatives which tend to offset beneficial outcomes. On the surface the urban voluntary sector is bland and benevolent, useful and worthy of public support. At the same time, it may have unintended consequences, aggravating the very problems that voluntary activity typically seeks to redress.

DEFINITION AND STRUCTURE OF THE URBAN VOLUNTARY SECTOR

The urban voluntary sector includes donors, donees, and passthrough organizations. Donors make cash and in-kind contributions, donees or recipient agencies procure or provide services for purposes other than profit, and passthrough or mediating organizations solicit and channel resources from donors to recipients (Weisbrod, 1977). Recipient organizations, in the process of producing various goods and services, generate employment and demand for intermediate goods (e.g., facilities, equipment), which in turn augment the private economy and donors. The flow of voluntary resources throughout the sector is illustrated in Figure 2-1.

This definition of the voluntary sector is very broad, subsuming what elsewhere is termed the non-profit sector, the charitable or philanthropic sector, the "third" sector, and the so-called independent sector. Under this definition fall an enormous number and variety of firms and organizations. On the donor side are foundations established by private families, communities, or corporations; bequests; corporations with giving programs; individual donors; and governmental contracting or grant-making agencies. Governmental "donations," of course, originate mainly in tax payments, and hence government is a "passthrough" of sorts.

Figure 2-1. The Flow of Voluntary Resources

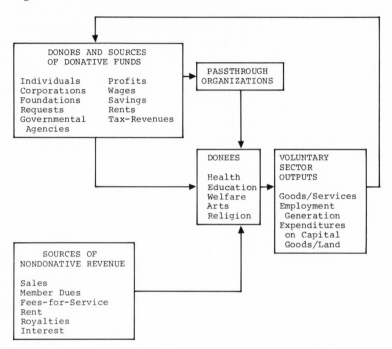

Taxpayers via the government provide approximately 60 percent of donee revenues from gifts and grants and about 30 percent of total revenues (United States Department of Treasury, 1977; Salamon and Abramson, 1982). Public support varies among sectors of interest—for example, health, education, welfare, the arts. In addition to direct dollars, the public sector subsidizes voluntary groups through tax expenditures in the form of deductibility allowances for charitable contributions, as well as income and property tax exemptions for non-profit donors and donees. Tax code provisions reduce the production costs for non-profit corporations, require foundation asset disbursement to donees, and have historically been effective incentives to private giving to voluntary organizations. Aside from government, national data on the relative size of donor groups indicate that individuals give the largest share of cash gifts—85 percent of non-governmental donations;

bequests, foundations, and corporations each contribute about 5 percent. Almost one-half of all individual gifts are targeted to religious purposes, while gifts to religious causes by other donor groups are negligible. Thus for non-religious activities, the relative importance of other donor groups is considerably greater; their share of total non-governmental donations rises to 10 percent each, and the share donated by individuals falls to about 70 percent (American Association of Fund Raising Officials, 1980). In addition to cash donations, all types of non-governmental donors (except bequests) provide in-kind services such as facilities, goods, and most importantly, labor. The case equivalent value of labor donated by individuals or through the corporate or foundation sector has been estimated to be approximately equivalent to cash donations (Weisbrod, 1977).

On the recipient side, service-providing organizations include archetypal voluntary institutions such as the church, the museum, the voluntary hospital, and the soup kitchen. In addition, there is a plethora of special interest agencies, not to mention innumerable civic groups, widows' funds, homeowners' associations, and recreation clubs. Recipient organizations can be characterized on the basis of their main purposes; common categorizations identify at least five groups: social welfare and community services, health, education, the arts, and religion. Nationwide, 10 percent of voluntary recipient organization revenues is targeted to social welfare and community services, 14 percent each to health and education, 6 percent to arts and culture, 47 percent to religion, and the remainder to miscellaneous civic and internationally oriented activities (American Association of Fund Raising Officials, 1980).

Recipients in each purpose category fall into two groups distinguished by sources of revenue. Some voluntary recipient organizations receive the bulk of their revenues from private and individual corporate donations, government and foundation grants, and allocations from passthrough agencies. This dependence on collective income to finance services to users not necessarily charged fees for services defines these organizations as philanthropies. In contrast, other organizations rely on fees and member dues, and other quasi-market sources of revenue such as the sale of goods, rents, and interest. These are member-benefit agencies, designed primarily for member or paying-user benefit. The philanthropy and member-benefit distinction is important but not clear-cut: some member-benefit organizations assess dues but use them to provide services to needy clients, while donors to philanthropies may derive direct benefits as well as tax savings from their contributions. Nonetheless, philanthropies tend to be more collective and redistributive than member-benefit organizations.

Donation patterns across cities may be quite different from what the national averages suggest. Unfortunately, urban data on donor activities are not available, so the identification of factors determining urban donation patterns is nearly impossible. However, fragmentary evidence indicates that the amounts given by various donor groups vary with the socioeconomic status and ethnicity of urban populations, urban industrial structure and health, and municipal traditions of private and public service provision. Compared to other groups, the affluent give much, as do certain religious orders, whites, blue-collar workers, and corporations in industry groups such as finance and manufacturing. Not surprisingly, corporate giving fluctuates with the prosperity of the times, and older cities with long philanthropic traditions have more donative funds than new cities more reliant on public provision (Feldstein, 1974; Reece, 1979; Schwartz, 1970; United States Department of Treasury, 1977).

In the small sample of cities where such data exist, targeting patterns mirror the nation, although there are fluctuations over time and differing patterns of change among cities. Thus far, no analyses have been done to illuminate the reasons for differences or similarities in urban targeting patterns. However, the general correspondence of patterns in cities with vastly divergent needs suggests that donor preferences for giving may diverge from the pattern suggested by population requirements. This is apt to be particularly true in newer cities, where donors lead the way in establishing initial priorities for young voluntary agencies dependent in their early years on private donations (Wolpert and Reiner, 1982).

CONTRIBUTIONS AND CONTRADICTIONS OF URBAN VOLUNTARY ACTIVITY

Research on voluntarism and the history of philanthropy reveals that voluntary activity can and has stimulated important improvements in the quality of urban life, and has generated new opportunities for urban residents. However, in almost every area in which the sector's activity augments the urban experience, certain aspects of voluntary structure and functioning create serious internal contradictions which can offset desirable effects. In this section, both positive and detrimental effects of urban voluntary activity are outlined, in realms of service provision, social interaction and structure, sociopolitical stability, metropolitan economic development, and redistribution.

Service Provision. Voluntary organization offers urban dwellers who are unsatisfied with local or central government provision of public services a way to adjust their consumption of collective resources (Weisbrod, 1977). If the levels or types of public sector services fall short of individual desires or community needs, voluntary action can create new sources of service supply or augment existing public programs. Voluntary association can thus be relied upon to fill the gap between service delivery and demands for services among the population, satisfying individual preferences. This is particularly true in cities where population demands for public services are extremely heterogeneous, because in this instance government cannot respond adequately to all of its constituencies. While voluntary activity may be useful as a consumption adjustment mechanism, everyone pays for the welfare gains of those who benefit from this voluntarism: the tax incentives to give that reduce the "price" of beneficence, as well as tax exemptions for non-profit organizations, are public expenditures which must be paid for by the entire community.

Social Interaction and Structure. Voluntary organizations are social environments where husbands meet wives, children of strangers become friends, and an internal social cohesion is created in the process of helping the larger society outside. This generates social networks, binding the community fabric. But, like the family and school, local voluntary organizations are powerful avenues of socialization and training, of forming group identities, and reinforcing notions of "us" and "them" (Sills, 1968). They often define communities of interest and of territory: their voluntary structure requires ready physical access to meeting places and agreement on common values, goals, and means for goals achievement. In residentially differentiated cities, these characteristics produce purposive, territorially based groups with homogeneous memberships ready to lobby for their respective causes. Such socio-spatial segmentation of voluntary association deepens metropolitan fragmentation along the lines of class, race, and culture, often in the name of reducing the efforts of such fragmentation.

Sociopolitical Stability. Voluntary organization allows people to shape their own environments and life changes, helping to sustain the American dream of success through individual, voluntary initiative, despite unfavorable market conditions or government action. Yet like conceptions of political pluralism, belief in the efficacy of voluntarism is and historically has been an important safety valve which buffers the market and the state from attacks on legitimacy and performance, preventing social unrest and dampening demands for greater social justice (Whitacker, 1974; Stedman-Jones, 1971).

Publicly subsidized donor and recipient organizations augment the range of collective goods and their level of supply, while being almost unassailable on grounds of accountability, effectiveness, or equity of distribution. The state implements many service programs through contracts with voluntary organizations, and in some cases creates new non-profit agencies to carry out state service delivery mandates (Salamon and Abramson, 1982). Conversely, the voluntary sector may map the future terrain of the state, initiating services that become necessary for social stability and control, but that remain outside the realm of historically defined state interests. As such services become recognized and accepted as essential for public welfare, they can be appropriated from the voluntary sector and brought under the legitimate aegis of government with a minimum of political controversy (Donzelot, 1979; Kramer, 1981; Ryan, 1976). Furthermore, the state can invisibly support, through tax favoritism, institutions whose very purpose is to maintain peace and social stability—for example, the church.

Freedom to organize for personal and social betterment is a powerful antidote for popular dissatisfaction created by reductions in public welfare benefits. As Piven and Cloward (1981) point out, governments that attempt to curtail relief for the poor in order to control labor supply more effectively and to increase capital accumulation risk widespread resistance as public income supports become viewed as entitlements by the population. Even where the potential for change is circumscribed by political-economic conditions and power relationships between social classes, the alternative of voluntary organization can soften resistance to cutbacks in collective provisions. By subtly "blaming the victims" and requiring that they shoulder the burden for change, challenges to the structure of social relations are averted.

Metropolitan Development. The voluntary sector is a major locus of resources, employment, and production activity. In addition, it is an important component of urban political structure and a determinant of urban development.

Evidence to support these contentions exists only in bits and pieces. Resources of voluntary organizations derive from local and non-local profits, wages, and rents, and indirectly from the state in the form of tax expenditures, grants, and contracts. But because voluntary production has remained outside formal accounting systems, there are no comprehensive data on the size, scope, and local economic impact of the voluntary sector. To compound difficulties, a significant but poorly known portion of voluntary resources takes the form of donated labor, services, and facilities, none of which can be readily monitored or priced.

The most indicative estimates of voluntary sector size are not urban but national in scope. They are far from satisfactory or consistent, but they clearly indicate that cash contributions from non-governmental resources constitute approximately 2 percent of GNP and over 2 percent of disposable personal income (American Association of Fund Raising Officials, 1980). Non-cash revenue estimates indicate that the annual donation of labor is of an approximately equivalent value (Weisbrod, 1977; Dye, 1980). According to some estimates, in 1977 the nation's more than 750,000 recipient organizations received approximately $165 billion, or 9 percent of GNP and 13 percent of disposable personal income. Lower-bound estimates of donee organization revenues for the same year are $85 billion, or 5 percent of GNP (Salamon and Abramson, 1981). Approximately 8 percent of the labor force is directly employed in the voluntary sector, but in some cities the voluntary sector employs up to 24 percent (Wolpert and Reiner, 1982; United States Department of Treasury, 1977). The combined assets of donor organizations, such as foundations and trusts, and recipient groups represent more than 15 percent of total U.S. private wealth (Weisbrod, 1977).

The local picture varies among cities but again indicates the consequential nature of the voluntary sector in the metropolitan economy. Estimates for a sample of voluntary recipient organizations in four metropolitan areas in 1976—Los Angeles, Houston, Philadelphia, and Minneapolis—are suggestive. These estimates do not include data for smaller organizations or religious organizations, so they represent a lower-bound approximation of voluntary sector size in each of the cities. Net revenues of this sample constituted between 2 and 6 percent of aggregate labor and proprietors' income received by area residents, while organizational assets ranged from 5 to 14 percent of the same base. Another sample for incorporated cities in Los Angeles County, accounting for more than 5000 voluntary organizations (foundations, trusts, and donee groups), offers a similar picture. This sample does not include churches, non-profit hospitals, or schools, but does include membership organizations and small organizations. For this segment of the voluntary sector, gross revenues constituted more than 4 percent of local aggregate labor and proprietors' income, while assets constituted more than 6 percent.[2]

While these are clearly crude, lower-bound estimates of urban voluntary sector size, they do highlight the direct contribution of the sector to metropolitan economies. Donors from within metropolitan areas and beyond are dumping resources into the local economy equivalent to those of a major industry. And, while there is no knowledge of local voluntary sector multipliers, they certainly exist.

Indirect contributions to urban economic development are perhaps of greater significance. First, the voluntary sector defines important regional characteristics influencing growth trajectories. It provides social capital and regional amenities which support, maintain, and enhance the quality of city life, and affect development chances (Richardson, 1973; Klaassen, 1968). For example, local non-profit educational institutions feed skilled labor and innovations into urban industrial sectors, building human capital and productivity potential. Local voluntary visual and performing arts centers are premier elements of a city's image—at least for the well-to-do—and are typically a focus of community life, as are parks and recreation facilities donated to cities. And social welfare and community services reduce social unrest and promote community stability.

Secondly, the voluntary sector plays a vital role in creating a favorable business climate for development. Donations by the business sector are tax-deductible purchases of community and employee goodwill, made in the enlightened self-interest of companies (Baumol, 1970). Local voluntary networks of health, social welfare, and community services constitute a "social wage" which can lower private wage bills and favorably influence negotiations over the distribution of income share between labor and capital. Moreover, many business leaders play dual roles as foundation directors and as board members, leaders of local united funds, and directors of major non-profit organizations such as universities, symphonies, and museums. These contributions of time expand their sphere of power and influence. Not surprisingly, what's good for the community often turns out to be good for their corporations. Giving may be used to enhance the lobbying power of politicians, managers, and planners, as well as vendors or other linked business interests, who can in turn facilitate production through land use, service delivery, public works decisions, and interfirm accommodations. At a lower level, many voluntary community service organizations are de facto business booster clubs working for better market conditions.

Unfortunately, the developmental role of voluntary activity is contradictory. Metropolitan areas in decline and most in need of development assistance are apt to have the least voluntary resources as incomes, profits, and rents falter. Growing areas, on the other hand, will have surpluses with which to build growth-enhancing social amenities and physical infrastructure. Moreover, the openness of urban economies means that voluntary resources are imported to and exported from regions; some regions are hence "hosts," others "parasites." Parasitic regions draw in voluntary resources from outside and experience a development boost at the expense of host areas unable to offset the outflow of voluntary funds with imports. Host status is often the outcome of metropolitan hardship, but it also accelerates deterioration; stocks of amenities and social income are depleted and disinvestment in local institutions, particularly on the part of corporations, signals to others a lack of community commitment, less-than-optimal business conditions, and perhaps an intention to migrate elsewhere (Wolpert, 1977). Unless such declining host regions have active voluntary organizations capable of maintaining resource levels, capital flight and population loss will create a local philanthropic crisis, harming those who remain (Reiner and Wolpert, 1981; Wolch, 1982). Thus, the voluntary sector, while working to enhance local economic conditions when regions are on the upswing, can in fact exacerbate interregional disparities in welfare and accelerate trends toward unbalanced regional growth.

Redistribution. Voluntarism satisfies individual desires for redistribution over and above the redistribution effected by government (Hochman and Rogers, 1973). Benefit distributions resulting from the donations may fall short of a social optimum (because of poor information concerning needs, inadequate resources of donors, and so on), but such redistribution can help meet needs close to home.

Can voluntary activity reduce inequalities in the long run? Redistribution benefits recipients, but it also benefits donors who see others assisted while retaining discretion over how and to whom their gifts are targeted (Becker, 1974). When philanthropic dollars and good deeds are bestowed only when donors target them to eligible or approved recipient groups, gifts cannot be given or received in anonymity. As Wolpert (1977) points out, "Anonymity implies adherence to a social contract which links donors and recipients who perform a service for one another in a symmetrical network. The network could be reversed. . . . The distinction between donors and recipients can be transitory" (p. 222). Lack of anonymity leads to asymmetry in social relations, to an implicit class relationship. In cities where the affluent fill their needs at the marketplace but the poor must rely on collective provision, giving is decidedly one-way, from rich donors to poorer recipients, reinforcing extant class distinctions. Since the poor cannot reciprocate, society establishes the quid pro quo, conferring upon donors prestige, community recognition, and an elevated position in the social hierarchy. Such an exchange thus reinforces the very imbalances in power, status, and opportunity that redistributive philanthropy and voluntarism seek to redress.

Despite such contradictions inherent in giving to promote greater social equity, we can ask the more pragmatic question: Is the spatial distribution of voluntary resources in cities equitable, and can local voluntarism effectively redistribute goods and services to needy communities?

Very little is known about the circulation patterns of voluntary resources in metropolitan areas, but per capita voluntary revenues in jurisdictions within metropolitan areas are vastly divergent and do not vary inversely with median community income.[3] This implies that although the (disproportionate) tax benefits from contributions accrue to residents of wealthier areas, donative funds either do not stray far from home or are exported from the region. They are not redistributed efficiently to less well-off communities, who nonetheless bear part of the burden of tax favoritism.

This inequitable outcome is not really surprising. The basic structure of voluntarism stands in the path of redistribution within cities. Voluntary organizations have a huge range of motives, typically related to benefactor wishes rather than community requirements. Furthermore, the sector is atomistic in that activities are rarely coordinated. Voluntary organizations face severe information problems in regard to who needs what, in locating potential donors, and in securing contributions. Even the largest donor and recipient organizations frequently have no systematic plan for assessing needs or allocating resources to people or places. In rapidly changing cities, inertia is the main guide to targeting efforts (Wolpert and Reiner, 1980).

The fragmentation of modern cities into exclusive enclaves, working-class districts, and ghettos also reduces the potential of the voluntary sector to meet the needs of city residents for collective goods. Residents can avoid both redistributive taxation and pressure to aid the needy voluntarily by forming homogeneous political units at the local level (Tiebout, 1956). As cities are fractured along lines of income, race, and class, social distance and distrust obstruct the flow of gifts between districts with differential resources. Isolation from those in need of assistance relieves the obligation to help, shifting the attention of donors to non-local problems.

Voluntary activity will therefore be neither equitable nor efficient in redressing disparities in the quality of life within cities. Urban voluntarism serves many vital functions but it clearly cannot be responsible for local redistribution. Its inability to perform such functions effectively is one reason that public social programs came to supplant the workhouse, the paternalistic donor, and the charity organization.

IMPLICATIONS OF RECENT PUBLIC POLICY SHIFTS

The Reagan administration has implemented cutbacks and elimi-
nation of many federally funded social service programs, reducing
the national social spending budget by over $12 billion (constant
1980 dollars) in 1982 (Salamon and Abramson, 1982). This was
accomplished through the tightening of eligibility rules, reductions
in cost-of-living increases for public aid recipients, and program
closures. The result for social services in 1982 was a 38 percent cut
in total spending (adjusted for inflation) from 1981 levels (Palmer
and Sawhill, 1982). These cuts caused a 43 percent drop in Title XX
social services funding, a 35 percent cut in child welfare programs,
a 27 percent reduction in programs for the elderly, a 42 percent cut
in rehabilitation funding, an 83 percent drop in community services
moneys, and a 38 percent reduction in other social services. Mental
health funds were reduced 29 percent during the 1980-1982 period,
and regulatory changes in Medicare and Medicaid implied reductions
in health care services to low-income and indigent groups. Budget
revisions for 1982 specified an additional $2 billion reduction in
AFDC and Foodstamp outlays, while new guidelines for the states
permitted local governments to discontinue targeting human service assistance to Supplemental Security Income and AFDC recipients to slash reporting requirements, to eliminate planning and
public participation requirements, and to allow states and localities
to employ their own income eligibility rules for some programs
(Palmer and Sawhill, 1982).

These cuts imposed significant losses on some segments of the
population. For example, 700,000 people lost all or part of their
welfare benefits, 1.1 million lost Foodstamp benefits, 900,000 lost
public service jobs, and an estimated 137,156 families are estimated
to have moved into poverty status (a 1.5 percent increase in the
number of poor families) because of AFDC and Foodstamp cuts
alone (Congressional Quarterly, Inc., 1982; Palmer and Sawhill,
1982).

This gutting of social programs has been accompanied by slogans
in praise of voluntary service. According to this rhetoric, "We've
let Government take away many things we once considered were
really ours to do voluntarily out of the goodness of our hearts and a
sense of community pride and neighborliness" (Ronald Reagan,

New York Times, September 27, 1981). No one would lose, according to this view, as welfare statism is overturned in favor of the tried and true American way of local self-sufficiency through voluntary action, and in fact the country should come out ahead. A governmental social safety net would be reinforced by private voluntary efforts to meet the needs of the aged, disabled, and poor, and the needs of the nation for cultural enrichment.

But the social safety net cannot be sewn at home. The reliance of the urban voluntary sector on public funds and indirect subsidies, and the inherent inability of the sector to redistribute resources effectively, belies the myth of voluntarism as a substitute for public action. The dependence of voluntary agencies on government assistance and private market prosperity obliterates any role they might have as an independent alternative to government supply. The integration of the voluntary sector into public and private spheres of economic activity exacerbates already severe cyclical problems, with downturns creating fiscal problems for government and reducing voluntary production—in turn promoting the downturn. Cutbacks in government philanthropy, the single largest source of voluntary sector funds, will not be replaced by private sources during periods of recession. To offset federal government cutbacks in grants and contracts to voluntary agencies, estimated to decrease total voluntary sector revenues by 27 percent by 1985, private giving would have to increase by 30 to 40 percent, or three to four times its historical rate. To fill the gap in public and voluntary services brought about by the federal cutbacks, private giving would have to increase by 90 to 100 percent, or eight times faster than its historical growth rate—highly unlikely during a boom, much less a deep recession (Salamon and Abramson, 1982). Instead of increasing incentives to private giving, recent tax cuts vastly reduce the corporate income tax, negating any tax-based incentives to business giving, and greatly ease inheritance gift taxes, which stimulated private giving in the past. The personal income tax cuts also curtail incentives to individual giving, by increasing the after-tax "price" of contributions and thus offsetting any increase in the rate of contributions occasioned by income gains (Clotfelter and Salamon, 1981).

Cutbacks in federal support do not affect all segments of the voluntary sector evenly: some areas are much more severely hurt than others. Social welfare services, community development, and the arts will lose more than 60 percent of their federal funds by 1985. Social service agencies lost almost $2 billion in 1982, accounting for more than 40 percent of the total cuts in federal support to nonprofit organizations during that fiscal year. Health care, on the other hand, will be less affected and is slated to capture 75 percent of all such federal support to voluntary organizations by 1985, reflecting a drastic shift in national social priorities (Salamon and Abramson, 1982).

The reduction in voluntary resources prompted by recession, fiscal austerity, and tax policy will hit cities hard, especially those already in decline. Localized downturns and public sector plight multiply population needs but reduce funds for voluntary groups now denied moneys from the federal government. Localities can raise fees for non-redistributive services (e.g., garbage), but locally initiated redistributive services will only reinforce urban decay and will not in any event be tolerated, as witnessed by the spreading fiscal limitations movements. Furthermore, the inefficiency of local voluntary redistribution impedes redress of growing income disparities within cities. Despite increasing levels of voluntary organization and action, the structure of urban areas is a major barrier to income redistribution. The poor will give to the still more impoverished in their own communities, but resources from the more affluent zones will either fail to flow to needy neighborhoods or will elude the region altogether.

Our understanding of the voluntary sector and its relationships to the state, market, and social groups is limited. In particular, the role of the voluntary sector in urban systems is only beginning to emerge. New theoretical frameworks are needed: to elucidate the spatial organization and dynamics of voluntary activities and revenue flows within cities and among regions, to delineate linkages between voluntary action and the agendas of competing interests in society, and to explicate the role of the voluntary sector as a "shadow state" used in subtle and complex ways by both the market and the state. Further, a wide range of historical and cross-sectional analysis is required to validate new theories of voluntarism as they emerge, and to enrich theoretical understanding of the voluntary sphere in regard to time, place, and culture.

Nonetheless, existing evidence provides important clues about the voluntary sector in cities. Voluntary organization and service provision are central to the quality and continuity of urban life, particularly in the United States. They provide health, welfare, educational, religious, community, environmental, and cultural services that are indispensable for social stability and a smoothly functioning economy. Despite the closeness of everyday existence, urban residents retain the freedom to give to those they know as well as to strangers, and to satisfy the needy through voluntary association and cooperative effort. They thereby augment governmental services and market goods, contributing to greater levels of social satisfaction. Moreover, voluntary services and amenities are key components of the urban economy. They stimulate metropolitan economic growth by providing jobs and income, by increasing the productivity of the urban labor force, and by creating physical and political conditions essential to urban development.

But at the same time, voluntary sector activity carries with it social costs. First, organizations claim voluntary non-profit status and therefore receive public subsidies, but in fact many of them produce quasi-market goods or are established to pursue political objectives. This calls into question the desirability of continued tax favoritism and raises the issue of equity losses and opportunity costs of the current blanket tax exemption rules. Second, voluntary activities can reinforce social and spatial inequality in cities. As defenders of local causes and prerogatives, territorially based voluntary agencies often serve to underscore social division. Moreover, they may redirect attention away from larger-scale issues that actually fuel local problems. Third, the interregional dynamics of the voluntary sector can heighten economic disparities among regions as social resources flow to growth areas, leaving hardpressed, declining regions to face shortages of collective goods. In sum, voluntary action can aggravate the very problems it seeks to remedy.

Intimate links to both the public sector and the private sector belie the notion that the voluntary sector is independent—indeed, it could be more appropriately dubbed the dependent sector. Voluntary organizations depend heavily on government grants, contracts, and programs, as well as relying on individual, foundation, and corporate donations for funds. Even member-benefit groups rely on general market conditions to enable members and users to purchase their goods and services. Thus, slogans heralding a return to local voluntary action to meet community needs are seriously misleading, because the capacity of the sector to maintain levels of service provision has been severely eroded by recession and by contraction of government social programs. The political rhetoric surrounding the voluntary sector serves only to blind the public to a harsh restructuring of American political and economic life.

3

Religious Groups and Institutions

The contemporary human service delivery systems of American religious communities have emerged from an array of models—benevolent societies, charity organizations, settlement houses, and mutual aid societies—developed in the nineteenth century and from their participation in a triangular partnership with government agencies and community agencies in the twentieth century. Elements of the nineteenth-century models continue in their delivery systems despite the substantial transformations brought about by involvement in the triangular partnership over the past 50 years.

While religious communities have achieved strong capabilities in their delivery systems since World War II, they are now stressed by shifts in financial resources, dramatic increases in the needs of client populations, rapid development of national and regional investor-owned and proprietary human service corporations, and public social policy ambiguities that emerged from the rhetoric of the 1980 presidential election campaign—a campaign that deeply aroused old conflicts in the American psyche about social responsibility for the vulnerable and the poor in our society. What remains constant, however, are the motivation and sustaining rationale of the Judaic ethic of charity, justice, and righteousness, the Christian gospel, and a humanitarian spirit born of the Judeo-Christian tradition that undergirds a commitment to human service systems.

In this chapter the development of the human service delivery systems of American religious communities, their contemporary forms and structures, and their probable futures will be examined. The focus will be on the complex dynamics of the triangular partnership of the past 50 years and on probable future developments in the American social welfare system.

NINETEENTH-CENTURY STRATEGIES

The processes of industrialization and urbanization dominated nineteenth-century America as successive waves of immigrants attracted by new opportunities in America came first from western and northern Europe and then from southern and eastern Europe. Vast numbers of immigrants crowded into the teeming urban centers, providing cheap, unskilled labor to burgeoning industries that, on the one hand, generated investment capital and great family fortunes but; on the other hand, created an industrial working class. Many workers were continuously confronted with economic and environmental conditions that made existence marginal, precarious, and hazardous.

Because the informal systems of assistance and surveillance and the networks of mutual assistance which had prevailed in colonial America no longer sufficed, new welfare strategies were necessary to cope with the social disorders and problems of the rapidly growing urban centers that were heavily affected by immigrants and industries.

In the first half of the century the two principal strategies were the creation of public institutions (e.g., poorhouses, insane asylums, reformatories, penitentiaries) as sanctuaries for paupers, orphans, and deviants, and the formation of voluntary benevolent societies that were often closely connected with local parishes or religious denominations and were supported by wealthy families and the philanthropy of an emerging middle class.[1]

While religious concerns informed many of their programs, benevolent societies became a very diverse group. The religious enthusiasm of the Second Great Awakening among Protestants brought about a fusion of evangelism and charity symbolized by the city mission. To resist Protestant influence in their Irish and

German parishes, Catholic leaders created special orders, some of which still exist. Some benevolent societies were organized to provide services to special constituencies. Others were the expression of the particular motives and beliefs of a single strong personality, as had been the founding of settlement houses in the post-Civil War period.

After the Civil War, massive waves of immigration brought tens of thousands of people, who settled in the old urban areas. Others came to new urban areas and the frontier lands. As newcomers, they moved with or sought out their own kind, and were sometimes forced through discrimination to do so. A principal result was the continuation of a pattern of relatively homogeneous ethnic-religious communities in both urban and rural areas. In this context indigenous networks of care and informal systems of mutual assistance developed as they had in the ethnic-religious communities prior to the Civil War.

The focus of the mutual aid model is the gemeinschaft quality of these networks and systems. Whether from western or northern Europe, or later from eastern and southern Europe, whether rural or urban, members of the ethnic-religious communities supported one another and their families through the vicissitudes of life together in America. Their shared cultural life and religious beliefs were cohesive forces that promoted the practice of mutual aid and assistance in every immigrant group throughout America.

Leadership was provided primarily by the educated clergy, who accompanied the immigrants to America or who arrived shortly after settlement was established. Sharing the people's social and cultural heritage as they usually did, the clergy identified with and nourished the language and customs of the people. Immigrants depended on them for counsel and assistance not only in their religious life, but also in civic and family matters. Thus, the clergy provided support services for all phases of coping with the New World.

Native-born clergy continued these roles in the ethnic-religious communities for several generations, adding hospitals, orphanages, community centers, settlement houses, and homes for the aged as institutional expressions of mutual aid. Out of their experiences with informal networks of mutual aid, the formation of mutual benefit societies and indigenous institutions emerged as the base for a more diversified service delivery system in the early decades of the twentieth century.

By and large the immigrants did not demand much for their welfare, even from local government. Public aid was a last resort and, in the latter part of the nineteenth century, both public aid and private charity became "mean and niggardly." If immigrants had a choice, they probably avoided the "truly needy" and "truly worthy" tests of eligibility that imposed a negative public image upon them and their families, preferring the social comfort and self-help possibilities of mutual aid in the ethnic-religious community.

In urban areas there were other major strategies. As Clarke Chambers points out, "By the turn of the century, some two hundred settlement (houses) were dotted about in immigrant, working-class neighborhoods . . . ; by 1911, with the founding of the National Federation of Settlements, they numbered nearly six hundred . . . ; they instituted informal opportunities for their immigrant neighbors to learn the English language and to pick up American habits and customs on their way to naturalized citizenship."[2]

In addition, as Chambers emphasizes, out of the initiatives of evangelical Protestantism to perform welfare work while engaged in religious missions came Goodwill Industries and Volunteers of America, a derivative of the Salvation Army. By the turn of the century, Goodwill also had begun a broad array of services in the prisons and the slums, among the down-and-out immigrants and the homeless, including those on skid row.[3] These were significant initiatives in urban America at the beginning of the twentieth century.

Given the array of strategies devised in the nineteenth century to alleviate all the human troubles spawned by rapid industrialization and urbanization among a largely immigrant population, it is not surprising that the leaders of the voluntary sector turned to coordination and to umbrella organizations. Before the turn of the century, charity leaders had created Charity Organization Societies in all of the major cities. Composed of diverse member agencies which would agree to coordinate their services through one agency, the COS became a strategy for screening applicants so that only the truly needy and the truly worthy would be served. This movement to organize charity did much, as Chambers notes, "to render private charity crabbed and niggardly and to retard the development of public policies leading to a welfare state."[4]

THE TRIANGULAR PARTNERSHIP OF THE
TWENTIETH CENTURY

The Great Depression of the 1930s was a watershed for American domestic policy, marking the end of small, passive government and the beginning of large-scale federal intervention in areas once considered the province of the private and voluntary sectors. The national response to the shattering experiences of the early 1930s was fashioned into significant legislative landmarks that, among other things, generated the planning and development of health, housing, and social service delivery systems for the next 50 years.

With the passage of the National Housing Act of 1934 and the creation of a comprehensive Social Security system in 1935, America was on its way to a half century dominated by federal and state funding of human services—particularly health, housing, and social service.

By 1930, the major religious groups (Catholic, Jewish, and Protestant) had established service delivery systems in all of these areas of human service. Despite the rapid acceleration of industrialization and urbanization, the ethnic-religious communities that developed throughout the country prior to World War I maintained their cultural and religious identities. As each passing generation within these communities advanced its economic well-being, the resources available for providing social services, building hospitals and orphanages, and establishing "national" homes increased under the clerical and lay leadership of these communities. The gemeinschaft character of the early mutual aid societies and associations continued to be at the foundation of these service delivery systems.

In response to the proliferation of agencies and institutions with specialized services and diverse structures, the leaders of the religious denominations had created national conferences and institutional arrangements for the coordination of services being developed by their congregations, synagogues, parishes, and dioceses. The National Conference of Catholic Charities, primarily an association of diocesan agencies, was formed in 1910. Within the Jewish community a large number of agencies and institutions developed in response to the mass immigrations of the late nineteenth and early twentieth centuries. These were coordinated in a number of ways—for example, the Jewish Family Service and the National Jewish Welfare Board. Later, the Council of Jewish Federations and Welfare Funds was formed as a voluntary association of central Jewish organizations throughout the country. Among Protestant denominations the move to national coordination was slower, being influenced by the scale of services developed, the variety of church polities, and the degree of participation of their constituencies in community or ecumenical agencies and institutions. Most of the national and regional associations of the Protestant denominations came into being after World War II.[5]

As religious communities formed their national strategies, they added social advocacy, social reform, and social action to their agendas. Both the Catholic and Jewish communities had strong traditions in these activities that they related to their social service systems. Given their different theological orientations, Protestant denominations tended to develop distinctive approaches to social advocacy, action, and reform separate from the social services system. Only recently have their efforts in this area become ecumenical through national umbrella organizations.

By the end of World War II, most of the health, housing, and social service systems of the major religious communities had achieved a sufficient maturity in organizational structure and management capability to enter into a partnership with federal and state governments and with the new community agencies spawned by the new federal bureaucracies. With few exceptions, the religious communities affirmed, in principle, the public policy goals embodied in early national social legislation and were prepared to integrate substantial public funding as well as corporate philanthropy into their strategies and systems for service delivery.

In the private sector, corporate America emerged larger and stronger from the Great Depression and World War II. Both industry and the unions prospered along with the growing middle class that had taken up residence in suburbia. Out of the tradition and practices of Charity Organization Societies, War Chests, and the Community Chest and Community Council movements, corporate American fashioned the United Way. The rationale was a quid pro quo in which the leaders of business and commerce, as well as the unions, hoped that "by coordinated fund raising and allotment, the base of philanthropic giving would be enlarged and they themselves would be spared the harassment of special appeals made by hundreds of agencies;" the leaders of social agencies hoped "to achieve more reliable bases for their own operations and to be able to raise the provision of services to higher levels of efficiency and effectiveness."[6]

In principle, the stage for the drama of the triangular partnership in human services for the next 30 years was then set. The Great Depression had radically shaken all the basic institutions of American society, and even though World War II brought the nation together, America had entered a new era in which health, housing, and social service needs would be responded to with massive federal and state funding, and, at the local level, by corporate and middle-class philanthropy and the religious communities. Both the governmental and community sectors wre to join with the religious communities and provide funding for their institutional and community-based human service delivery systems.

IMPACT OF THE TRIANGULAR PARTNERSHIP

The past 50 years since the Great Depression have profoundly shaped the character of the social welfare programs of all major religious groups in America. Out of partnership with the public and community sectors, the religious communities have established a comprehensive spectrum of human services for which they expend millions of dollars from their own funds, corporate philanthropy, United Way, government grants, third party payments, and client charges. The 1981 annual reports of two diverse national organizations, based on a complete reporting of services and expenditures by their constituent units, are illustrative.

The National Benevolent Association of the Christian Church (Disciples of Christ), established in St. Louis in 1877, now provides oversight and management for 55 local service units in 24 states for children, older adults, and people who are mentally retarded. NBA reported operational expenditures of $39,370,054 in 1981 by all of its units.[7]

The Society of St. Vincent de Paul, which is essentially a neighborhood center operation involving members of the Society as volunteers in a variety of localized services across the country, reported total expenditures of $47,467,862 in 1981.[8]

The total value of social services rendered by the religious communities can be only grossly estimated because many social service agencies and institutions that are related to religious denominations report only to their particular local constituency. In addition, many individual congregations, parishes, or synagogues which directly provide social services in their communities by using a member of their staff and/or volunteers from their membership are not likely to report even summary data to either a regional or national office. If complete data were available from all the denominations, religious orders, ecumenical organizations, congregations, parishes, and synagogues, the total current value—cash and in kind—of the human services would undoubtedly be higher than any of the estimates made by even those most knowledgeable about organized religion.[9]

Diversified Multi-Funding Base

Until the dramatic shift to federal funding of public assistance and social welfare in the 1930s, public funding for income maintenance and social services was largely a function of state and local government. The level of funding was limited and varied greatly from state to state and locality to locality. Welfare strategies of the nineteenth century and the early twentieth century continued to prevail. What changed in the twentieth century was the role of organized private charity and its successors, the community chests and the United Way and, of course, the role of the federal government in social welfare. As religious agencies and institutions entered the partnership with the governmental and community sectors, they depended less on constituent support and private philanthropy and more on funding from governmental entities and community organizations, such as United Way.

Today the percentage distribution of income for a large multi-program social service agency would be similar to that summarized in Table 3-1 by the National Conference of Catholic Charities on the basis of reports from dioceses representing approximately 77 percent of the total membership of NCCC.

Operating units such as hospitals, nursing homes, and residential treatment centers would, of course, have different profiles of income sources, but on the average 35 percent or more of their total income would probably be from the public sector. No matter what the mix of services, the range of public funding for most agencies

Table 3-1.
Income Sources Reported

CATEGORY	AMOUNT	% OF CASH INCOME
TOTAL CASH INCOME	$474,522,755	100.0
1. United Funds	43,903,049	9.3
2. Government Fees and Grants	246,642,076	52.0
3. Foundation Grants	2,663,509	0.6
4. Investment Income	12,896,876	2.7
5. Program Service Fees	79,585,896	16.8
6. Catholic Charities Appeal	21,183,171	4.4
7. Diocesan Grants	29,318,051	6.2
8. Other Contributions	16,426,707	3.4
9. Fund raising	3,876,340	0.8
10. Other	18,026,990	3.8
TOTAL IN-KIND INCOME	$ 15,693,649	100.0
11. In-Kind Salary Contributions (priests and religious)	8,071,735	51.4
12. In-Kind Space and Facilities Contributions ($ value)	4,943,523	31.5
13. Other In-Kind Contributions	2,678,391	17.1
TOTAL CASH AND IN-KIND INCOME	$490,216,404	

and institutions of the religious communities is probably from 35 to 80 percent, with 10 to 20 percent from United Way and other local community sources, and 5 to 25 percent from the membership of the supporting denominations and their congregations, parishes, or synagogues.

Organizational Structure and Delivery Systems

In order to qualify for government funding (federal, state, and local) and community funding (e.g., United Way and foundations), non-profit agencies often found it necessary to modify their organizational structures and to enhance their management capability. The eligibility criteria and the accountability requirements developed by both the government and community funding agencies were much more stringent than those with which the religious communities had previously dealt. The structural adaptations and modifications were diverse and complex, but they allowed management to develop a capability for competent response to the new funding available. For the most part, the new professional managerial personnel and professionally trained program staff from graduate and undergraduate schools increased the efficiency and effectiveness of the social service delivery systems. In many instances it decreased the percentage of clergy in management and increased the percentage of minority people and paraprofessionals in program management and direct client services.

Out of organizational and management responses such as these to substantial increases in government and community funding, the religious communities have developed a complex of local, regional, and national delivery systems during the past 30 years. Throughout the structures of the religious communities—national, regional, and local—there emerged human service programs within the context of religious belief and value systems.

Congregations, parishes, and synagogues—particularly those which had expanded their non-worship facilities in the 1950s and early 1960s—established child care centers, senior citizen centers, counseling programs, neighborhood community organizations, group and home-delivered meals for elderly and handicapped people, prisoner release and community reentry programs, and sponsorship for refugees.

In addition to these programs, congregations, parishes, and synagogues also formed either denominational and ecumenical coalitions or not-for-profit corporations to build nursing homes and group care facilities for the elderly, group homes for retarded people, and residential treatment centers for children. Other programs included efforts to expand hospital facilities, neighborhood centers, day-care centers for children and adults, and housing for low-income families, people with handicaps, and the elderly. Currently, a growing number of these micro-level delivery systems are under the stress of substantial shifts in the triangular pattern of funding now taking place throughout the country and may need to move to a larger-scale organizational structure to survive.

Concurrent with the development of micro-level systems since World War II was the development of regional and national organizational structures. Such structures were not new to this period. Catholic religious orders, Jewish federations, and smaller Protestant denominations had been operating regional and national programs which they expanded in the post-World War II period. Within this context congruent developments took place. By consolidating existing systems into regional systems and organizing statewide delivery systems, religious denominations created larger-scale organizations with commensurate management capability. In contrast to local micro-systems, these larger systems acquired professional and technical middle-management personnel who, along with competent chief executive officers, created systems of financial, personnel, program, and resource management that were necessary to the growth and stability of these systems.

Nationally, the religious communities did not tend to establish macro-delivery systems. There were notable exceptions. Following World War II, the religious communities cooperated with the federal government in the resettlement of European refugees by establishing national organizations. Major Lutheran denominations organized a joint agency called Lutheran Immigration and Refugee Services; other mainline Protestant denominations came together and formed Church World Service, to which they also assigned other international programs; the National Conference of Catholic Charities assumed similar functions for refugee resettlement, and so did the Jewish national community. These national organizations have continued these functions in the resettlement of refugees from Southeast Asia, Ethiopia, Eastern Europe, Central America, and the Caribbean countries.

Another notable exception is leadership in advocacy and public social policy. In these areas the responsibility has usually been assumed by or assigned to a national office of the denomination or an ecumenical organization. Examples are the U.S. Catholic Conference, the National Council of Christian Churches, and the Lutheran Council in the United States of America.

For the most part, however, the national role has been one of support to regional and local service delivery systems. The kind and range of supportive roles performed varies considerably among the religious communities, depending primarily on the polity of the denomination and the organization of its delivery systems. For example, national fund raising in support of agencies and institutions may be undertaken in one or more of the following ways: annual national campaigns (e.g., the One Great Hour of Sharing, the Campaign for Human Development), coordinated Campaigns of Units (e.g., Jewish Federation), special appeals (e.g., domestic and world hunger), capital funds appeal for a network of institutions (e.g., National Benevolent Association), or inclusion in the campaign for the denomination's national budget for human services, money which is distributed as grants or subsidies. As religious communities continue their commitment to health, housing, and social services as a necessary and appropriate function of the churches and synagogues, they will probably intensify and expand their supportive roles well beyond what they are now.

Program Development

In a partnership where one of the partners supplies the major funding it is said—perhaps simplistically—that programs go where the money is. Three observations may, however, be somewhat corrective. First, the religious communities that accessed the massive public funds were already involved in health, housing, and social services that were supported from within the ethnic-religious community by middle-class constituencies and wealthier members. Though on a lesser scale than in the Catholic and Jewish communities, major Protestant denominations had also built hospitals, homes for the elderly, institutions for people who were mentally handicapped, and organized agencies for non-institutional services to families, youths, and children. In principle, therefore, all three religious communities welcomed the new public and community funding and supported the goals of social legislation because these goals were congruent with their long-standing commitments and past efforts.

Second, while social service legislation specified target populations and desired outcomes, it was possible to propose other than conventional methods to produce the usual outcomes. This allowed for implementation of alternative methodologies and therapies. In consultation with specialists, social service agencies developed innovative programs that introduced and tested alternatives, many of which have become accepted in social service practice.

Finally, if for theological or moral reasons a religious community did not accept the policies or objectives of a particular program, it did not seek the funding available. Some denominations, such as the Wisconsin Evangelical Lutheran Synod, did not use government funds even though their services to children, families, and older adults were eligible for such funds.

Nevertheless, the cumulative development by religious communities of a comprehensive spectrum of human services during the decades following World War II was stimulated by accessibility to government and community funds. These funds were accompanied by program designs and regulations which, in turn, brought about considerable similarity in the populations served, the profiles of services rendered, and the delivery systems used. For example, a comparative review of the annual reports and surveys of the United Church of Christ, the United Methodist Church, the Christian Church (Disciples of Christ), the National Conference of Catholic Charities, and the Lutheran Social Service System indicates the following.[10] All provide services to families and children, youths, the aged, the mentally and physically ill or handicapped, and populations at "high risk." While the proportion of all services that each population group receives varies considerably among these five denominations, the profiles of services rendered are very similar: institutional care, group home care, foster care, day care, housing, emergency assistance, counseling, and information/referral. As the profile of services indicates, the delivery systems are also similar, varying primarily in the locus of management and administrative control.

A description of the dynamics of the triangular partnership involved in these developments is beyond the scope of this chapter, but the partnership's role has been significant.

Volunteerism

Volunteerism has been characteristic of non-profit agencies since the organization of benevolence societies, settlement houses, and charity organizations in the nineteenth century. People motivated by the Judaic ethic of charity, justice and righteousness, the Christian gospel, or a humanitarian spirit of reform were crucial to their development. With the rapid expansion of the health, housing, and social service systems of religious communities after World War II, it was necessary to recruit not only professionals and paraprofessionals, but also volunteers.

At the micro-level, volunteers were often critical—and still are—to the social service programs of congregations, parishes, and synagogues. Program directors soon discovered that by careful selection and systematic training, they could more adequately staff client services and maintain the quality of their delivery systems. In recent years, the management of volunteer resources has become more important as the pool of potential volunteers has decreased; a higher proportion of women have entered the nation's work force, and men have not been actively recruited as volunteers.

Advocacy, Social Reform, Social Action

The involvement of large cadres of volunteers, board members, and supporting constituencies in health, housing, and social service delivery systems has dramatically raised the consciousness of religious communities about public social policy and social legislation. Again, the significance of the triangular partnership must be recognized. As increasing numbers of people from religious communities participated in the formation of delivery systems, in policy-making, in fund raising, and in serving clients, and encountered the many issues and problems that emerged from the new partnership, it was inevitable that advocacy, social reform, and social action would find their way to the agendas of religious communities.

The priorities given specific issues were not the same, even though the Judaic-Christian ethos was shared by Catholics, Jews, and Protestants. In the 1950s and early 1960s, the emphasis on denominational growth and establishment in a postwar period of prosperity diminished the attention given to social issues. But the emerging civil rights movement, the war on poverty, and the Vietnam War persistently changed the social context in the 1960s and 1970s. The social activism of this period compelled even the most reluctant denominational groups to address the issues. Coalitions among denominations and social movement groups created a more general consensus on social reform than had previously existed.

The current threat to the triangular partnership, however, may revise the agenda on advocacy, social reform, and social action. The essentially liberal consensus on goals that was formed in the last two decades is still intact, but the strategies that were in place are not. Perhaps the current theological dialogues and ecumenical practices in which the religious communities are engaged will lead to new formulations regarding the social ministry and political responsibility of the churches and synagogues.[11]

Corporate Structure and Governance

An exception to the extensive impact of the triangular partnership on the human service organizations of religious communities has been the component of structure and governance. In general, each of the religious communities retained the basic corporate structure and governance system that it had already developed before entering the partnership. Several reasons for this essential continuity with the past can be identified.

Religious communities established their human service organizations in the context of their theology of social ministry. They intended them to be integral to their mission and ministry. To accomplish this, the religious communities developed human service programs and policies consistent with their religious beliefs and value systems.

The integrity of the organizations as ministries of the religious communities was further secured by establishing ownership and governance through incorporation within or by the religious communities. Generally, the result was that the structure and governance of the human service organization paralleled the structure and polity of the religious community. This was most clearly so in the development of Catholic charity organizations as diocesan agencies and institutions within the basic governance system of the church.

If, however, the polity of the religious community was congregational, then a variety of corporate structures and governance systems were possible. Thus, for example, Lutheran social ministry organizations were organized as non-profit corporations whose membership could be (1) a single congregation, (2) a single regional judicatory which itself was an association of congregations, (3) several congregations or several judicatories, or (4) the national church body. In addition, whatever the form of corporate ownership, the elected/appointed governing board had policy-making authority and management oversight responsibility.

The complex—and sometimes confusing—array of corporate structures and governance systems under which human service organizations of the religious communities operate has not been a barrier to partnership with the public and community sectors.

During the past 30 years, the human service organizations of religious communities have developed stronger organizational structures and management capability. They have created more diversified funding bases for more sophisticated service delivery systems. Generally, the quality of their services has continued to enjoy public confidence and the support of their constituencies. As the religious communities enter the next decades, these significant developments in the planning, management, and delivery of human services will be of great value to them.

ENTERING THE 1980s

Whether the election of 1980 was a watershed event in American history remains a matter for historical judgment, but the rhetoric of the campaign aroused the old conflicts in the American psyche about social responsibility for the vulnerable and the poor in our society. All of the major presuppositions of the previous strategies surfaced at all levels in the political campaigns and in the accompanying public debates and private discussions. The outcomes of the elections and the first two years of the Reagan administration made it abundantly clear that the demise of the liberal consensus of the 1960s had come.

What is not clear is whether a new model of social welfare will emerge in the next decades. The current administration seems to be dedicated to a radical reduction of the federal role in the triangular partnership. But during the third year of the Reagan administration, Congress indicated that it would hold the line on some federal programs and did, in some instances, increase funding. Among leading state governors there was some support for the partnership model—with certain revisions—if for no other reason than to slow down the shift of funding to state governments.

In a recent essay,[12] Stuart Eisenstadt, formerly chief domestic policy advisor to President Carter, and Paul Kahn, former law clerk to Supreme Court Justice White, elaborate a revisionist position based on conscious adjustments in the underlying structure—not on revolution. The adjustments are to be guided by principles that should govern the division of public responsibilities if a non-ideological, pragmatic version of a "new" federalism is to be achieved:

In developing a new federalism concept, it is time to end the ideological battle over federal and state roles and look rather at the practical questions of which level of government can best deliver a particular government service. Economic and political reality have long since matured well beyond the political rhetoric of the federalism debate. This is 1983 not 1776. Federal, state, and local governments operate in a complicated web of relationships, sharing responsibilities for setting policies, and for funding, administering, and regulating countless programs. No modification of the existing interrelationships is possible if based on the premise that the federal government and the states are locked in opposition. Sound change is impossible if one assumes a polarity or antagonism between the national and state governments; both are necessary to serve the public.[13]

As the debate on public social policy continues, so do the basic economic and social changes that must be addressed by that policy. Even a rational federalism must eventually also deal with the human consequences of profound demographic, economic, and social changes that continuously occur in society.

Family Income and Poverty

The debate is intensified today by the human consequences of dramatic changes that are occurring in the economy, with effects such as the following. (1) Median family income in 1982 decreased for the third consecutive year. This decline took place for families in large metropolitan areas, married couples, families with a wife in the paid labor force, two-earner families, and three-person families. (2) The decline in real money income between 1981 and 1982 was accompanied by an increase in the number and percentage of people below the poverty level. There were 34.4 million people classified as poor in 1982, an increase of 2.6 million over 1981, raising the poverty rate from 14.0 percent to 15.0 percent, the highest since 1966. This increase in poverty affected many segments of the population. All of the lower age groups, up to age 55, experienced increases in poverty. All of the four major regions had more poor people in 1982 than in 1981, with the highest rate (18.1 percent) in the South. There were increases in the poverty rate for each family type: married couples, male householders with no wife present, and female householders with no husband present. About half of all families below the poverty level in 1982 were maintained by women with no husband present.[14]

Reductions in Federal Funding

Coupled with the decline in real family income and the increase in poverty is the withdrawal of federal funding, at a time when the discrepancy between the demands for social welfare and the availability of funds to meet these demands is growing. State and local governments have limited capability to cover the loss of federal funding. United Way has apparently reached a plateau and increasingly falls short of campaign goals. Corporate philanthropy has not significantly increased, and foundations are moving to economic development as a preferred category of funding.

Growth of Proprietaries and Investor-Owned Human Service Corporations

Given the continuing demand for health, housing, and social services, the corporate growth of the proprietary sector in human services is not surprising. There is a profitable market in human services among those who have the necessary personal resources or from whom third-party pay is available. With aggressive entrepreneurial leadership, proprietary and investor-owned corporations have created national and regional systems of hospitals, nursing homes, retirement centers, home health care, day care for children and adults, counseling centers for families and individuals, and group homes for people who are developmentally disabled.

Included in the emerging array of such corporate systems are some rapidly growing enterprises.

Recently, *Fortune* magazine reported the following on Beverly Enterprises, now the largest nursing home chain in the United States:

Since 1976, Beverly has increased its revenues 12 times over, largely through acquisitions. In 1982 alone sales rose a steep 68% to $186 million, making it the second fastest growing company in *Fortune's* ranking of the largest diversified service companies. Net income climbed, too, by 62% to $26 million. This year Beverly estimates it will gross over $1.1 billion, most of it from 75,000 nursing home beds in 643 homes.

Moreover, "Beverly has taken off so fast that it now represents 7% of the investor-owned industry—more than twice as many beds as its nearest competitor, National Medical Enterprises' Hillhaven Corp."

Parallel to Beverly Enterprises is the Hospital Corporation of America, the largest operator of proprietary hospitals. With revenues of $3.5 billion, HCA has holdings of 18 percent in Beverly Enterprises, making it Beverly's largest shareholder, a connection that will soon prove beneficial in an important way:

On October 1 (1983), Medicare's new "prospective payment plan," which Congress tacked onto the Social Security Bill, will go into effect. Instead of being paid on an inflationary cost-reimbursement basis as in the past, hospitals will be paid fixed fees based on national and regional averages for various illnesses. Since the fee will be the same whether the patient recuperates in one week or three, hospitals will have an incentive to move patients out to convalescent centers like Beverly's, where they can be cared for at a fraction of the cost.[15]

A variation of the corporate development of human services is the creation of employee assistance programs. Corporations have found that it is profitable for them to provide employment-related services and, in some instances, have marketed their most successful services to other corporations. In 1974, Control Data Corporation started with one alcoholism counselor and has now expanded its employee assistance program to cover its 57,000 employees

worldwide with a budget of $750,000, an expenditure that it esti-
mates to save CDC approximately $15 million annually. Because
the services of Life Extension Institute contracted by CDC were so
successful, CDC purchased the Institute and now markets it to
other businesses at an annual rate of $25 per employee.

Constraints on Advocacy

The commitment to a social ministry which encompasses the vulnerable and powerless in society on the basis of both charity and
justice requires the inclusion of advocacy in the ministry's implementation. As was noted previously, participation in the partnership with the government and community sectors led to the development of advocacy programs and practices by many churches and
synagogues. They seek to continue these programs in support of
their inclusive ministries, but recent proposals by two different
federal agencies suggest strong intentions to constrain the advocacy
programs of non-profit corporations.

In January 1983, the Office of Budget and Management
proposed to broaden the definition of "political advocacy,"
restricting the attempts of organizations to influence a wide range
of governmental decisions, ranging from program guidelines, to
licensing, to rate setting, to public interest lawsuits. The proposal
would have restricted employees of non-profit organizations from
engaging in these broadly defined political advocacy activities, even
on their own time. Organizations would have risked losing government money if they used communications equipment, meetings,
conferences, or publications—even in part—for political advocacy.
Similarly, the proposed revision of current rules that disallow use
of federal money for lobbying would have disallowed money for
building and office space when 5 percent or more of the space was
devoted to political advocacy. Following intense opposition by
organizations and strong congressional reaction, the proposal was
later withdrawn, but OBM intended to reissue essentially the same
regulations in the fall of 1983.

In February 1983, the U.S. Office of Personnel Management,
which is administratively responsible for the Combined Federal
Campaign that raises thousands of dollars from federal employees
for charities across the country, proposed regulations making

ineligible any charity agency which spent more than 15 percent of its total funds for the following activities:

1. Attempts to influence legislation (lobbying) at any level of government
2. Attempts to influence administrative rule making at any level of government
3. Any litigation, except the legal aid type of "self-defense" litigation
4. Any service or activity not in a limited list of acceptable health and welfare services.

This 15% expenditure limitation on a combination of lobbying, advocacy on rule-making, litigation, and other activities went well beyond the existing limitation on lobbying that Congress enacted in 1976 for 501 (c) (3) organizations, which included no restrictions on influencing rule-making or litigation, nor restrictions on any other activities that are charitable, educational, religious, or scientific.[16]

On July 15, a federal district court judge declared unconstitutional major portions of the February executive order on which the proposed CFC rules were based. But the issues involved are not yet settled.

EMERGING ISSUES

The religious communities in the 1980s are not only encountering dramatic changes in the composition and characteristics of the populations they have traditionally served, but are also encountering new populations whose human needs are the result of recent and rapid changes in our economy. Changes are equally dramatic in the sources of funding available to their human service organizations as they seek to maintain both the quality and quantity of services delivered. Operating in a changing corporate environment, they are challenged to revise their own relatively small-scale delivery systems. Moreover, the ambiguities and ambivalence in public social policy at all levels create great uncertainty in both the short term and long term for those who want to act responsibly and for those who are most vulnerable in our society.

It is difficult to predict what new patterns of economic, political, and social development will occur in the final two decades of this century. But certain issues such as the following, which are already confronting the religious communities, will probably be exacerbated in the near future.

Inclusive Social Ministry

Historically, religious communities have had a strong commitment to inclusive social ministry. On the basis of their religious and moral values they have included the poor, the vulnerable, and the powerless in their ministries of service to all people. To accomplish this mission, they have called upon their constituencies for human and financial resources to establish what has become a comprehensive array of human services. These services reach those least able, or even unable, to pay.

However, it may be difficult to maintain this inclusive ministry. In a recent survey of non-profit agencies,[17] the Urban Institute found that more than 50 percent of the responding agencies (3,411) suffered decreases in government funding; almost the same percentage reported having reduced services or increased fees for service; and more than 30 percent reported increased use of volunteers, some of whom replaced paid professional staff, to cope with diminished resources. The Urban Institute projects that federal spending will decrease by $107.6 billion below FY 1980 levels for FY 1982-1986, after adjustment for inflation. This includes a 52 percent decrease in constant dollars by 1986 for social services and a 48 percent decrease for community development. How will the religious communities maintain their inclusive ministries?

In the short term, congregations, parishes, and synagogues are increasing their financial support of their agencies and institutions and are also responding with their own efforts, such as food and clothing distribution, basements converted into shelters for homeless people, soup kitchens, rent subsidies for the very poor, and client advocacy at the local welfare office. It has been necessary to return to mutual aid and assistance to meet the survival needs of fellow members and neighbors. But in the long term such needs far exceed the resources that can be generated out of the mutual aid model, as was learned in the Great Depression of the 1930s.

Nothing so clearly sets the rest of the agenda for the religious communities' human service delivery systems as the commitment of the communities to inclusive social ministry. It compels them to consider allocation of available resources, design and management of delivery systems, maintenance of a viable autonomy, and strategies for advocacy.

Allocation of Resources

Out of the mix of resources available during the past 30 years, the religious communities have heavily invested in institutional facilities such as housing, hospitals, nursing homes, residential treatment centers, and community centers, all of which depend on public reimbursement for client care and treatment. Should the reimbursement rates not meet the costs of care and treatment, religious communities will need to secure larger outlays of financial support from their constituencies. For their non-institutional social service programs this may mean a reduced allocation of resources for serving those least able, or unable, to pay. Since constituency contributions are now usually in a range of 5 to 15 percent of the total operational budget, a substantial increase would be required to recover losses in public funding even in efficient operations.

Problems such as these already confront both institutional and community-based programs. Some nursing homes have already reduced the percentage of Medicaid patients that they will accept, in order to balance their budgets. Moreover, less costly non-institutional services have forced some residential treatment centers to close. Even if in the future resources were no less scarce than they have recently become, priority decisions in support of inclusive social ministries would be as difficult as they are now, if not more so.

Design and Management of Service Delivery Systems

A large majority of agencies and institutions of religious communities are still relatively small-scale systems operated independently of each other—even in the same religious group. Managers of non-institutional systems may have the advantage of program and staff flexibility; managers of large institutional programs usually do not. But both are confronted with the growing presence of investor-owned and proprietary corporations in the human services area.

Prototypes of large-scale systems already exist in the religious communities: hospital systems owned and operated by Catholic religious orders; health care and residential facilities for the elderly, such as Ohio Presbyterian Homes; and a combination of housing, health care institutions, and social service area offices, such as Lutheran Social Service of Illinois, a statewide non-profit corporation. Three years ago a group of Catholic religious orders established the Catholic Health Corporation, which now manages 21 hospitals. More recently, the Lutheran Institute of Human Ecology, which operates Lutheran General Hospital in the Chicago area, diversified its corporate structure to include the establishment of a for-profit subsidiary (Parkside Medical Services) to provide alcoholism treatment programs throughout the country. These corporate developments signal a move from microsystems to macrosystems in institutional programs in the next decades.

While small-scale, multi-service systems have been more viable than larger single-function institutions, recent reductions in nonentitlement program funds have caused many of them to become marginal operations. Highly diversified, multi-site, large-scale systems such as statewide or regional social service agencies appear to be more capable of adjusting to changes in funding sources. Again, the move to macro-systems seems probable.

The trend to large-scale operations is disturbing to many members and leaders of religious communities. Unlike the congregation, parish, or synagogue in which they personally participate, the separately incorporated agency or institutional complex is often perceived as large and remote. Viewing it as "our own," as in the mutual aid model of an earlier time, becomes more difficult as the scale of operation increases. Questions about mission and accountability are raised. So, while economy of scale may be demonstrable, its achievement may change the image of the agency or institution as a mission and ministry of the religious community and reduce constituency support.

Viable Autonomy

Religious communities entered the triangular partnership from historical positions on church and state relationships. Most of them decided that, in principle, the acceptance of government and community funding did not compromise the autonomy of their agencies and institutions. This reflected a general consensus expressed in the phrase, "institutional separation and functional interaction."

The concept of institutional separation is derived from the belief that God is the sole Lord of life, whether He rules people as members of the religious community (the church) or as citizens of the state. The distinctive mission of the religious community (the church) is to proclaim the Word of the Lord in preaching and sacraments, worship and evangelism, and educational and social ministry. The distinctive mission of the state is to establish civil justice through the maintenance of law and order, the protection of constitutional rights, and the promotion of the general welfare of the total citizenry. In view of the religious and cultural pluralism which has prevailed in America since the colonial days, this institutional separation of church and state appears to be the most equitable arrangement. It guarantees each institution the freedom to perform its own God-ordained tasks for the common good.

While recognizing the institutional separation of church and state, religious communities also recognize that church and state can interact without being united, and can remain distinct without being divorced. There are many ways by which the state, simply by fulfilling the duties of a just state, is also helpful to the church. For example, the state promotes the interests of the church by providing funding on a non-preferential basis to church agencies engaged in the performance of social services which are also of secular benefit to the community. On the other hand, there are many ways in which the church, solely through the free exercise of its divine mandate, also helps the state. For example, the religious communities champion human rights by encouraging the state to guarantee to all citizens equal justice under civil law, and by creating a moral and legal consensus that supports the state in promoting the common good of all citizens.

There are a growing number of areas in which the state and the church have a common interest. Federal and state governments continue to be willing to reimburse the agencies and institutions of religious communities for many health, housing, and social services which are primarily of secular benefit to the community and which the government itself might otherwise provide. But even where such state financing is constitutionally legal, it may not always be socially desirable or ethically advisable for the religious community to seek or accept public financing. To maintain a viable autonomy within the framework of "functional interaction," each religious community and its agencies and institutions will need to continue to decide in each case (1) if their integrity requires that they support the service, (2) if their autonomy is jeopardized by public funding and regulatory requirements, and (3) if they consider a particular service to be the responsibility of the state alone. As public social policy is developed in the next two decades, it is almost inevitable that new program designs and new regulations in social legislation will require these same considerations if a viable autonomy in relation to the state is to be maintained.

Advocacy and Social Justice

Advocacy is integral to most religious communities' missions and ministries, particularly social ministry. Historically, this is most clearly so in the Jewish and Catholic communities, and more recently in mainline Protestantism. In the last 50 years, most religious communities have, individually or in coalitions, vigorously involved themselves at the national, state, and local levels in programs of advocacy that addressed the problems of impoverishment and social injustice in our society. In the prior era of the mutual aid model, their focus was on support services for their own kind. In that time the "spearheads of reform" were, as Chambers points out, the settlement houses and community centers, which played prominent roles in initiating organizations such as the Urban League, NAACP, and ACLU; they also agitated for a whole series of specific reforms at the municipal, state, and national levels.[18] There were prominent religious people among the leaders of these social reform movements, but it was participation in the triangular partnership that generated the involvement of religious communities in advocacy for social justice and human rights. As religious communities interacted with government they more clearly defined their institutional relationship to the state and their role in promoting the general welfare and establishing a more just society. They also became aware that the rapid changes in our economic, political, and social life required new strategies for advocacy and social action. How to continue as effective advocates for those who suffer from social injustice will be a central issue for religious communities and their human service organizations.

The human service delivery systems of the religious communities have evolved out of the interaction of the religious communities with the government and community sectors. Their evolution through a succession of strategies reflects the interplay of the missions of the religious communities with the changing patterns— demographic, economic, political, and sociocultural—of our national life since the colonial period.

Within the framework of American pluralism, the religious communities eventually created a formula of institutional separation and functional interaction that served as a model for their involvement with the government and community sectors in the establishment of service delivery systems. The partnership has satisfactorily implemented both the missions and ministries of the religious communities and the mission of the state and its citizens.

The political campaigns of 1980 indicated that the complex interactive system that had been developed in the triangular partnership of the last 50 years would be put to the test. That is now occurring through reduction of federal and state funding, the plateauing of corporate and community funding, the emergence of investor-owned corporations in the human service delivery system, and the great uncertainties about public social policy in the next decades.

In the short term, religious communities and their congregations, parishes, and synagogues are returning to mutual aid to meet the survival needs of their fellow members and neighbors. But for the long term, religious communities are keenly aware that their Judeo-Christian commitment to inclusive social ministry will require intensive planning of resource allocation, design and management of service delivery systems, maintenance of a viable autonomy, and new strategies for advocacy and social justice. Since major revisions of American social welfare will probably occur in the next decades, this is a demanding agenda for the religious communities and their health, housing, and social service systems.

4

Serving the Needs of Children:
Child Care in the Voluntary Sector

FRANCES L. HOFFMANN

The child care debate in the U.S. has attracted strange bedfellows. Diverse agendas, often having little to do with the care of children, have been put forward in defense of or in opposition to expansion of child care services. Feminists interested in expanding opportunities for women, profamily groups concerned with strengthening family ties, child advocates interested in the welfare of the under-five population, and policymakers committed to addressing the problems of poverty and unemployment all have a stake in the debate—a debate rife with contradictory, emotionally charged, and exaggerated claims.

There is little dispute that expanded child care services will be needed in the coming decade as growing numbers of women with children under five enter the labor force. Women have entered the labor force in increasing proportion since the 1940s; the labor force participation rates of women with preschool children are rising faster than those for any other category of women. All available projections indicate no abatement in this trend.[1]

On the other hand, responsibility for the care of preschool children is a matter of intense debate. The purpose of this article is to bring the insights of current feminist and child development scholarship to bear on the question of the relative responsibility of governments, volunteer agencies, employers, and individual parents for the provision of child care services.

FEMINIST THEORY

Feminist theory and research generated in the early years of the contemporary women's movement focussed on family roles as major impediments to women's equality in occupational and political structures. The early feminist scholarship paid little attention to parenting as an activity with intrinsic worth for either men or women—indeed, analyses of mothering as full-time work emphasized its negative consequences for both mother and child. Feminists also criticized the glorification and mystification of motherhood that were prevalent in American culture, pointing to the more mundane and less fulfilling aspects of the care of the young which comprise a significant proportion of a caretaker's time with children.

Public child care, an early and central concern of the women's movement, was promoted essentially as a means to relieve women of full-time child care responsibilities and to address the needs of working-class and poor women. Advocates stressed the need for quality, parent-controlled, cooperative centers accessible to low-income as well as middle-income families, and many communities experimented with such arrangements. The National Organization for Women's Bill of Rights, adopted at NOW's first conference in Washington, D.C., contained the following demands, typical of the feminist approach to child care at that time:

IV Immediate revision of the laws to permit the deduction of home and child care expenses for working parents.

V That child care facilities be established by law on the same basis as parks, libraries, and public schools, adequate to the needs of children from the preschool years through adolescence as a community resource to be used by all citizens from all income levels.[2]

Feminists also called for the increased participation of men in child-rearing. Fathers have both abdicated and been prevented from meaningful involvement in the day-to-day care of their children, feminists argued, and have some obligation for (and would benefit from) assuming a fair share of the work entailed in rearing children. With shared child-rearing responsibilities, feminists assumed, it would be easier for women to enter the public domain.

Demands such as NOW's for extensive child care centers were

grandiose. They assumed a parental preference for group care—an assumption that has since proved problematic. These early proposals nonetheless articulated values that are important to preserve as the child care debate continues. Equal access across class and racial lines, parental involvement in the delivery of services, affirmation of the relationship between expanding opportunities for women and provision of child care services, emphasis on gains accruing for children and parents with increased involvement of fathers, and the recognition of the significance of varied forms of public support for community-based child care programs and services remain valid principles to be built into any proposal for expanded child care services in this country.

The early feminist visions, while exposing the limitations in assigning one category of people, mothers, sole responsibility for the care of preschool children, came close to throwing the baby out with the bathwater. In their enthusiasm for freeing women from the constraints of a societally imposed role (imposed by implication if not by design), they denigrated that role and paid too little attention to the experiences of the children they were sending off to daycare centers. Most recent feminist scholarship,[3] building on the insights of the early works, has sought to reexamine parenting, particularly mothering, in light of women's expanding roles in society. Rather than calling for the emancipation of women from the isolation of family responsibilities, this new scholarship seeks a reconceptualization of family life which affirms its centrality to people's lives and its relationship to broader economic and political structures.

A ground-breaking analysis of this sort, Alice Rossi's 1977 "A Biosocial Perspective on Parenting," critiqued early feminist emphasis on integrating women into economic and political institutions, calling instead for restructuring of these institutions to allow for, if not encourage, meaningful and enduring family ties and involvements. Notwithstanding Rossi's controversial arguments about biological and evolutionary differences between males and females in their parenting aptitudes, her discussion of mothering and fathering as important activities was placed squarely on the feminist agenda and spawned debates about and analyses of the nature of parenting and the needs of children. Thus were children and parents reintroduced into feminist discourse.

Rossi was foresighted in recognizing that the feminists' major solutions to the problem of child-rearing—i.e., greater involvement by fathers and expanded day-care facilities—while valid, were by no means a panacea. Equally essential were fundamental changes in work structures and employers' attitudes toward family concerns, without which even the best-intentioned of fathers and working mothers would find it difficult to expand significantly the time for involvement with their children. The expansion of day-care services is similarly more complex than was initially believed, for as Rossi warned, "In recent years, we have seen too many social programs end up crippled by inadequate funding, bureaucratic red tape, and corruption to advocate putting all energies in child care institutions."[4]

The problem of family life in contemporary society goes beyond simply finding someone to care for the children as women enter the public domain. Strictly private approaches (the integration of fathers into child-rearing activities) or public ones (the construction of day-care centers on a large scale) provide only a part of the solution. What is missing from these proposals is recognition of the *interrelatedness* of family and work place concerns. Family life is typically seen as private, separable from work place activity, and as needing to accommodate to the work place, rather than the reverse. More participation of fathers in parenting and the construction of more day-care centers would do little to change this pattern. What is needed are systematic analyses of costs and benefits of transforming work place structures and values to enhance family life. Such analyses are central to the child care debate as well.

Those who argue that the family is the sphere of the private, the "haven in a heartless world,"[5] the only niche left in which nurturance, bonding, and intimacy occur, and which, therefore, must be protected from encroachments of the so-called public domain, fail to recognize the embedment of family life in broader institutional frameworks and the degree to which its structures and functioning are determined by governmental and economic policies. Family life is far more influenced by the demands of the family members' occupations and by the governmental policies which undergird the economic order than the reverse. Far from constituting havens, families are often arenas for the conflicts of the broader institutional order. Those who seek to enhance the quality of family life would do well to start by focussing on economic and political arrangements which constrain the abilities of family members to function as family members.

On the other hand, those who argue for the integration of women into public life and for the creation of large-scale, publicly funded and operated child care centers fail to take into sufficient account the need for intimacy and nurturance, qualities at least theoretically available through family interactions and more difficult to attain in large-scale organizations.

Current discourse separates the private and public spheres, failing to address the potential for transcending their separation, to recognize their interrelatedness, and to develop strategies for restructuring work place, family, and public institutions in ways which would enable family and community members to support and nurture one another.

The feminists' insights regarding the contradictions inherent in family life and women's liberation in the context of modern capitalist organizations should inform the child care debate and the proposals for child care policies. As Thorne argues, summarizing the arguments of historian and feminist Linda Gordon, "We must keep the oppressive dimensions of modern families clearly in view and struggle against them, while also recognizing their supportive possibilities, which may point to a larger vision of human community."[6]

Parents, both mothers and fathers, need to be able to parent as well as to be productive members of the economic and political worlds. Child care arrangements should allow and empower people to be effective as parents and as members of the community. Such arrangements should also meet the developmental and emotional needs of children.

THE NEEDS OF CHILDREN

In the voluminous literature about child care needs in the U.S., surprisingly little attention is given to the needs of the child, because child care has so often been proposed to serve other ends (e.g., permitting women access to the labor force, encouraging welfare mothers to get off welfare, employing unemployed teachers or welfare mothers). Research design difficulties have prevented scho-

larly attention from focussing in any systematic way on the effects
of diverse child care arrangements on children, not to mention the
effects on parents and family life in general. Much is claimed by
child care advocates and foes, but little is documented.

Notable exceptions to this pattern include Belsky and Steinberg's
review of the literature on the effects of day care,[7] Kagan's extensive cross-cultural and national research on child development,[8]
Steven's reviews of the National Day Care Home Study and the
New York City Infant Day-Care Study,[9] and Suransky's provocative analysis of the day-to-day experiences of children in day-care
centers.[10]

Belsky and Steinberg point to major methodological problems in
research to date on effects of child care on children's development.
Most research is conducted on high-quality, group care, typically
child care centers affiliated with universities; it is a type of care
received by a small minority of children involved with alternative
child care arrangements. Most research relies on standardized cognitive and social adjustment measures whose utility is widely ques-
tioned, and most research deals with direct effects of child care on
children, paying little attention to interactions among child care
arrangements and children, parents, and the work place. Few
studies provide comparable methods of inquiry and scope of analysis, making generalizations beyond individual investigations
extremely difficult. Suffice it to say that something is known about
the direct effects of high-quality group care on children; precious
little is known about the effects of child care in other contexts on
anything else.

According to Belsky and Steinberg, "Experience in high quality,
center-based care (1) has neither salutary nor deleterious effects
upon the intellectual development of the child, (2) is not disruptive
of the child's emotional bond with his mother, and (3) increases the
degree to which the child interacts, both positively and negatively,
with peers."[11] Most studies of the effects of group care on cognitive
development find no differences between non-disadvantaged day-
care children and matched controls; what differences are noted
disappear shortly after the children leave the program. Group care
programs that focus on enrichment do seem to alleviate, but do not
eliminate, some of the measured differences in IQ between economically disadvantaged and middle-class children.

Taken as a whole, the research provides little fuel for child care advocates who argue the enriching potential of day-care experiences for children in general; and just as importantly, it provides little fuel for the day-care opponents who warn of deleterious effects.

This conclusion is generally supported by the New York City Infant Day-Care Study,[12] an examination of differences between group and family day-care settings as far as the health and the social and cognitive development of infants. Four hundred infants divided among group care settings, licensed family day-care homes, and home settings were observed and tested at 18 and 36 months of age along a variety of dimensions. The infants were primarily from moderate- or low-income families. The study found that group care centers provided more enriching physical environments and equipment than family-based care, and greater support for intellectual development. In keeping with the findings summarized by Belsky and Steinberg, group care infants scored significantly higher on measures of cognitive development at 36 months than infants in family- or home-based care—reinforcement of the findings that enriched group care attenuates the effects of disadvantaged home backgrounds. No differences were found among any of the groups of infants in health or in social or emotional functioning.

The extensive research of Jerome Kagan and associates sheds further light on the effects of day care on children's development. Kagan's studies of Caucasian and Chinese children in American day care and Israeli children on kibbutzim found that, even in contexts in which children spend most of their waking hours with substitute caretakers, the parents (typically the mother) remain the preferred attachment object for the children. Thus, placed in anxiety-producing situations with a choice of adults for comfort, all of the children studied, whether home-reared or in day care, chose the mother. Caretakers were sought only in the absence of the mother. Kagan concludes,

A child can be attached to more than one caretaker, and most children have a stable hierarchy of preference that is tied to the quality of interaction rather than to its duration . . . the biological parent in the Western nuclear family . . . remain[s] the preferred target of attachment, even for young children who spend a considerable amount of time with substitute caretakers outside the homes.[13]

Though uncertain about the dynamics through which this attachment is generated, Kagan offers some provocative contrasts between the behavior of the caretaker and that of the mother, through the perspective of the child. For Kagan, the caretaker's relative lack of deep emotional attachment to the child, along with the routinization of group care, results in treatment of the child which is more predictable than the mother's and allows for a greater latitude in the child's behavior. The mother, on the other hand, is deeply involved in the child's growth and development, and strongly attached emotionally to the child. Mother and child interact with less predictability, more emotionally. Mother is a greater source of uncertainty for the child. The child experiences, then, more passion in his or her relationship with the mother—more joy, excitement, and reassurance, as well as more uncertainty, guilt, and unhappiness.

Whatever the dynamics, the research appears at this point unequivocal in finding that children are able to sustain close relationships with more than one caretaker and that their primary attachment, even with many hours of separation, remains with their mothers.[14] Further, if Kagan's contention that caretakers offer more predictability and tolerance of broader ranges of behavior and diversity among children is accurate, positive benefits may indeed accrue to children from this kind of interaction with caring adults. Much has been written about the negative consequences to mother and child of maternal over-identification with the child during its development. Kagan's research should reassure those who fear that time spent away from the mother will result in a disruption of the mother-child bond. The conclusion that association with a caring and competent caretaker may in fact benefit the child remains speculative, but is not ruled out by current research findings.

Although the fear that day care disrupts parent-child relationships is unfounded, other fears of opponents of alternative forms of day care deserve attention. Typically, opponents argue that only parents are capable of instilling the values they cherish in their children, and that other caretakers are inadequate for the task. Further, there is often an unstated assumption that children will feel abandoned or rejected—"farmed out"—if left to alternative forms of child care. None of the available research supports the first argument. Since Western societies place a premium on parental love and acceptance as preconditions to adult mental health, the latter fear is a serious one indeed, and deserves empirical attention.

Kagan's cross-class and cross-cultural research makes clear that there is no automatic relationship between a particular set of parental behaviors and the child's sense of being accepted and loved. Behaviors regarded by middle-class parents as punitive and rejecting, such as the greater use of physical punishment among working and lower-class parents or the practice among Utka parents of treating children's aggression with silence and seeming indifference, are not necessarily (and in fact not usually) regarded as such by the recipients of the behavior, the children. A child's interpretations of parental behaviors depends on the environment in which they occur and the meaning the child imposes on them. As Kagan argues: "Evaluating a parent as rejecting or accepting cannot be based solely on the parent's behavior; for rejection, like pleasure, pain, or beauty, is not a fixed quality; it is in the mind of the rejectee. It is a belief held by the child, not an act performed by the parent."[15]

The *fact* of child care participation, then, carries with it no automatic perception on the part of the child of either parental rejection or acceptance. The child's interpretation of his or her experience depends on a complex of factors, the most important of which seem to be whether child care is used by a majority of children in the community or by very few, whether child care is taken for granted as a means of child-rearing or as an undesirable deviation from a more desirable norm, and whether the parents themselves use day care reluctantly and with guilt or embrace it as beneficial for themselves and their children.

As Baxandall[16] cogently argues, American culture has always viewed child care with ambivalence at best, or open hostility at worst. Americans have traditionally associated day care with socialism, with remedial programs for the poor and otherwise disadvantaged, and with maternal deprivation—and have viewed the ideal (not to say morally superior) form of child-rearing as the private preserve of the nuclear family, with the mother devoted full-time to the care and rearing of the family's children.

As increasing numbers of women with children enter the labor force, this ideal becomes increasingly difficult to attain. Nonetheless, bedrock values lag behind social changes, and Americans continue to feel a great deal of anxiety and ambivalence about children in child care settings. (This ambivalence is, I think, directly related to the continued cultural ambivalence about whether women *should* be in the labor force. While the nation has committed itself to equitable treatment of women in the labor force, it has by no means committed itself to bringing them into that sphere.) While public polls[17] indicate that Americans generally support the creation of more child care facilities and tax breaks for child care costs, a large majority also believes that the increased number of families in which both parents work outside of the home has had a negative effect on family life. Thus, Americans seem to feel that, as long as the reality of working parents is with us, child care alternatives should be supported. The preference, however, would be to change that reality. The strength of the opposition to various pieces of child care legislation introduced throughout the 1970s is testimony to the deep rootedness of those beliefs.

The child in day care receives conflicting messages from society and from his or her parents as to the appropriateness of his or her being there. The lesson here is that children's experience of child care is not restricted to the quality of particular arrangements, but is grounded in the larger culture. Without profound changes in the prevailing national sentiment regarding the nature and extent of women's participation in the labor force, the nature of family life, and the relationship between public policy and child-rearing practices, the ambivalences experienced by parents and communicated, however subtly, to children, will undoubtedly affect the quality of day care. Changes in attitude may indeed come as the entrance of large numbers of women into the labor force becomes a fait accompli. Those changes have not occurred to date, however, and child care advocates remain on the defensive, unable as yet to generate a convincing ideology to counter the private, nuclear family, mother-in-the-home value system.

If the data on the effects of day care on children reviewed thus far have been at least minimally reassuring to day-care advocates, a note of caution is sounded in Valerie Suransky's observation of five different day-care settings.[18] Suransky offers a feminist theory critical of contemporary feminists' omission of "the voice of the child" from their analyses of the family and of child development theorists' rationalization of childhood. She examines the "landscape'' of a variety of day-care settings from the perspective of the child. Sensitive to changing historical conceptions of the nature of childhood, yet not succumbing to a radical cultural relativism, Suransky is deeply troubled by current images and organization of childhood:

But today, having separated children from the world of work, having infantilized their perceptions and moral sensibilities with insidious moral inventories and taxonomies, having circumscribed their lives in schooling institutions where their experiences, intellect, and state of being are constantly measured, quantified and evaluated we have perhaps rediscovered childhood but in so doing eroded its very ontology as a life phase.[19]

Over a two-year period, Suransky observed children attending a nursery school in a Jewish Community Center; a Montessori program; a profit-run day-care center; a federally funded, low-income, innercity day-care center; and a private, non-profit "free school." She provides detailed accounts of the day-to-day lives of the children in these centers, their interaction with peers and staff, the nature and quality of their work and play. What she finds gives pause to those advocating group care on a large scale, and to those who see the private sector as the appropriate provider of that care. In three of the centers,

the spontaneous, moving, energetic, playing being of the child presented a threat to [these] organizational structures and hence needed to be contained. The untrained, mischievous toddler constituted a problem because playfulness, physical exploration, and curiosity were anti-norms detrimental to the imposed spatial and temporal structure. Children were not free to create their own landscape; to significantly imprint their mark upon the environment. They were denied their own history-making power, which as *becoming beings* is an existentially vital theme.[20]

The for-profit center was characterized by high staff turnover; more than 100 children in the center; impersonal, authoritarian staff-child interaction; highly structured, fragmented, and routinized use of space and time; and frequent use of physical and humiliating verbal reprimands. Over time the children became isolated, anomic, angry, cowed. Though Suransky's portrayal of this center is grim, it cannot be written off as an exception to day care in general. Now expanded into four centers run by a husband-wife team corporation, it is probably more typical than not of the 40 percent of all day-care centers which are run for profit. For example, Keyserling's 1972 survey of centers and day-care homes across the nation rated only 1 percent of the for-profit centers as superior, 15 percent as good, 35 percent as fair (rendering custodial care), and more than 50 percent as poor in quality of care provided.[21]

Only two of the centers observed by Suransky provided flexibility (and thereby spontaneity) in time and spatial arrangements; warm, caring, and enduring staff-child relationships; and the potential for purposeful play initiated and structured by the child, undistinguished from "work." It is no accident, according to Suransky, that these two centers were counter-cultural in ideology —in one case, in the commitment to affirmation of black cultural tradition, in the other, in the ideological commitment to deinstitutionalizing or "deschooling" childhood experience. They represent a small minority of child care centers, atypical in theory and practice.

The two centers, albeit marginal cases, do hold out the promise of quality group care for children in other than university settings. They also provide standards by which other centers may be judged. For example, are parents involved with policy and program formulation? Are the values of the constituencies preserved? Is the staff committed, child-oriented, enthusiastic, responsive to individual children? Are the children the focus of staff time and activity? Does the staff play with the children? Does the staff respond to the developmental capabilities, interests, and needs of the children or to its own agendas? Are the children happy, enthusiastic, and permitted to express their feelings? These attributes are clearly not met by the majority of currently operating child care centers. Not unlike the work places of the parents they serve, child care centers commonly sacrifice parental and community involvement, flexibility, spontaneity, and tolerance of diversity for efficiency, predictability, and control.

One should not, then, be hopeful about the expansion of child care centers in this society. Experience to date should warn that they would most likely become extensions of an already overinstitutionalized, bureaucratized social world. To concede the point, however, is to make even more forcefully the case of the feminists that the broader institutional world needs to be informed by the values traditionally seen as the province of the family. That being the case, the values epitomized by Suransky's marginal cases would transform the work place and political life, creating community-oriented, participatory, and flexible institutional structures, including child care facilities. If there is to be meaningful participation of parents in the creation of such child care services, some understanding of current parent preferences is needed.

CURRENT TRENDS: PARENT PREFERENCES, PUBLIC POLICY, PRIVATE SOLUTIONS

The issue of parent preferences for alternative child care arrangements is complex. Utilization data provide some information on the pattern of choices parents make in selecting child care from available options. There is little information about parents' preferences in the context of currently unavailable options.[22] We do know that utilization patterns have changed over the past 25 years. For example, in 1958, 57 percent of children under six of full-time working women were cared for in the child's home, 27 percent in another's home, 4.5 percent in group care centers. In 1977, utilization of group care centers had increased to 15 percent, care in another's home to 47 percent, and care in the child's home declined to 28 percent.[23]

These trends notwithstanding, researchers find no clear pattern of child care utilization. That is, parents' choices of child care arrangements run the gamut of available options, with no type of care gaining ascendancy. Age of children, presence of older siblings, family income, region, ethnicity, availability of relatives, and educational level of parents all influence choice of child care arrangements.

Further, research reporting on criteria used by parents in choosing among day-care arrangements is contradictory. Woolsey,[24] summarizing the Westal survey of 1970, found closeness to home, cost, convenience of hours, sick-child care, and program to be salient factors. On the other hand, the National Childcare Consumer Study of 1975[25] reported that the parents it surveyed cited child-oriented rather than cost or convenience rationales for selection among child care alternatives.

Finally, research on parent preference and utilization patterns typically focusses on *types* of care selected (e.g., at-home, family care, group care) and pays little or no attention to supplemental services which might be provided (community child care referral services, child care benefit programs by employers, family care provider training programs, and so on). As a result, little is known, for example, about choices parents would make if family care providers were trained, if referral services were available, if employers provided child-care–related benefits such as flex time, shared appointments, and on-site care.

The General Mills American Family Report[26] touches these issues in one of the items in its survey of 1503 family members. Respondents were asked to rate the degree of usefulness to them of "benefits that might help balance family and work responsibilities." Again, no clear patterns emerge—the degree of usefulness of child-care–related services reported by respondents varied widely. For example, 45 percent of working mothers surveyed rated "Child Care at the place you or your spouse works" as benefitting them a great deal or somewhat, 44 percent as hardly or not at all.

Taken together, what emerges from parent preference and utilization research is a diversity of needs and preferences, specific to specific situations. That is, paid personal leave for paternity is desired by some families, part-time work by others. Family care is preferred by many parents of very young children, a combination of care arrangements for the three-to-five-year-old population, and group care by many of the others. Numbers and ages of children, type of employment of both parents, region, availability of relatives, economic considerations, and personal characteristics all affect selection of child care arrangements in ways which do not, at least as yet, allow prediction of utilization patterns for planning purposes. These observations underscore the arguments against broad-scale expansion of group care facilities mentioned earlier, and reinforce Hill's[27] conclusion that public policies should be neutral with regard to the mode of care promoted, with goals of equity across income levels and also with the availability of a diversity of options tailored to particular circumstances of individual families. Before suggesting such a model, it is useful to examine briefly the nature and extent of federal support for child care to date.

Federal support for child care has been sporadic at best, reflecting deeply rooted beliefs that the rearing of children (at least the rearing of middle-class, mainstream children) is a private concern, the province of parents rather than of government. Economic and political crises have brought some government action in the provision of day-care services, but these services have never maintained their quality or scale after the resolution of the crisis. Current federal child care programs, as has been the case historically, serve other agendas, are disconnected philosophically, and are uneven in terms of constituencies served. Major legislative initiatives of the past decade for expanded provision of child care services by the federal government (notably the Economic Opportunity Amendments of 1971, the Child and Family Services Act of 1975, and the more modest Child-Care Act of 1971) were either vetoed by the executive branch or failed in Congress. In each case widespread opposition from conservative groups was effectively marshalled. The opposition to expanded federal involvement in child care has successfully defined the terms of the debate, arguing for the sanctity of the family and against a federal intervention in private concerns.

In sum, the federal government is minimally involved in provision of any kind of child care services, and there is little on the horizon which would give one hope that its role will be expanded in the coming years. The successful assaults on broad-scale federal involvement in child care services left in their wake a few discrete programs, currently struggling to maintain funding and eligibility levels. Title XX of the Social Security Act provides approximately 750,000 children from low- and moderate-income families with subsidized care in licensed centers and homes. Head Start provides educational, medical, nutritional, and social services for approximately 372,000 children from low-income families. The AFDC Child Care Disregard provides AFDC mothers seeking employment or training up to $160 a month per child for child care costs. The Child Care Tax Credit, of benefit primarily to middle- and upper middle-class families, provides a tax credit to working parents on a sliding scale of from 30 percent to 20 percent of child care costs, up to $2,400 per child.[28]

Programs for disadvantaged children and moderate tax breaks comprise the extent of federal involvement in child care. In 1979, Kamerman and Kahn declared, ''After many years of controversy, day-care legislation in Washington is dead, at least for now.''[29] The Children's Defense Fund[30] analysis of the Reagan administration's stance toward child care legislation indicates that the situation is worse than that: not only are no initiatives in the works, but existing legislation is under active assault. Poor and working-class families are most seriously affected by the cuts in child care food subsidies, in Title XX block grants, and in AFDC child care supports. The only child care legislation in which benefits were expanded, the Child Care Tax Credit, assists primarily middle- and upper-income families. Because it is a non-refundable credit, it is of no benefit to those families whose incomes are too low to owe income tax. Further, though the change from a 20 percent of child care expense credit to a sliding 30/20 percent scale theoretically benefits lower-income families, cuts in other areas such as food supplements in many cases offset the tax credit benefit.

With public attention focussed on economic and international concerns, child care remains, in C. Wright Mills' terms, a private trouble for millions of working parents. Though the inadequacy, costs, and inaccessibility of quality child care alternatives cause considerable stress for affected families, no consensus is emerging that federal action is appropriate or necessary.

The feminist and child development scholarship reviewed earlier suggests the outlines of a model of child care services, a model that would respond to parental preferences and needs. Given the very limited role of the federal government in the provision of these services, is it likely that the voluntary sector can fill the void?

What implications for this question can be drawn from current feminist and child development research regarding an appropriate model of child care services? Such a model would begin with a restructuring and democratization of family life, with fathers assuming greater responsibility in child care. It would entail the creation of diverse services which would provide parents with a variety of child care settings from which to choose. These might include home-based family care, neighborhood group care, employer-sponsored child care programs, parent-run cooperatives. Programs would encourage parent involvement and be responsive to the needs of the communities they served. Services would be available to all, regardless of income, and selection of particular programs or combinations of programs would be a parental prerogative. Programs would be responsive to the developmental needs of children, allowing for flexibility, spontaneity, child-initiated activity, "child friendly" staff. Training programs and resource services would be available to child care providers. The overarching goals of all programs would be concern for the welfare of the children served and commitment to enabling parents to fulfill their parenting responsibilities more effectively. The latter goal is as much a problem of restructuring work place expectations as it is the creation of diverse child care services.

The problem of child care in the U.S. goes well beyond establishing more child care programs in which to place children while parents are at work. In Suransky's terms, "Public and social policy must provide support time for parenting, for if everyone works full time . . . how do you keep a society going?"[31] Public policy needs to provide incentives for efforts by employers to create flexible options for working parents. Fringe benefits should include such provisions as child care allowances, flex time, shared appointments, on-site care where feasible, referral services, subsidized care in community programs, and sick-child leave time.[32] In short, family and work life must be reciprocally accommodating, with benefit programs tailored to the changing needs of employees.

Finally, however, it is the ideological climate surrounding child care and family life in the U.S. which is the core of the child care problem. The changes called for above, particularly the structural transformation of the family, are conceivable only in a context in which family life is less isolated and mystified, in which the integration of women into the economic and political life of the society is embraced, and in which the care of children is seen as a social issue and public responsibility.

The voluntary sector has an important role to play in the delivery of some of the many services called for above. Its potential contribution lies in its ability to provide programs for the care of children and assistance to parents. Some of these might include referral services; parent and child care provider training programs; group care programs sponsored by churches, neighborhood centers, or other non-profit agencies; and crisis intervention services.

The voluntary sector does not, however, have the moral force to transform the ideological context within which the child care debate is currently conducted. Nor can the legal, economic, organizational, and political resources necessary to transform employer-employee relations be mobilized under purely private or voluntary auspices. Restructuring work expectations, integrating the care of children into broader institutional frameworks, and transforming the complex of values surrounding family life in this society are tasks beyond the scope of the voluntary sector. The enhancement of family life as here suggested is a task requiring the material and moral resources of state and federal governments, in partnership with private enterprise. Only the public sector can provide the financial incentives for active employer interest in this issue and the resources for coordinating and funding voluntary sector services. The voluntary sector can bring pressure to bear upon governments to accomplish these ends, but it cannot take the place of government if the kinds of changes in American institutional life proposed here are ever to be realized.

5

The Politics of the Voluntary Sector

E. TERRENCE JONES

What voluntary agencies want, American governments often have. A group of working parents seeks more financial support for day-care centers from Congress and state legislatures because the parents themselves cannot afford to pay the entire cost. Several black neighborhood organizations try to convince a city's mayor to reopen a full-service hospital because many members of the black community do not have ready access to adequate health care. A senior citizens association wants the state social services agency to enforce more stringently nursing home safety regulations in order to protect the residents' lives. A group concerned about women's freedoms and population growth asks a federal court to overturn a state law limiting abortions, on the grounds that the statute violates an individual's constitutional rights.

What all of these situations have in common is that the voluntary group lacks the money or the legitimacy or the authority to accomplish its goal: better day-care centers, more accessible health care, safer nursing homes, or greater freedom to choose to have an abortion. Government, at some level (federal, state, regional, or local) and within some branch (legislative, executive, judicial), has what the voluntary element needs to achieve its objective. Moreover, since voluntary groups often address a socially desirable goal, governments are sometimes predisposed to assist them.

Consequently, voluntary groups frequently find themselves

trying to convince one or more parts of government to help them. If these groups want to co-opt government in their overall plan, they must understand the most effective ways to approach the American polity's different levels and branches. After sounding a few discouraging general notes about some key underlying features of American government, this chapter will discuss maxims for the voluntary sector in lobbying government.

OBSTACLES

Convincing American governments to mend their ways is not an easy task. Several obstacles lie between the hope that new policies will be adopted and the achievement of change. Four major problems are governmental fragmentation, the upper-class bias in most public policies, the antigovernment motif in the American ethos, and the peculiar calculus which underlies participation in lobbying efforts.

When they set out to restructure American government, the Founding Fathers wanted to prevent tyranny by setting "ambition against ambition." Their solution was to disperse power among many governments, giving each some say but none a controlling interest. Their scheme—typically labelled "separation of powers" and "checks and balances"—has succeeded with a vengeance. Like any successful innovation, this one has been widely imitated as American government has expanded. Not only, for example, is power dispersed among major branches (e.g., Congress and the president), but it also is fragmented within individual institutions at all levels of government.

The practical impact of this fragmentation is inertia. In order to accomplish even modest change, numerous units—a legislative subcommittee here, an executive agency there—must concur. Any of these entities (and there may be as many as ten involved) can scuttle the whole effort by doing nothing: a subcommittee might not find the time to get it on its calendar this session, an agency might not have the resources to fit it into its budget this year, an elected executive might not be able to include it in his or her new initiatives this term. More often than not, attempts to make new public policy in the United States are not killed by some governmental body's formal action; instead, they are ignored to death.

Many Americans manage to subscribe simultaneously to two contradictory propositions. On the one hand, they believe that any individual or group can try to alter public policy and that, therefore, lobbying is an equal opportunity enterprise. On the other hand, these same people assume that money and status matter and that, therefore, wealthier and more established interests will dominate the policy fray. This apparent inconsistency reflects the American tendency not to have one's ideology cloud one's practical sense.

The fact is, to adapt George Orwell's phrase, that some Americans are more equal than others. Or, as E. E. Schattschneider wrote in his path-breaking *The Semisovereign People*, "The flaw in the pluralist heaven is that the heavenly chorus sings with a strong upper-class accent."[1] Upper-class people are more apt to be in office, better able to contribute to campaigns, more likely to hire the most skilled attorneys, and so forth.

Since a large portion of voluntary group attempts to rewrite public policies involves some type of redistribution from the rich to the poor, this upward tilt in American political reality is a serious problem. The upper and middle classes often applaud the voluntary groups' intentions, but seldom wish to see government tax them to provide funds needed to underwrite the programs.

During the past fifteen years, all the leading national public opinion surveys have reflected a growing disillusionment with government.[2] People are more cynical about government's practices and less confident about government's effectiveness. The last two presidents—Carter and Reagan—have won election by capitalizing on these sentiments and running against government. They and other politicians are sensitive to the public mood, and they tend to interpret opinion as being that people want less rather than more government.

Since voluntary groups often are requesting that government take on additional responsibilities and initiate new programs, they are swimming against the opinion tide in the 1980s. Elected officials are predisposed to believe that the public does not support expanded government, and appointed bureaucrats are preoccupied with protecting their existing turf. Hence, those asking them for more are not bringing happy news.

Finally, voluntary organizations pursuing collective goals are beset by the "free rider" problem. As Mancur Olson first noted, voluntary efforts have the problematic mix of individual costs (e.g., paying dues or contributing time) and collective benefits (e.g., a new program for *all* senior citizens) producing an over-abundance of "free riders"—those who cannot be prevented from consuming the benefits, but cannot be coerced into contributing to the costs.[3]

This means that voluntary groups pursuing public policies for the good of the entire class must often struggle to get members of that class (often themselves from the lower economic strata) to partici-pate either financially or personally in the process. Not only do individuals frequently have limited time and money, but they also calculate that the lobbying effort might very well succeed without their personal involvement.[4]

MAXIMS

The following ten pieces of advice are a mixture of theory and practice, science and art. The study of politics extends back to the Greeks and beyond, and Plato and Aristotle were among the first to attempt to summarize government's underlying principles. But only so much of reality can be encapsulated; the rest squishes over. Although these points are based on much research and practice, they are more a guide than a formula.

There Can't Be a Solution Until There's a Problem

Sometimes the principal task for a new voluntary association is gaining recognition that their area of interest actually represents a problem. In addition, groups which have already had their issues placed on the societal agenda need to work hard to keep them sa-lient in the public consciousness. In a political world where the demand to do something greatly exceeds the supply to get some-thing done, only the problems perceived to be highly important are apt to receive much attention.[5]

How does a group go about getting exposure for its concerns? The answer, in short, is usually by manipulating the mass media.[6] There has been much research during the past fifteen years about each medium's everyday routines.[7] These studies have amply demonstrated that print and electronic journalists have established procedures for defining and obtaining news. Groups wishing to have their problems and issues stay in the public eye must exploit these media routines. Some are well known, such as television's penchant for stories which have interesting visual dimensions. Others are more subtle, such as the need to link (peg, in journalism jargon) some timeless problem to a recent event.

Find Champions

Lobbying Congress or state or local legislatures will not be totally successful if it is done completely from the outside. Even a persistent, timely, and well-coordinated campaign typically needs one or more legislators who are fully committed to the cause and are willing to champion it. Probably the most vigorous and effective advocate for the aged in the United States, for example, is not the head of some senior citizens group, but Claude Pepper, the long-time Democratic congressman from Florida.

The biggest obstacle in any legislature is making sure that one's bill gets considered. Out of the hundreds of proposed laws introduced each session, only a small proportion are seriously deliberated. The rest are rarely voted down, but instead get lost somewhere along the way. The principal reason they are pigeonholed is that some legislator was not there to move them along at critical junctures, such as committee assignment (the bill should go to a committee where it will receive a friendly reception), committee scheduling (the earlier in the session it is heard, the better its chances), and floor scheduling (again, sooner is usually better than later).

Legislators are best able to make all of these things happen, not only because they are there (lobbyists can pay close attention to the legislative process) but, more important, because only they possess legislative currency: the ability to trade their committee or floor vote for another representative's support.

Where They Stand Depends on Where They're Headed

Although legislative champions can sometimes be recruited for altruistic reasons, most productive relationships between voluntary associations and elected or appointed government officials are based on some mutually satisfactory exchange. Voluntary groups know what they want from government. What might politicians or bureaucrats like to have in return?

The best single way to answer this question is to find out how the officials define their careers: where have they been, how do they interpret their current roles, and where do they want to go? Most ambitious people have a personal plan, a ladder they are climbing. A group seeking to enlist an official in its cause needs to know where the ladder is based, where the person is now, and what the next rung is.

For example, most state legislatures have several members who eye themselves as potential governors. Part of their political game plan includes getting themselves and their work known outside of their immediate districts. One good way to make this happen is to persuade the legislator to take the lead in promoting the voluntary group's program both by helping to dramatize the problem (State Senator X inspects the nursing home) and by allowing the legislator to take credit for the solution (X introduces nursing home reform bill which, in fact, has been written by the voluntary association).

Although the search for ambition will take longer in most bureaucracies than it would in the typical legislature, many appointed officials—especially at the middle and upper levels of government agencies—also have high aspirations. Either because they define their own success in terms of policy accomplishments or because they are seeking more prestigious posts (the two goals, of course, are not mutually exclusive), they are open to innovative programs which will bring them opportunity to break new ground.

Don't Tell No Lies, Don't Make No Threats

Milton Rakove's insightful analysis of the Daley machine is entitled, *Don't Make No Waves, Don't Back No Losers.*[8] This pithy advice capsulized the marching orders for the ward and precinct captains in Chicago. Another bluntly worded aphorism for lobbyists would be this: Don't tell no lies, don't make no threats.

Lobbyists and legislators have a symbiotic relationship: they need and rely on each other. One way in which legislators use lobbyists is as a source of information. Especially at the state and local levels, legislators are very much understaffed and, therefore, do not have the ability to gather and process background data and arguments for their policy proposals. Organizations whose goals are being served by these bills can help the legislator by doing the required research.

In this process, the voluntary group might be tempted (after all, the legislator would not know) to skew the statistics or to invent phony examples. Once the legislator uses the material, however, he or she accepts responsibility for its accuracy, and if a vigorous opponent or an enterprising reporter uncovers its weaknesses, the official will not be able to pass all of the public blame back onto the group which supplied it. Voluntary organizations rarely get more than one chance to make such a mistake; a reputation for bad research circulates quickly among legislators, and lobbyists who have distributed the tainted data are no longer welcome.[9]

When an elected official is an especially stubborn obstacle in the way of an organization's policy objectives, someone usually suggests that the group try to defeat the politician at his or her next election. This suggestion should be resisted, since such threats rarely work and often are counterproductive.

Lobbying Is Not for Lone Rangers

Logrolling ("you scratch my back and I'll scratch yours") is a time-honored tradition at all levels of American politics. It is highly unlikely that any single voluntary association can unilaterally produce major shifts in public policymaking. To be most effective, one must seek political allies.

Although coalitions escalate the bargaining that must be done (the members, after all, rarely have identical goals, and each wishes to gain more from the coalition than it gives), they are an essential element in accomplishing significant changes in a decentralized polity.[10] As has already been noted, most American political structures favor the status quo, and it typically requires a supramajority to overcome policy inertia.

In forming coalitions, groups must not be overly picky about their political partners. More often than not, the unions are temporary alliances and not permanent relationships. The emphasis should be on similarities rather than differences. For example, groups aiming to provide more public dollars for the physically disabled should seek out businesses which produce equipment or construct facilities for the disabled. More generally, having some business interests working with you often neutralizes other corporate opposition by making it more difficult to characterize the issue as the haves versus the have-nots.

Don't Leave Lobbying to the Lobbyists

In many organizations, lobbying is left almost entirely to one or two staff members. Once a policy agenda has been established, the executive director or, in larger groups, the governmental relations specialist takes almost complete responsibility for planning and implementing a lobbying strategy.

Such total reliance on a small number of individuals underplays the voluntary association's hand. Political strength typically lies in numbers and diversity. Even though those charged with the major daily responsibility for working with government might sometimes jealously guard their prerogative as the sole link between the organization and the polity, they should not be allowed to monopolize lobbying.

More of the association's entourage—especially other members of the boards of directors, chapter presidents, middle managers, and so forth—should be actively involved. This means, of course, that the process for arriving at the group's program must be more open and more elaborate. People are not apt to eagerly execute a plan for greater governmental assistance unless they have had some role in formulating it.

If You Didn't Like the Law,
Maybe You'll Love the Regulations

A great many statutes written and passed by Congress and by state legislatures are vague. Gaining consensus can be very difficult, and yet, when the legislators perceive that the public demands action (or at least the appearance of action), they feel that some bill must be passed. One common way out of this apparent impasse is to make the law's language very general, thereby allowing individual legislators and lobbyists to read different meanings into the same words.[11] Thus, there can be agreement on the bill's passage, even though there may be disagreement about its meaning.

The buck is then passed to the bureaucracy which, in most cases, does not like ambiguous statutes. Charged with implementing the law in an evenhanded and consistent fashion, and interested in protecting itself from charges of being arbitrary and capricious, the bureaucracy usually writes regulations which transform the general language into more specific requirements.

Voluntary organizatons must be prepared to intervene in the regulation-drafting process. Such an intervention requires knowing a good deal about the organizational routines of the agency responsible for administering the law and having some sensitivity to the values of the individuals staffing that agency. Since there is much less publicity associated with writing regulations than with passing legislation, it is very important that the lobbying effort begin too early rather than too late.

Courts Make Laws, Too

Although a naive version of American political mythology claims that the courts only interpret what is in the law and do not substitute their judgment for that of elected officials, even a cursory review of U.S. political history shows that judges have frequently been active in the lawmaking process. Hence, voluntary groups which have not been successful in lobbying elected officials or bureaucracies might find a sympathetic ear in the courts.

The National Association for the Advancement of Colored People (NAACP) is an example of an organization which has had great success in pursuing its objectives through the courts. Thwarted by insensitivity and lack of representation in the elected branches of federal and state government, the NAACP began to concentrate on the courts as the instrument for achieving policy change in the 1930s. For the next 30 years, the NAACP won one landmark case after another. Among its triumphs was putting a legal end to white primaries, restrictive covenants, and school segregation.

Courts, of course, must be lobbied very differently from legislatures and executives.[12] Certain things, such as wining and dining judges, are simply not done. Instead of personal contact and informal persuasion, voluntary groups seeking victories through the judiciary must carefully plan a strategy which creatively blends legal elements (e.g., constitutional precedent) with drama: a particular case which clearly demonstrates the voluntary group's cause.

Don't Forget: Expenditures Usually Require Revenues

As various groups lobby one or another government for appropriations, it is often easy to forget that how much a program receives depends both on its share of the existing revenues and the overall change in total receipts. Organizations which focus entirely on getting the same fraction might find themselves, in an era of shrinking government, obtaining the same proportional slice of a smaller and smaller pie.

With all levels of government finding it more difficult to raise taxes and more politically palatable to cut outlays, groups must devote some attention to revenue policies if they are to maintain current public support, much less obtain additional resources. Since one state after another (the number now exceeds twenty) passed some type of fiscal limitation measure during the past decade, the proponents of less government have had a relatively easy time of it, in part because the advocates for more government have not organized to support existing revenues.[13] Instead, the more common reaction has been for each voluntary association to finesse the tax issue and hope to survive by getting a larger share of a smaller pot. This beggar-thy-neighbor approach has doubtful validity in the short run and is disastrous in the long run.

Policy Success Equals a Few Big Winners and Many Small Losers

Given the status quo bias in the American political system, the difficulty of recruiting support for a cause, and the fact that, at any given time, only a modest amount of slack public resources are probably available for new policy initiatives, what is the obvious conclusion?

The logic chain goes like this.[14] First, because of government inertia, it will take a substantial push to make something happen. Second, people are not likely to join a push unless it promises large rewards for them. Third, since unclaimed tax dollars are limited, large rewards can be obtained only if the benefits go to a relative few. Ergo, the most likely policy successes occur when the benefits will be received by a small number and the costs are spread (typically through the tax system) among the many.

By the same reasoning, the least likely policy proposals to be adopted are those which distribute the benefits widely and concentrate the cost. Both consumer protection and gun control are excellent examples of this proposition. Even though public opinion polls steadily show that a clear majority support tougher controls on handguns, few executives propose and even fewer legislatures adopt effective gun control laws. Why? The benefits to the many are small: a modest reduction in the already minute probability that an innocent person will be killed or injured by a handgun. The costs to the few are high: individuals involved in the production, distribution, and use of handguns would either have their livelihood disrupted or their personal hobby hampered. Organized through a very effective lobby (the National Rifle Association), the intense minority has easily held off the apathetic majority.

Lobbying government never ends. Each attempt to gain some additional resource from the public sector or to prevent some loss from an existing program should be viewed as one episode in a continuing struggle. Although the matter at hand is usually important and merits close attention, it should always be placed in a larger context. Most elected and appointed officials tend to stay in public life for decades, and it is sometimes prudent to lose gracefully today in order to win decisively tomorrow. Voluntary groups will accomplish more of their political objectives if they adopt a long-range perspective on their lobbying efforts.

What would a long-range lobbying plan include? The following six points provide a framework on which to hang a fully developed strategy.

First, determine what the voluntary association wants from government and specify which units (e.g., level and branch) have the actual or potential authority to provide it. If the group's goals will require significant additional dollars from government, then the present climate of a steady state public sector suggests that one of the goals will need to involve revenue policy.

Second, determine what opinions among which publics will support the efforts to have the key government units adopt and implement the desired programs. The analysis of opinion should include salience (e.g., that this is an important problem) as well as direction (e.g., support for more government action to solve the problem). The key publics will probably vary by level of government and by the type of government unit.

Third, identify and recruit champions in the target governmental units. Once these individuals have established their credentials, support them even when it has some costs for secondary objectives. Do not abandon your best legislative ally, for example, when he or she is under attack for some alleged wrongdoing.

Fourth, involve most of the voluntary association's staff and members in the lobbying process. Implement a program to educate the internal group about the lobbying effort's goals and objectives, devise specific roles for each person, and assign management positions for coordinating everyone's lobbying actions.

Fifth, develop coalitions with other groups. Some of these coalitions will be relatively permanent, while others will be ad hoc. Devote adequate staff time and association resources to maintaining the coalitions.

Sixth, monitor and update the entire plan. Regularly scan the political environment for important changes in structure (e.g., shifts in functions between governmental levels, bureaucratic agencies, or legislative committees), personnel (e.g., rising stars that necessitate repositioning the group's wagon accordingly), and climate (e.g., shifts in public opinion).

6

The Domain of Private Social Welfare: Comparisons between the Public Sector and the Voluntary Sector

MICHAEL SOSIN

Voluntary social welfare agencies dispense many social services in the United States, and researchers have recently begun to reexamine their contribution (Gibleman, 1981; Kramer, 1981; Terrell, 1979; Wendel et al., 1979; Young and Finch, 1977). A common focus is the *domain* of the voluntary sector—the social problems or issues covered, services rendered, and client population served (Thompson, 1967; Levine and White, 1961). A key hypothesis is that voluntary agencies tend to differentiate their domain from public ones, continually altering their service network as public responsibilities expand (Grønbjerg 1982; Manser and Cass, 1976).

The differentiation hypothesis has important implications for students of social welfare. At the level of theory, it implies that it is now best to view voluntary agencies more as reactors to the public sector than as organizations that respond to many local demands. The implication at a planning level is that public policy is an important determinant of the reduction in the domain of the voluntary sector.

Unfortunately, contemporary empirical work on the presumed differentiation across the entire network of social service agencies in the United States does not exist. It is even difficult to locate a survey of the activities of the voluntary sector as a whole or a concise theoretical argument that can be used to test hypotheses. Accordingly, this paper presents a discussion of the issue. It develops alternate theoretical views concerning the differences in domain between the voluntary and public sectors, presents empirical tests of the views, and discusses the implications of the results for a characterization of the voluntary social welfare network and for planning.

THEORY AND HYPOTHESIS

A complete theoretical conceptualization would be quite useful in comparing the domain of the voluntary sector to that of the public sector. Such a theory would specify exactly what types of differences to expect and also to list causal mechanisms, so that one would have a way of interpreting results of the data analysis. Although such a complete theory does not exist, Grønbjerg (1982) presents a partial theoretical formulation of the differentiation thesis that, while peripheral to her argument, is a useful place to begin the analysis.

Dealing more with philanthropy than with social welfare, Grønbjerg argues that the domain of the voluntary sector must be understood in the contemporary political context. She claims that the United States has witnessed the growth of a "mass society," which involves an expansion of political rights among citizens. "Mass society" implies that all citizens have a right to participate in society, and as a result the public sector is expected to guarantee economic survival. Public agencies thus have come to provide for basic needs such as income maintenance, and to dispense tangible, material social services that relate to basic needs. Grønbjerg also argues that the belief in equality leads to universalism in the provision of services by government, ensuring that individuals are not selected on the basis of ascriptive characteristics.

Grønbjerg's major point is that the mass society also affects voluntary agencies. She believes that they have become somewhat more like the public sector in their level of bureaucracy and their desire to appeal to the mass rather than to particular subgroups. This major point is not at issue here. But she also cites more controversial differences in domains. She claims that voluntary agencies once also provided for basic needs but that they have been forced to differentiate themselves from these new public responsibilities because they cannot legitimate overlapping domains. To obtain funds from government, as a response to community-wide and national funding, and to convince the public that they play a useful role, voluntary agencies have come to focus on supplementary "quality of life" problems, such as those demanding family counselling. They have also attempted to demonstrate their efficacy by turning to professional services. Finally, although as a result of the mass society movement the trend is toward universalism, voluntary agencies have retained something of their traditional propensity to select clients according to such criteria as race, religion, and age.

While Grønbjerg's view might seem convincing, it contradicts some organizational theories. Many talk of common processes that affect all organizations and that might be expected to reduce differences between the two sectors. Thus, one perspective suggests that the availability of resources affects the services that agencies deliver (Brittain and Freeman, 1980; Pennings, 1980; Stinchcombe, 1975), and another points out that organizations usually ensure that they receive sufficient resources to survive by meeting community demands for a specific domain (Scott, 1967; Clark, 1956; Selznick, 1949). Because public and voluntary agencies are faced with similar sets of local cultural beliefs and community demands, one implication is that the problems, services, and clients dealt with in each sector might be quite similar. (Indeed, as has been mentioned, Grønbjerg sees such similarities in organization but not in domain.) In short, according to this view there is less differentiation by sectors because the welfare system responds to specific group demands rather than to a widespread belief in government-sponsored social citizenship.

To date, these alternate views about domains have not been tested. For example, Grønbjerg's (1982) own data concern philanthropy as a whole rather than social welfare agencies, speak as much of historical trends as of current patterns, and view the results in light of various additional points, such as the entire size of the voluntary network. No other empirical study of the issue could be located.

This paper tests three hypotheses derived from Grønbjerg that concern social welfare organizations: that voluntary agencies are differentiated from public agencies in the problems covered and focus on quality-of-life problems rather than basic needs; that they stress different services from the public sector, particularly professional as opposed to tangible services; and that they are more particularistic than the public agencies. In assessing these hypotheses, the alternate view, stressing similarities in the domains of agencies in the two sectors, is kept in mind.

DATA AND METHODS

The data in this paper are part of a pilot study concerning the nature of the local social welfare network in six counties. The counties were selected from a sampling frame developed in another research project, an examination of public emergency assistance programs (Handler and Sosin, 1983). The project selected counties on the basis of a stratified design. There were six strata, developed on a state level according to the size of public welfare benefits as a whole (low or high) and the size of emergency assistance benefits (low, medium, or high). States, and counties within them, were selected in a way that resulted in an approximately equal chance of selection for each county in the nation with a population of over 25,000. For the current study, one county in each cell was selected randomly.

The six randomly selected counties seemed fairly representative of the nation as a whole. They varied in size from a population of 100,000 to a population of 500,000. They also varied geographically, as they included representatives from the Northeast, South, Southwest, Midwest, and West.[1]

In each county, the main source of data was the social service directory. Data were collected for 675 agencies, both voluntary and public. Agencies not normally defined as involving social welfare services, including hospitals, schools, and legal aid clinics, were excluded (Kahn, 1973). The directories were unusually comprehensive and included apparently complete information concerning all of the relevant variables.[2]

The coding scheme differentiated between public and voluntary agencies. The criterion for differentiation was auspices; that is, the type of unit that had direct administrative control. Public agencies were defined as agencies administered by a government agency. Voluntary agencies were agencies under the auspices of a religious group, a national non-profit entity (such as the Red Cross), or a non-profit local and secular board of directors. They might also be proprietary in nature. Data were collected for 570 voluntary agencies and 105 public agencies.

The nature of the population served by each agency was also coded from the directories. Focus was placed on whether an agency claimed to specialize in a particular age group, ethnic group, religion, sex, or in a group with a particular income.

A key task was developing measures of the problem and service domains from the directories. The specific items were not developed solely to test the mass society view, but were to be as comprehensive as possible. Twenty-four categories of problems and nineteen categories of services were developed.[3] These generally parallel specializations in social welfare. Tables 6-1 and 6-2 list the items. (The tables present the tests of the first two hypotheses, as will be discussed below.)

To test the specifics of the mass society view from this data, one must specify which of the categories involve basic needs as opposed to quality-of-life problems, and tangible as opposed to professional services. Grønbjerg (1982) offers few examples and fails to define her terms in detail. It is thus necessary to estimate which items might match her views.

Basic need problems apparently are those that threaten the normal survival of clients. Needs for continuing material aid, emergency assistance, disaster aid, shelter, or transportation are the clearest examples. For children and the dependent, special care might also be a basic need. Neglect and dependency and the need for special protection and care thus may be fringe basic need problems.

Quality-of-life problems appear to involve improving or extending life. Grønbjerg implies that health issues fit this category— although we will quarrel with her on this at a later point. She also includes family problems and education. Coded problems fitting the category thus involve health, individual and family life, and the need for day care. Apparently, special deficiencies or life-stage issues are also included, which translate into areas such as aging, school problems, development disabilities, mental health needs, alcoholism, drug abuse, and family planning.

A few problems do not appear to fit either category. These

Table 6-1.

Comparison of Problems Covered in Voluntary and Public Social Welfare Agencies—by Rank and Frequency

Problem	Voluntary Agency (N = 570)		Public Agency (N = 105)	
	Rank	Frequency	Rank	Frequency
Individual and family life	1	25.8%	3	11.4%*
Health	2	17.2	9.5	6.7*
Need for day care	3	15.8	9.5	6.7*
Physical handicap	4	9.8	5	10.5
Aging	5	9.1	7.5	7.6
Developmental disability	6	8.4	6	8.6
Mental health	7	7.9	18.5	2.9
Financial emergency	8.5	7.4	18.5	2.9
Alcoholism	8.5	7.2	13	4.8
Nonfinancial emergency	10	6.7	13	4.8
Unemployment	11	6.0	1	30.5*
Homelessness	12.5	3.9	11	5.7
Need for family planning	12.5	3.9	13	4.8
Continued financial need	14	3.3	2	25.7*
Drug abuse	15	2.6	16	3.8
Dependency and neglect	16	2.5	7.5	7.6*
Criminal justice	17	2.3	4	12.4*
Need for transportation	18	1.9	22	1.0
Natural disaster	19	1.8	22	1.0
Discrimination	20	.9	18.5	2.9
Protection and care	21	.5	15	4.7*
School problem	22	.4	18.5	2.9*
Consumer complaint	23	.2	22	1.0
Landlord-tenant problem	24	.1	24	0

$r_{(s)} = .54$ *p < .05 (comparing frequencies)

Ranks are averaged in the case of ties.

Table 6-2.
Comparison of Services Rendered in Voluntary and Public
Social Welfare Agencies—by Rank and Frequency

Service	Voluntary Agency (N = 570)		Public Agency (N = 105)	
	Rank	Frequency	Rank	Frequency
Education	1	33.9%	2	32.4%
Counseling	2	28.4	1	42.9*
Information and referral	3	18.4	4	29.5*
Day care	4	17.0	7.5	13.5
Recreation	5	15.3	7.5	13.3
Medical care	6	12.5	11	7.8
Advocacy	7	10.9	12	6.7
Material assistance	8	10.5	5	26.7*
Rehabilitation-residential	9	8.4	9.5	8.6
Employment and training	10	8.1	3	31.4*
General social services	11	6.3	6	17.1*
Transportation	12	5.6	9.5	8.6
Maintenance-residential	13	3.7	17.5	1.9
Rehabilitation-day	14	2.5	13.5	5.7
Chore	15	2.1	13.5	5.7*
Adoption	16	1.9	15.5	3.8
Foster care	17	1.4	15.5	3.8
Community organization	18	.9	17.5	1.7
Developmental-residential	19	.7	19	0

$r_{(s)}$ = .84   *p < .05 (comparing frequencies)

Ranks are averaged in the case of ties.

involve such issues as unemployment, criminal justice, and discrimination. Thus, the mass society view does not necessarily make
predictions about such problems.

A similar rough division can be made among services. Tangible
services might include material assistance, transportation, chore

service, information and referral, unemployment, adoption, foster care, recreation, and perhaps advocacy. Professional services might include education, counselling, health care, rehabilitative services (institutional care and day care are separated), developmental services, and perhaps maintenance services. Again, certain items, such as general social services, day care, and community organization do not clearly fit either category.

Some problems with the mass society distinctions are apparent from these differentiations. In certain cases one can make alternate arguments for the choice of categories. For example, health needs may involve difficulties related to life-threatening problems, such as cancer. Is this really a quality-of-life as opposed to a basic need issue? Further, as has been mentioned, certain items do not fit the categories.

The ambiguity of categories suggests that we must not rely on them too heavily in analyzing the data; they may not be accurate enough in representing agency domains. Therefore, rather than relying on indicators that combine items, this analysis looks at each problem and service (as well as population category) separately. It estimates how closely patterns of differentiation between the public and voluntary sectors follow the mass society theory, but it also looks for other explanations for whatever differences (and similarities) between sectors turn up.

PLAN OF ANALYSIS

Differences in frequencies are calculated to determine whether each element of the domain is more common in the public or voluntary sector. The independent variable is auspices—public or voluntary—while the dependent variable is the frequency with which each problem, service, or population group is in the domain of the agencies. Two statistical tests are appropriate for this task: t-test comparisons and the chi-squared test (Huntsberger, 1967). Because the t-test comparisons directly use frequencies and are simpler to report, they are presented in the text. A level of statistical significance of .05 and the two-tailed test are used. It should be noted that the chi-squared statistics were also computed. The statistical results obtained with this test are similar to those reported in the text; the only difference is that three statistically significant t-test results involving specific age groups would not be statistically significant according to chi-squared.

The number of statistically significant differences is also a measure of the level of differentiation between the sectors as a whole, but it may be too dependent on the number of cases to be valid. Thus, while the lack of comparable items disallows drawing conclusions about the population served, differences in the ranks of problems and services between the two sectors are also presented. Rank order correlations that compare the stress placed on problems or services in the two sectors are calculated; a positive correlation implies overlap in the emphasis by each sector, while a negative correlation indicates differentiation. Strictly speaking, only a statistically significant negative correlation supports the view that the two sectors tend to focus on distinct domains. A statistically significant positive correlation supports the alternate view.

RESULTS

Tables 6-1 and 6-2 (presented earlier) and 6-3 (to follow the analyses of the first two tables) present the analyses that test the three hypotheses. Because no overview of the voluntary service network exists, the information is useful for considering the patterns in the voluntary sector, as are the comparisons with the public sector. Owing to the complicated nature of the results and the need for such a detailed analysis, results for each hypothesis and table are reported separately.

Problems Covered

Table 6-1 reports information concerning the problems covered in the agencies. The left-hand side of the table lists the categories of problems and their ranks in the voluntary sector. It also reports the frequency with which each problem is covered. The right-hand side of the table reports comparative information for agencies in the public sector.

One issue is the emphasis the voluntary sector places on each social problem. Looking at the left-hand side of the table, it appears that problems which might be considered quality-of-life issues dominate. The items ranking one through seven are consistent with the quality-of-life definition: individual and family life, health, the need for day care, physical handicap, aging, developmental disabilities, and mental health. The problems are dealt with in between 25.8 percent and 7.9 percent of the voluntary agencies; taken together, they account for a good deal of what voluntary agencies in the sample contribute to the welfare network. Only three issues involving the quality of life rank lower: alcoholism, ranking eighth (a tie), family planning, tied for twelfth, and school problems, ranking twenty-second.

Basic needs items seem to share middle and lower ranks. The highest rank for a problem in this group is a tie for eighth, held by financial emergency. Homelessness is tied for twelfth, a need for transportation ranks eighteenth, and a natural disaster ranks nineteenth. Dependency and neglect, and protection and care—possible basic needs items—rank sixteenth and twenty-first, respectively.

Middle and lower ranks are also common for issues that do not fit the categories. For example, unemployment ranks eleventh, while criminal justice ranks seventeenth. Legal problems involving consumer complaints and landlord-tenant problems are at the bottom of the list.

As the mass society view posits, quality-of-life problems appear to rank highly. However, the key issue for this paper is comparative areas of concentration between sectors. This may be assessed by comparing the frequency with which each problem is stressed in the voluntary sector with its stress in the public sector.

Asterisks on Table 6-1 report statistically significant differences in frequencies between the two sectors. Thus, according to the table, in this sample voluntary agencies are more likely to stress—to a statistically significant degree—individual and family life, health, and day care. Public agencies demonstrate statistically significant tendencies to deal more frequently with unemployment, continuing financial need, dependency and neglect, criminal justice, protection and care, and school problems.

These results help assess the mass society view. One core tenet of the view is that quality-of-life items are more commonly the focus of voluntary agencies than of public agencies. This seems to be supported by the data for selected items. Voluntary agencies are thus more likely to be involved with the three problems ranked highest: health, individual and family life, and the need for day care.

However, the level of differentiation is selective; many other quality-of-life items are not stressed differently by the two sectors to a statistically significant degree. Items not differentiated include physical handicaps, aging, developmental disabilities, and drug abuse. School problems, which may represent a quality-of-life issue, are even less likely to be a voluntary responsibility to a statistically significant degree.

A mixed pattern also arises from the basic needs items. Some items stressed less heavily by voluntary agencies according to the frequencies seem to deal with basic needs. These include continuing financial needs, neglect and dependency, and the need for protection and care. However, many items are stressed similarly, such as disaster problems, emergency financial need, and the need for transportation.

Two statistically significant differences involve items about which the mass society view is silent: voluntary agencies do not focus as often on unemployment and criminal justice. To be sure, one might attempt to stretch the definition of basic needs to cover these items. One might say that unemployment can lead to a material problem, or that criminal justice services cover the basic need of protection. But such a definition would also include as basic needs nearly every problem; a very large segment can indirectly contribute to survival. A more likely explanation is that both items involve "social control" issues—encouraging work or discouraging crime. The differential involving school problems may be described similarly. Apparently social control is also an area in which voluntary agencies are likely to be underrepresented. This was not anticipated by the mass society view.

Looking at all of the patterns, it must be concluded that similarities are more common than the differences the mass society view claims. Only the nine items mentioned above demonstrate statistically significant differences, and this is a small minority of the 24 items. Further, there is also a moderate, statistically significant positive correlation between the two sets of ranks, 0.54. This indicates that the ranks of problems in voluntary and public agencies exhibit similarity to a statistically significant degree.

In sum, although voluntary agencies clearly stress items Grønbjerg might call quality-of-life problems, while less frequently dealing with basic needs, a comparison with public responsibilities demonstrates only selective differences. For some highly stressed problems these differences are consistent, but other differences are not consistent. Overall, similarities dominate differences.

Services Rendered

Table 6.2 presents information about the services rendered. It lists all of the services in order of their rank in the voluntary sector, reports the frequency with which each service is offered in this sector, and compares ranks and frequencies to those in the public sector.

One issue is whether there is any pattern of services within the voluntary sector. For example, Grønbjerg appears to believe that professional services dominate, and that tangible services are provided less often. From the ranks of items in the voluntary sector in Table 6-2, no clear pattern involving the professional service-tangible service distinction emerges. For example, the two highest-ranking items, education and counselling, may be professional services. But other items in the professional category, such as rehabilitation and development, rank quite low. Similarly, information and referral, and recreation—two tangible services—rank third and fifth, while other tangible services, such as chore service, rank quite low. Services that are difficult to categorize, such as day care or employment and training, also vary greatly in rank.

Again, the most important issue is the comparison between the public and voluntary sectors. The mass society view predicts vast differences and a relatively strong emphasis on professional services in voluntary agencies, along with a relative lack of emphasis on material services.

According to Table 6-2, only a small number of differences in frequencies reach statistical significance. All differences involve less emphasis on specific services in the voluntary sector than in the public sector. Voluntary agencies are less likely to focus on counselling, material assistance, unemployment services, information and referral, chore services, and general social services.

These results indicate that in keeping with the mass society view, five items that appear to represent tangible services are less likely to be in the domain of voluntary agencies than of public agencies. These items include material assistance, unemployment services, information and referral, chore services, and (more questionably a tangible service) general social services. Thus, there is some support for the mass society view that the voluntary sector shies away from basic needs. But support is very selective. Other items that might be tangible services, such as transportation or emergency financial aid, do not demonstrate such statistically significant differences.

The claim that voluntary agencies are more likely to provide professional services is not supported. Voluntary agencies are not more likely (to a statistically significant degree) to stress such professional services as rehabilitation and medical care. More telling, Table 6-2 reports that they are actually less likely to provide a core professional service, namely counselling.

Overall, because there are only six significant differences out of nineteen items, similarities appear to outweigh differences. Similarities are indeed striking when ranks are considered. The rank order correlation between services in the two sectors is quite large, positive, and statistically significant, 0.83.

In opposition to the mass society view, there are more similarities than differences between the two sectors. Voluntary agencies stress only selective professional services and often provide them no more frequently (or even less frequently) than public agencies. Only a few items support a differentiation concerning tangible services. The hypothesized distinction between the sectors thus rarely develops.

Population Covered

Another set of issues involves the client population served. Grønbjerg's (1982) view is that voluntary agencies tend to be more particularistic than public agencies, although the tendency is toward universalism in both sectors. The alternate theory suggests similarities.

Table 6-3 reports results that include the population served, focussing on sex, race, religion, age, and the existence of a means test. It reports the frequency with which these factors are used as selection criteria in voluntary agencies and compares them to similar frequencies for public agencies.

According to the frequencies for voluntary agencies alone, universalism appears to be the dominant mode, as both theories

Table 6–3.
Comparison of Populations Served in Voluntary and
Public Social Welfare Agencies

Population Served	Frequency Served	
	Voluntary Agency (N = 570)	Public Agency (N = 105)
Population Group		
Males only	4.2%	1.0%*
Females only	2.5	0.0
One religious group	1.4	0.0
Below a given income (means test)	4.7	21.9*
Race		
Whites	98.2	100.0
Blacks	98.2	100.0
Native Americans	99.5	100.0
Asian Americans (various groups)	99.5	100.0
Spanish speaking (various groups)	98.6	100.0
Age		
Less than 5	59.3	56.2
5–12	50.7	52.4
13–17	62.8	67.6
18–21	66.3	76.2*
22–54	64.6	75.2*
55–59	70.0	79.1
60–64	70.7	80.0*
65 or over	70.7	80.0*
All ages	39.8	43.8

*$p < .05$

predict. According to Table 6-3, just 4.2 percent of the agencies serve only males, and just 2.1 percent serve only females. Very small percentages rely on racial or religious selectivity. The means test is also uncommon, used in 4.7 percent of the voluntary agencies. Forty percent of the voluntary agencies have no age restrictions, and each of the listed age groups is covered by a majority of the voluntary programs. Thus, while age selectivity is not universal, a large percentage of the agencies seems to select a portion of the population to serve.

Nevertheless, the mass society view predicts that voluntary agencies are more selective than public agencies. Even though the distribution of many items about the population served might minimize differences, some statistically significant results occur and are reported in Table 6-3. Voluntary agencies are less likely to have a means test. Public agencies are less likely to serve only males, to serve only individuals 18 to 54, or to focus only on those 60 and over.

One of these results, that public agencies are much more likely than voluntary agencies to have means tests, contradicts the mass society view. But this may be an artifact, consistent with the public agencies' focus on financial problems, which is in effect a means test. Voluntary agencies that dispense financial aid are also more likely to have means tests.[4]

The difference is not great, but the theory is supported by the fact that voluntary agencies are indeed somewhat more particularistic than public agencies in other ways. They are thus more restrictive in terms of age. According to Table 6-3, they are less likely to serve groups of 18-21 year olds and 22-54 year olds, and are also somewhat more selective (not to a statistically significant degree) with older individuals. The relation occurs even though voluntary agencies are only slightly less likely to serve all age groups; apparently, these agencies target somewhat smaller ranges among adults and the elderly in general than do public agencies.

Given the near universalism of race, religion, and sex domains, one might not expect voluntary agencies to be less universalistic on these measures. Within the limits of selectivity, however, the particularism of these agencies, which Grønbjerg predicts, is also apparent in this case. According to Table 6-3, voluntary agencies are slightly less likely to serve males, and they demonstrate more selectivity on racial and religious grounds (this is not statistically significant). As might be expected, no public agencies exclude racial or religious groups.

There is thus some support for the mass society view concerning the population served; voluntary agencies are indeed more selective than public agencies (except for the existence of a means test). Perhaps there is some historical continuity, as many voluntary services traditionally have had a mission of limited focus. But in general, both types of agencies have universalistic orientations and accept a wide range of clients. The notable tendency of agencies to become more universalistic—acknowledged in virtually all views of the voluntary sector—is quite evident.

VOLUNTARY DOMAINS AND PUBLIC
FINANCIAL SUPPORT

Many of the results seem to indicate at least a moderate degree of overlap between the domains of the two sectors, bringing the mass society view into question to some degree. But the view implies that the differentiation is in part due to the way public agencies fund the voluntary sector. Public agencies are said primarily to fund voluntary agencies that are willing to differentiate their problems and services from those of public agencies, so that overlap is avoided. Thus, it is important to determine whether the predicted pattern is more apparent in voluntary agencies that are funded by government. It is also claimed that public agencies demand that the voluntary agencies they fund be universalistic.

Again, there is an alternate hypothesis (for problems and services): perhaps public agencies fund agencies that are much like themselves. Contracting may occur when there is an overload of clients, or when public agencies in a specific community wish to make use of the voluntary sector to deliver services that are normally public priorities. Thus, to test the theories more completely, a key quesiton emerges: Do voluntary agencies that are funded by government tend to represent more completely the pattern Grønbjerg hypothesizes? This section examines that possibility.

Methods

In theory, it is possible to test predictions concerning the impact of public funding by relating the acceptance of governmental support by voluntary agencies to all of the variables described in Tables 6-1, 6-2, and 6-3. Unfortunately, the tables provide too much information. Such an extensive series of comparisons would be too confusing to discuss.

As an alternative, a few key variables can be analyzed. Funding from the government is related to seven problems: individual and family life, health, day care, continuing financial need, unemployment, drug dependency, and criminal justice. Services to be tested include counselling, medical care, employment and training, day care, day rehabilitation, residential rehabilitation, continuing financial support, and advocacy.

Most of these variables are items for which differences in emphasis between voluntary and public agencies were discovered from comparisons of frequencies in Tables 6-1 and 6-2. Thus, further analysis will help discover if public funding leads to the determined division of labor. A few of the included variables signify problems and services that voluntary and public agencies are about equally likely to provide. In each case, however, the aspects of the domain relate to important hypotheses. Thus, many believe that public funding might decrease advocacy, an activity that is not considered professional (Kramer, 1981), while the mass society argument seems to be that public funding would increase the emphasis of voluntary agencies on rehabilitation, a professional service.

Public financial support will be related to all aspects of the population served, including ages, race restrictions, religious restrictions, sex restrictions, and the existence of a means test. Grønbjerg seems to imply that public funding should reduce restrictions and thus increase the universalism of services in all cases. The results are reported in Table 6-4.

Comparisons

As Table 6-4 points out, 183 of the voluntary agencies receive public funding from one or more levels of government. As the table reports, voluntary agencies receiving public funds are more likely to emphasize mental health, drug problems, unemployment, criminal justice, in-patient rehabilitation, employment and training, continuing financial support, and all religious groups to statistically significant degrees. They are less likely to emphasize health, day care, and a number of specific age groups; they are also less likely to serve all racial groups.

The relations in Table 6-4 involving problems are quite obviously in opposition to the mass society claims. While the argument is that quality-of-life issues are stressed more when voluntary agencies receive public funding, this does not seem to be the case. According to the table, individual and family problems are neither more nor less common when voluntary agencies receive public funding; in direct opposition to this point of view, day care and health problems are less common in the domain of the voluntary agencies with such support.

Table 6-4.

Frequencies and *t*-Tests Concerning the Domain of Voluntary Agencies; Public Funding and No Public Funding

	Frequencies	
	Public Funding (N = 183)	No Public Funding (N = 387)
Problem		
Individual and family life	27.3%	25.2%
Health	8.7	21.2
Day care	11.4	17.8
Continuing financial need	3.3	3.4
Employment	15.3	1.6*
Mental health	12.6	5.7*
Drug dependency	3.3	2.3*
Criminal justice	4.3	1.3*
Service		
Counseling	27.5	27.9
Rehabilitation-day	3.8	1.8
In-patient rehabilitation	14.8	5.4*
Medical care	10.4	13.4
Employment and training	18.6	3.1*
Day care	14.8	18.1
Advocacy	12.0	10.3
Continuing financial support	0.0	2.2*
Age		
Under 5	47.5	64.9*
6-12	39.9	55.8*
13-17	56.8	65.6*
18-21	63.4	67.7
22-54	61.8	65.9
55-59	72.1	69.0
60-64	73.8	69.3
Over 65	73.2	69.5
All ages	30.1	44.2*
Males	94.5	96.4
Females	97.8	97.9
Whites	96.2	100.0*
Blacks	96.2	100.0*
Asians	97.8	100.0*
Hispanics	95.6	100.0*
Native Americans	98.4	100.0*
All religious groups	100.0	99.7*
Means test	5.5	4.4

*p < .05

In most ways, the relations seem to support the alternate hypothesis: public agencies are actually more likely to fund voluntary agencies that share the special concerns of the public sector. Unemployment is a public agency responsibility more frequently than a voluntary sector one (according to Table 6-1), and voluntary agencies receiving public funds focus on this problem more often than voluntary agencies not receiving public funds. Criminal justice follows the same pattern. In contrast, when issues involve areas in which voluntary agencies are more active than public agencies, such as individual and family life, health, and day care, public support does not relate to a voluntary agency emphasis on these problems.[5]

Relations involving services are also inconsistent with the mass society view, as there seems to be little evidence for the claim that public funds promote more professionalism on the part of voluntary agencies. Four services that might seem particularly professional—counselling, day rehabilitation, medical care, and residential rehabilitation—are included in the table, and only residential rehabilitation seems more common when there is public funding. Yet, in this case, one can make a more specific hypothesis: residential rehabilitation services may be largely supported by state and federal health and rehabilitation funds. The reliance in the United States on public support for private providers rather than on a national health care system seems to explain the relation best (a reliance that seems to be more due to lobbying from various medical groups than to a public desire to fund voluntary services that are particularly professional).

Table 6-4 reveals that services that do not seem highly professional, such as advocacy, employment and training, and day care, are not less common among voluntary agencies that are funded by government to a statistically significant degree. This is in opposition to mass society theory. Indeed, employment and training services are more common when there is public funding. As was mentioned with respect to the problem served, this may indicate that public agencies fund services that are public priorities.

One finding in Table 6-4 is inconsistent with this description. Agencies receiving public funds are less likely to focus on continuing financial support than are other voluntary agencies, even though continuing financial support is normally stressed in the public sector. Since the New Deal, the notion that financial problems are a governmental responsibility has spread. Perhaps public agencies are not likely to fund voluntary agencies that seem to duplicate this service. Contracting out financial services to private agencies is usually illegal (in order to ensure equal treatment), thus limiting the role of the voluntary sector. Nevertheless, except in the very important case of financial aid, the general picture is of public agencies funding voluntary services that are similar to, rather than different from, public services.

Even if one confines the discussion to statistically significant differences, the results in Table 6-4 concerning population groups are unexpected. In many ways public funding seems to encourage particularism, not universalism. Thus, voluntary agencies receiving public funds serve all age groups less often and focus on the young to a slightly lesser degree. The findings appear to contradict the claim that public funding encourages universalism, and they also contradict a similar claim based on the alternative hypothesis. Perhaps the relation occurs because public agencies are legally constrained from specializing in an age group; when services to a specific age are desired, the agencies apparently most often contract the services out to a voluntary agency.

The use of voluntary agencies to provide particularized services is also apparent in the statistical relations involving race. In direct opposition to the claim that public funding promotes universal coverage, voluntary agencies that receive public funds are somewhat more likely than those that don't to exclude some ethnic group. Again, this appears to be a function of the way public agencies use voluntary agencies to be more particularistic than public agencies can be. Government officials may at times believe that certain ethnic groups, such as Native Americans, need a separate service. It apparently is not appropriate for public agencies to have ethnic criteria; rather, they seem to rely on voluntary agencies to provide such services. Publicly funded voluntary agencies are the only organizations in our sample that have formal racial criteria.

The only relations that are consistent with the mass society view involve religion. Table 6-4 reveals that all of the publicly funded agencies serve all religious groups. There is a strong constitutional mandate, backed by many years of public discussion, that the government cannot support sectarian causes. This mandate seems to be carried out in public dealings with voluntary agencies. The agencies apparently cannot both receive public funds and exclude any religious group.

DISCUSSION

These data cannot completely refute or support Grønbjerg (1982). She considers the voluntary sector as a whole and is tuned more toward positing a reduction in the unique organization of voluntary sector agencies than dealing with the domain. Nevertheless, she cites distinctions between public and voluntary agencies as early as her second paragraph. These are questionable for social welfare, according to the data.

The strongest refutation involves services. There are few significant differences in frequencies, and there is a high rank order correlation between items in the two sectors; such similarities contradict the mass society view. To be sure, the stress in the voluntary sector on a few items such as material assistance and information and referral may be consistent with the mass society view, but these differences are such a small fraction of all relevant items that the mass society interpretation is questionable. Differences can even go the other way; voluntary agencies are less likely to rely on counselling, a core professional service.

The results concerning problems offer a bit more support for the mass society view, but also in a selective, incomplete way. The greater emphasis in the voluntary sector on health, individual and family life, and day care might support claims about the stress on quality-of-life problems, while the private sector does focus less often than the public on some basic needs, such as material needs. However, the view is supported only for some items. And certain differences, such as the lack of emphasis in the private sector on criminal justice, unemployment, and school problems, are not anticipated by a mass society argument. In my opinion, support of the mass society view with respect to problems caused, as well as services rendered, is so selective as to bring into question its validity as a framework for understanding trends in the voluntary sector. Only data involving the population served seem consistent.

The patterns are complicated, but because the majority of relations imply similarity rather than differences there is some support for the alternate theory. Indeed, it seems that this approach, if modified somewhat, explains the results best. In part, the similarities in frequencies may indicate that the alternate theory's stress on demands of interest groups is accurate. Interest groups may make demands on the voluntary sector to have a domain similar to the public sector's. Thus, there may be strong interest in covering physical handicaps and avoiding drug abuse; certain issues, such as family problems, may be considered to deserve agency services while others, such as homelessness, might have a weaker following.

The nearly universal coverage as far as race and sex and the high coverage of age groups may also indicate that many coalitions make demands on both sectors. Agencies may find it to their advantage to be universal in order to attract widespread financial support and to assume legitimacy (rather than to be consistent with a view of social citizenship, as the mass society argues). Only limited particularism thus remains.

As presented in the introduction, this framework does not explain differences in emphasis between the two sectors. However, a view based generally on community demands—albeit a more complicated one—might explain differences uncovered by the research more adequately than the mass society view does. For example, an examination of the problems stressed by the voluntary sector (not at this point comparing it to the public sector) reveals a rough order based on two criteria: the extent to which all members of the community might need the service (and for less widely dispersed needs), and the extent to which the client group has historically been considered to be deserving. Thus, the three most widely stressed problems (health, individual and family life, and the need for day care) in theory affect a wide segment of the community—particularly since individual and family life issues involve recreational activities as well as counselling (the two are about equally distributed). Many of the items ranked in the next group involve problems that are less common but that appear to be normally considered beyond the control of clients, and thus more deserving of support, such as developmental disabilities. Many items ranked lower, such as drug abuse, are probably considered more morally questionable. This ordering seems to imply that community members are more likely to support (by fees or donations) activities they need or that they believe deal with legitimate needs of others.

Differences between sectors may occur because the public sector has more resources and can stress some problems for which community support is not as complete, but for which there is some demand. For example, due to the rather large cost of meeting material needs, combined with the fact that the government can tax and, thus, deal with expensive issues that the community does not grant high legitimacy, the public sector is involved more heavily in this area. One cannot easily claim that this support is consistent with the mass society view that all are guaranteed basic needs; the coverage of material needs is not that complete in the public sector. Emergency needs of many individuals and basic needs of adults who are not elderly, disabled, or living with children are often not covered (Handler and Sosin, 1983). At best one can argue that public support responds to a lack of private support for this issue and some belief that the government has a special role to play in meeting the needs of certain groups.

Other results of the data analysis can be similarly explained. Public agencies may stress health, individual and family life, or day care less often because of the existence of many voluntary agencies. The stress in the public sector on chore services might stem from the large expense this service entails relative to the community's interest in the service. Most other differences in stress on services seem to follow from variations in the problems covered.[6] Similarities between the activities of the public sector and the domain of those voluntary agencies the government supports suggest that the government directly acts to increase the ability of voluntary agencies to deliver services for which community support is limited. The patterns of difference probably have more to do with patterns of community desires relative to the expense of certain activities than with a society-wide growth in political equality and social citizenship.

Certainly, these explanations move far beyond the alternate theory. They appear to combine an explanation based on community interest with a small dose of the mass society view. In particular, there appear to be special pressures on public agencies—although the explanation based on a belief in social citizenship is questionable.

Given the distance between the original two theories and the offered explanations, there is a need for additional research that verifies the analysis. Nevertheless, the results offer many insights even when interpreted narrowly. For example, they imply that many specific differences and similarities in services, problems, and population groups between the public and voluntary agencies must be taken into account in understanding the role of the voluntary sector. Common pressures on all agencies, differences in resources between the two sectors, and special demands placed on each type of agency all seem to play a role. A clear lesson is that any simple one-dimensional view of the domain of voluntary agencies cannot explain a great deal of the agencies' behavior. Sometimes the domain appears to represent a reaction to government; at times it appears to respond to similar forces. Funding from government appears generally to support similarities between the sectors, but occasionally to support differences. Voluntary agencies appear to be affected by a variety of social forces and must be analyzed from a perspective that takes many of them into account.

Given the tentative nature of the findings, any policy implications can only be speculative. Nevertheless, the results do offer some cautions for current policies. At present, the federal government is reducing its investment in social programs. One apparent rationale is that the voluntary sector will step in to increase its efforts and thus compensate for the reductions. Indeed, some believe that the voluntary sector would be much more active if it were not for the existence of government programs.

One of the assumptions of this movement is that voluntary efforts have been forced out of existence by governmental ones. But this key tenet of the mass society view is challenged by the data. The great overlaps in services, problems, and population groups indicate that the domain in one sector does not completely dictate the domain in the other. Rather, many other issues, such as the popularity of serving a given group or problem, are also important. Given that the domain of voluntary agencies does not completely depend on that of the public sector, it is questionable that the voluntary sector will dramatically change its domain as public priorities change.

One might argue that in those areas in which there is a much larger effort in the public than in the voluntary sector, the latter has reduced its effort because of public policies and might expand as public priorities change. In particular, perhaps in areas such as income maintenance the voluntary effort will expand when competition from the public sector is reduced. This is a possibility, but the great disparities in the sizes of the two sectors indicate that a complete compensation is not possible. Further, as the last section indicated, it is possible that public provision has reacted to a lack of voluntary effort, so that a reduction in the former will not change the priorities of the latter.

Current policies also include a reduction in total social service funds, and thus a limit on the financial support of the voluntary sector by the public sector. While the current data cannot speak to the effect of the reduction on the size of the voluntary sector, they may imply something about the range of services offered. The data indicate that public funds often support activities that are otherwise rare in the voluntary sector. Thus, agencies receiving funds from government are more likely to deal with drug problems or criminal justice problems and to focus on a radical minority.

Given the unpopularity of such issues, it seems very likely that when support from government is reduced, voluntary agencies will not be able to compensate completely for the loss. Thus, a reduction of voluntary effort in these areas might ensue. In other words, the least popular problems, services, or client groups, those that cannot easily be supported through typical funding mechanisms of voluntary agencies, might be jettisoned as funds from government are reduced. It is thus possible that a reduction of support will result in a focus in voluntary agencies on those elements of the domain that do not depend as heavily on public support, such as health, individual and family life, and perhaps day care. One current policy question must be whether this is the type of focus that is desirable in the voluntary sector.

It is important again to stress the tentative nature of these conclusions. It may be possible to document the implications of changes in policy only after the fact. The bulk of the evidence, though, signals caution more than it encourages further reductions in the public sector. The voluntary sector may not have the level and type of legitimacy and financial support to compensate for reductions in government support.

7

The Role of City Government

WILLIAM DONALD SCHAEFER

I do not speak for other American cities, but I can speak about Baltimore. The challenges we face and how we meet those challenges may be of use elsewhere. The issue of this chapter is what role city government can, should, and will play in meeting the social service needs of its people. How does local government interact with the voluntary service sector? How much can be realistically expected of local government?

Baltimore has an international reputation as a city on the move. The renaissance of Baltimore is a renaissance of downtown, a renaissance of business, a renaissance of arts and culture, a renaissance of neighborhoods, and a renaissance of people. The downtown renewal gets the most media attention. Our abandoned waterfront has been transformed into a mecca for our own people as well as for tourists. Open space, marinas, shops, restaurants, hotels, renovated nineteenth-century townhouses, offices, and a convention center ring the harbor at the heart of downtown. Renewal and growth radiate from the harbor area to office and financial districts, the retail district, and historic residential neighborhoods.

Tourism is bringing millions of dollars a year to Baltimore, creating hundreds of new businesses and thousands of new jobs. New theaters, restaurants, and night spots make downtown streets as busy at night and on weekends as during weekday business hours.

But the renaissance is also a city-wide renewal, as dozens of neighborhood commercial centers have been revitalized. Each commercial revitalization project is an exciting partnership between the city and neighborhood merchants, showing that Baltimore has developed and perfected local commercial revitalization. The real story of Baltimore's success is the revitalization of its neighborhoods. Homesteading has brought hundreds if not thousands of the middle class back to the city to rehabilitate and occupy historic townhouses in many neighborhoods. Private reinvestment is going on across the city.

The revitalization of Baltimore does not mean that the poor have disappeared. We have as many poor people as we ever had. We have more elderly people and more single-parent families than we ever had before. Over a fifth of our people live in poverty. Many more are unemployed. And they look to the city for help. The city provides all of the help it can. Over 70 percent of our operating budget is for direct services to people.

The purpose of all of the renewal, rebuilding, business development, neighborhood development, and tourism is to provide a better place for our people to live, work, prosper, and raise families. The task of city government is to build up the city in every way possible for the benefit of our people. To do that, we must be as efficient, innovative, and creative as possible. And we must work in intimate partnership with neighborhoods, institutions, citizen groups, businesses, other government sectors, charitable and philanthropic groups, and private service providers. Baltimore works only because these many partnerships work.

For our partnerships with the voluntary and philanthropic sectors to work, there must be mutual respect and recognition of each partner's strengths and limitations. Specifically, the private service sector needs to recognize, as it largely does in Baltimore, what local government can and cannot do.

WHAT LOCAL GOVERNMENT CANNOT DO

First of all, the city cannot create new pots of money. Every tolerable tax that can be levied has been levied. There is no new untapped revenue source for local government to exploit. As with most large cities, Baltimore's real property tax rate is already twice the rate of surrounding suburbs. But then, one cent on the suburbs' tax rate generates twice the revenue that a penny on the city's tax rate does.

Secondly, the city cannot get out of its role as the center of the metropolitan area, a role that involves many costs. We cannot ignore the importance of our museums, our zoo, symphony, ballet, and theaters, which serve the entire state and are imperative for the economic and cultural life of both the city and the state.

People from across the state come to the city to work, conduct business, be educated, and be entertained. A large portion of the cost of maintaining this heart of the metropolitan area falls to the city. To increase the flow of resources back to the city from the suburbs and countryside we must continue our strategy of attracting more people into the city for business, shopping, culture, education, and entertainment. We cannot allow the city to stagnate.

The city cannot ignore the need to continue the revitalization and rebuilding of the downtown areas, or the need for business retention and new business development. Ultimately, it is the rejuvenation of the inner city that will provide the jobs, the opportunities, and the revenues that will allow us to continue to address the needs of the dependent and disadvantaged. Only a vital city can be a place of opportunity for the disadvantaged.

Nor can the city focus only on our downtown and our visitors. The city must and does place a high priority on helping the neighborhoods maintain, improve, and renew their homes and local commercial areas. Amenities in old neighborhoods, new neighborhoods, and renewing neighborhoods require continued city investment.

But most of all, the city cannot ignore the needs of its people. A disproportionate share of Maryland's elderly, poor, unemployed, and homeless are concentrated in the city. The city must and does assist them. The city is not only where they find the most help and acceptance, but also where the poor have always found the greatest opportunities. With 20,000 units of public housing (as many units as in the rest of the state), the programs to assist the homeless and the hungry, to provide meals for the elderly and fuel for the poor, to provide home repairs, weatherization, medical care, and literacy instruction, we do everything we can to assist those in need.

But with all of these things the city cannot stop doing, needs the city cannot ignore, the city also cannot generate new sums of money with new taxes. Nor can the city compel corporations to contribute more money to services for the dependent and disadvantaged. If the city has major responsibilities that cannot be ignored, and yet the resources to meet those responsibilities are limited, what can the city do?

WHAT LOCAL GOVERNMENT CAN DO

If there are many things local government cannot do and cannot stop doing in spite of loss of federal funds and support, there are also things it *can* do. The city obviously can and has tightened the local budget belt, thus stretching dollars, cutting fat, and pinching pennies. The city can and must do less *for*, and do more *with* people, organizations, and neighborhoods. Our partnership with the voluntary sector must continue to expand.

We are trying every possible way to find new sources of money for essential services; to divest ourselves of liabilities; to reduce cost by more frugal purchasing, by reduction in services, by increase in productivity, or by the transfer or sharing of fiscal responsibility; and to increase the taxable base of real property, business activity, and personal income.

Baltimore has moved to reduce costs by such strategies as buying one-year-old rental cars rather than new cars for its fleet needs. The city has effectively reduced its liabilities by a very simple process of selling city-owned vacant lots and houses at $100 and $200 each, respectively. Larger vacant buildings, such as former schools, libraries, fire stations, and police stations, have been aggressively marketed for housing as well as commercial uses. Of greater significance, however, are recent efforts to enlist individuals, neighborhoods, and businesses to assume responsibilities for functions formerly seen as city tasks.

A "Wish List for Baltimore" campaign catalogued a list two newspaper pages long of services, equipment, and supplies needed by city agencies but not affordable under current budget constraints. Both individuals and companies responded with unexpected generosity, offering everything from office furniture and equipment to volunteered professional skills, to landscaping, to a neighborhood group which volunteered to completely restore a historic pagoda in one of our oldest parks.

In other volunteer and private sector efforts, the city's school children raised $55,000 to buy a new elephant for the zoo. Building contractors responded immediately when the city asked for assistance in clearing ice-clogged storm sewer inlets after a heavy snowfall. Residents of a historic neighborhood volunteered their own labor to restore their streets to cobblestone. Individuals, neighborhood groups, and businesses have adopted many of the city's flower beds in parks and highway median strips.

The semiannual spring and fall cleanup in every neighborhood across the city is a totally volunteer effort using trucks and drivers provided by individual citizens, contractors, and local companies. City employees also volunteer time on weekends to clean along major approachways into the city.

Local corporate executives, on a volunteer basis, teach job-finding and interviewing skills in the city's manpower program. The city library's adult literacy program has become virtually all-volunteer in its staff. Businesses, individuals, and city employees raised money for a new non-profit foundation to employ over 4,000 teenagers in the summer after the federal government cut the summer youth employment program from 10,000 slots to 1,700. We call our program "Blue Chip In." Laid-off industrial workers volunteer their time in city schools in return for food vouchers. City employees donate tons of food to the city's soup kitchens. New partnerships have been created with neighborhood organizations to get residents to assume more responsibility for cleaning up, fixing up, and keeping up their neighborhood's alleys, streets, parks, schools, and other public buildings.

The most problematic aspects of the recent loss of funding have been the direct cuts in crucial services to people in need, and the continuing concentration of the needy people in the central city. New strategies are needed to stretch and maximize the impact of very limited resources, and to tap heretofore unused resources. The most promising of such strategies seems to be increased provision of vitally needed services by the private sector, and cooperative efforts between the city and the private sector.

Instigated by the city, several major downtown employers formed a non-profit corporation to establish a preschool day-care

center in downtown Baltimore. Major employers have supported
the day-care center with start-up grants and numerous in-kind staff
services. Staff support and technical assistance have been contributed by the city's Department of Law, Finance, and Social
Services.

Desperate need for shelters for the homeless resulted in a private-
public partnership in 1981. The city contributed a vacant former
school building, most of the furnishings, utilities, and some staff.
Businesses and private non-profit social service agencies contributed sleeping bags, furnishings, and casework staff.

With widespread support by businesses, by volunteers, and by
private and city agencies, the Maryland Food Bank collects, ware-
houses, and distributes surplus food donated by shippers, manufacturers, wholesalers, and retail food chains. At a cost of only a
few cents per pound, surplus food is sent to shelters, soup kitchens,
and neighborhood food cupboards.

Baltimore has an exceptionally good relationship with its business
community. Businesses here are very supportive of the city's
renewal efforts and of the city's cultural institutions and events.
When the city requests business support for other kinds of human
need, however, the response is best when the request is for goods
and services rather than for cash contributions. Businesses are willing to make much larger contributions of staff time, technical
assistance, equipment loans, and other fixed-expense items for
which the marginal cost is very low. Contributions of equipment
and manpower also have much more public visibility and public
relations effect than a cash contribution.

Further, Baltimore has found businesses more likely to respond
to a specific task than to general appeals for cash or to long-term
commitments. Businesses will respond quickly and positively to
requests to provide trucks and drivers for a city-wide weekend
cleanup, but they are sometimes hesitant and less responsive to
appeals to employ the disadvantaged. The state of the economy is a
factor in this.

While the cooperation between local government and the private
and voluntary sectors is improving, and the above examples show
how cooperation is possible and working, the voluntary and other
private sector agencies must become more realistic about local governments' resources. It is unrealistic for private sector agencies to
think that local governments can magically create millions of

dollars to replace federal funds cut from this program or that agency's budget.

Local government funds are generated by taxes and fees paid by local people and businesses. If cities are to raise more tax money to meet local needs, local people and businesses will be the ones to pay those taxes. City administrators constantly hear special interest groups claiming that the city government has lots of money if only it would spend the money on their favorite project or program. They seem to be saying, "I don't care where you get the money, who you tax, or what other services you cut out—just get the money *I* want for the program *I* want!" Cities have to balance a multitude of needs and constraints. Advocates for specific programs and services must be realistic about the constraints under which local governments operate.

HOW THE VOLUNTARY SECTOR CAN WORK WITH CITY GOVERNMENT

The only way to make a city work is for local government, the voluntary sector, business, industry, and citizen groups to work together. Voluntary organizations that want to work effectively with local government need to be willing to be partners in solving problems with the limited resources that are available.

Bring us solutions, plans for dealing with problems, schemes that can link limited public and private resources, proposals that are carefully and completely thought out. We do not need to be told about the problems. We know people are sick and unemployed and homeless and hungry. We do not need to be told to spend money we do not have, start programs we cannot pay for, supply services we do not have, or hire staff we cannot afford.

We need partners, not adversaries. We need partners from voluntary and religious groups, from business, from neighborhoods. We need partners who will help us find new solutions that will work. We need partners who can pull together the scattered resources in government, voluntary institutions, businesses, and neighborhoods. Bring us specific and concrete proposals. Bring us your best thinking. Bring us a willingness to work together. Don't tell us about a problem unless you can also tell us a realistic and workable solution.

The needs of Baltimore are great and continue to grow. The

resources available to us are finite. It is unproductive to wring our hands and whine about what we don't have, what we can't do, what somebody else should do for us. Baltimore does not need those who say what we cannot do, but more people who focus on what we can do.

Most importantly, we have to focus on what we can do together. Local government, business, philanthropies, voluntary agencies, neighborhoods, and the people are all partners in making the city a better place for everyone. Only as we work together to strengthen and build up the partnership will the city and all of its people and components prosper. Baltimore is working because the city works in partnership with everyone, building a city that works for everyone.

PART II

Planning in the Voluntary Sector

8

Ethics in Planning
in the Voluntary Sector

GARY A. TOBIN

The adoption of an ethical framework for planners in the voluntary sector ought to be simple, but often is just the opposite. First, many individuals who are employed as planners in the voluntary sector have little or no rigorous training in either religious or humanist ethical frameworks. Sunday schools and parochial schools, in the precollege years, and an occasional course in philosophy at the undergraduate or graduate level do not constitute the intellectual basis for complex decision-making for their planning tasks. Where ethics are applied, it will often be in an ad hoc way, which is often as fruitless as having no ethical framework at all.

Planning in the voluntary sector seems to be more concerned than ever with management techniques, political roles, and career advancement. All of these are fundamentally part of professional life for the planner, and should be so. All have languages of their own, and the language of politics is substantially different from the language of management. Each has its purpose, and each has its limits. As these facets of the planning system are expanded, the ethical framework in which all decisions are made seems to be discussed less, understood less, and the awareness that ethics are a concern at all seems not to touch some decisions, individuals, or institutions.

The move toward management and efficiency, of course, has its roots in the criticisms from lay leaders (often business people), government funders, and others who believe that the voluntary sector has been dominated too long by the "social work" mentality, that it is too client-oriented and not management-oriented enough. Critics argue that large-scale organizations must be managed by managers, and run more like businesses. Discussions in boardrooms, committee meetings, and planning sessions sometimes are void of the ethical concerns that justify the existence of most voluntary organizations.

This chapter discusses the necessity for a keen awareness of the ethical framework for planning in the voluntary sector. It cannot prescribe such a framework, nor should it, but rather the issues involved in discussing ethics in this field are outlined. For a discussion of the importance of ethics, see Rachels' essay "Can Ethics Provide Answers?" from *Ethics in Hard Times*, pp. 1-30. Indeed, one of the major points of this chapter is that ethical discussions at all are rare, much less a definition of the codes, principles, and traditions that should guide planning decisions. Moreover, it is wrong to assume that these ethical guides are implicitly understood, or universally known and accepted. Such assumptions weaken the ability to reaffirm and explore ethical decisions, because serious discussions and debate of the moral character of planning problems and dilemmas are precluded.

This chapter proceeds by stating a number of propositions and discussing them in some detail. These propositions are the following:

1. All planning is an ethical activity.
2. Planning and politics are not the same.
3. A good planner uses skills of the trade to operate within the political system. The planner must be in the political system, but not of it.
4. Professionals have a moral calling, but the guides for behavior are not likely to be found in the profession.
5. The language and therefore the actions of planners in the voluntary sector must be formulated and based within the pluralistic tradition of American planning, calling upon the distinct customs, traditions, and laws of different religions and other active groups.

Each of these propositions is discussed in some detail in the following sections.

All planning is an ethical activity. All planning is, by definition, goal-oriented; it is a set of activities designed to achieve desired outcomes. Goals are usually an expression of a set of values which distinguish and calibrate relative worth. It is through systems of ethics, the disciplines that deal with good and bad, and moral duties and obligations, that values are determined. Either an absolute standard of "goodness" or a hierarchy of goods is the means by which morality is determined, a moral order to the universe, a spiritual or mystic confirmation of that which is good or bad.

Goals and values are usually part of the language that is associated with planning, rather than moral duties or definitions of goodness. Yet the "good," the public good, the religious good, the social good, are the guiding forces of all planning.

The deliberate aspect of planning, along with a sense of the "good," is a key component in this activity. All planning, in addition to being "good-seeking," is purposeful. That is to say that the achievement of good outcomes is the consequence of deliberate action. While a moral order is assumed to be attainable, it is not to be so without purposeful effort. Planning must be purposeful; otherwise, it has no direction and no logical conclusion. If good outcomes are achieved by random wandering, this cannot be described as planning, even if we get somewhere by doing something long enough.

Being both purposeful and future-oriented, planning may be characterized as utopia-seeking, and planners as utopian builders. Since we do not live in a utopian world, nor is it very likely to be achieved in the near future, planners are of necessity in the position of advocating unrealistic goals. That is not to say that the goals are unachievable, but rather that they are not likely to be achieved within existing frameworks, either theoretical or structural:

> There . . . are ideological currents within planning, those linked to its utopian aspects, which tend to challenge the limits of the system by posing basic alternatives and *unrealistic* goals, unrealistic because they cannot be achieved within the limits of prevailing structures. There are also social forces challenging structural features of each social system. (Marcuse, 1976, p. 272)

All planning has utopian aspects, and all planning takes place in a political world. We must have some sense of the unreal or impossible. Clearly, planning must be system challenging or there is little, if any, need to plan. Planners could be system maintaining if utopia were ultimately achieved.

Yet often planners believe that in order to be effective, they must pose only realistic goals, or there is no hope of success. Such a posture confuses a number of issues. First, it fails to distinguish between planning and politics, which is the subject of the next section. Second, it assumes that realistic planning looks only at the more barren aspects of either a situation or system, an equation of rationality and harshness, or a real world view that considers only matters of efficiency. Benveniste, in his treatise *The Politics of Expertise*, which considers the role of the planner, notes:

When experts undertake analysis, they often adopt the posture of "realists." Reality, in this context, is "hardnosed" reality; it usually involves a simplified image of humanity, say "economic" man and woman or "exchange and power" man and woman. Since experts still think they are agents of efficiency instead of inventors of the future, their calculus of rationality reflects theories of behavior that are necessarily simplified.

In planning, evaluation, or policy analysis, this results in down-grading certain concepts such as aesthetic norms, love, or even ideologies.

Disregard for love, poetry, art, ideology, or other cultural attachments results in images of the future in which love, poetry, and art play a minimal part. (They may be an item of consumption in the economy but not a principle central to explaining preferences.) Since images of the future serve to orient action and thus become self-fulfilling prophecies, the architects of the future assume less than is wanted or possible. The social edifice is gradually built on limited assumptions, and, increasingly, a limited and possibly quite unattractive social world is created. (Benveniste, 1977, p. 225)

The institutionalization of many planning practices can be limiting. They are often devoid of moral or aesthetic content, and can lead to self-fulfilling stilted visions.

Indeed, a planner must avoid the limiting and ultimately stifling practice of beginning the planning process by looking first at the real constraints, and at what cannot be done. Such efforts are dangerously restrictive in terms of intellectual growth or social change. Planning, if it is directed toward definitions of good, must be characterized first by notions of what ought to be.

Furthermore, it is easy to make the transition from limited vision to visions that are devoid of any moral content at all. An equation can develop between "it cannot be done," or "it is politically impossible," to "it does not matter if it is done." Conversation and action, if prelimited to what is possible or what is real, may eliminate discussions, or actions directed toward what *should* be done, or what should be attempted to achieve "good outcomes." Fear of the unknown outcome, or maintenance of the system as it is, may choke dealing with issues as an ethical matter. But this does not imply that an activity may be ethically neutral. The maintenance of a system or the rejection of change is in itself a statement of a set of moral decisions. Bolan states that "action is in no sense neutral—it is grounded in intentions, goals, or aims" (Bolan, 1980, p. 261). The choice to limit planning decisions to "hard-nosed realities" is in itself an extremely powerful statement of beliefs that limits individuals, institutions, and programs.

As choices are made, the planner must help direct the systems in which decisions are made. Planning is summarized by Benveniste as policy analysis, programming, and evaluation (Benveniste, 1977, pp. 8-9). Each of these activities must have standards that guide them and moral frameworks in which to judge them. Evaluation, for example, uses established and standard criteria for assessment, but the criteria themselves are determined by desired outcomes. What is it that we wish to achieve? What we wish to achieve is set in the planning framework. How it is to be achieved is a political issue, and the difference between the two modes of conceptualizing and behaving are analyzed in the next section.

Planning and politics are not the same. Politics is where agendas are chosen; planning is where agendas are formulated. While the political system is designed as an arena for coordinating diverse and antagonistic interests "and sublimating the private interests by furthering principles with the general interest" (Beckman, 1964, p. 324), planning a priori defines what that general interest, or public good, must be. Some analysts of the political system would argue that the public good is the sum of the outcomes of the political process. Planning for a utopian vision of the public good supports the notion that some political outcomes are counterproductive to the public good, and some political processes ensure the absence of true planning. For a discussion of planning and politics, see *Speaking Truth to Power*, Wildavsky, 1979, pp. 114-139.

On the other hand, true planning must include carefully orchestrated and conceptualized excursions into the political process. Planning cannot simply be exercises in visionary, imaginary worlds, but the combination of vision and action. Action, of course, takes place in the political arena and requires political force, technique, and constraints. This point is made by Peattie when she notes that "planning without a political force behind it becomes a paper exercise and politics without planning becomes a politics of symbols or personalities" (Peattie, in Burchell and Sternlieb, eds., 1978, p. 84). Forester confirms this point, noting that "if planners ignore those in power, they assure their own powerlessness" (Forester, 1982, p. 67). The planner must operate and create within the political system; but what role should be played? How can the planner be most effective? What tools should be used? What differentiates the planner from the politician? When, as in the final scenes of Orwell's *Animal Farm*, do the clients look from the pigs to the humans and from the humans to the pigs, unable to distinguish the difference between the two? And, most importantly, what roles do ethical concerns play in the planner's intervention and participation in the political process? In a system of moral conflicts and ethical diversity, where interest groups, institutions, and groups of constituents compete for different goals and moral orders, some form of social coercion is finally necessary. Horowitz stresses this point when he notes that planning requires power:

> Where disagreement over social goals or policies exists, as it must, there can be no planning without the ability to make other people act differently than they otherwise might. There would be no need to plan if people were going to do spontaneously what the plan insisted they do authoritatively. Planning assumes power. Planning requires the power to maintain the pre-eminence of the future in the present. [Quotation from Aaron Wildavsky: Discussion of planners] (Horowitz, in Burchell and Sternlieb, eds., 1978, p. 55)

Even where interests converge, the definition of the good society is by no means monolithic. A hierarchy of goods comprises the greater good, and a host of political, religious, and philosophical systems combine to define this good society. The pursuit of the utopian vision can be fraught with danger, as discussed by Webber:

First off, *who* is to formulate the goals that social engineers are to serve? The notion that "society" can formulate a purposive statement is peculiar at best and pernicious at worst. Only persons are equipped to do that, and so we are unavoidably led to ask *which* persons are to set the agenda. Is it the majority of voters? the legislatures? the more-powerful interest groups? individual consumers? professional planners? Obviously an old and persistently troubling question. But a terribly important one for the planner, because what he does might be consequential. What he proposes might matter. The ends he works for may be those his employers seek; but they may simultaneously be antithetical to other people's purposes. The specter of Eichmann is the constant companion of the wary planner. (Webber, in Burchell and Sternlieb, eds., 1978, p. 154)

Thus, the planning system continually pushes against the political constraints that may restrict progress toward utopian vision, but it also serves as brakes upon excursions into *negative* utopias, those visions that violate the moral order. This sense supercedes decisions in the political system and allows us to say that a political outcome is not a *good* one. At some point, it may even force us to challenge those outcomes and argue that Eichmann should not have executed bad laws because they violated a higher moral authority. This remains the chief differentiating factor between planning and politics. Where this definition of higher authority comes from is discussed in the final section of this paper.

A good planner uses skills of the trade to operate within the political system. The planner must be in the political system, but not of it. A good planner possesses both planning skill and political savoir faire. It is difficult to say how one learns the latter set of skills. Some people seem to learn it through experience. In some people it seems to be innate. Some people imitate it. It seems that some people can never learn effective political skills. They usually are not very successful planners, since they are easily unmasked and not very effective in persuasion or organization.

Planners' sources of power, which are discussed below, can lead to considerable influence. Three points, however, should be emphasized. First, planners who do acquire power should not be surprised when they are resented. People who acquire power through non-elective processes tend to be looked upon as usurpers by individuals who are making decisions. Planners who actually make decisions are often believed to have no right to do so. Second, the planner's power base is never secure. Planners are appointed, and can be dismissed. They must walk a fine line when political roles are played. Third, planners should keep their political roles as discreet as possible.

It is interesting to attend professional conferences and hear comments like, "He's very political." Sometimes it is said with admiration, noting that this is somebody to watch out for because he is on his way. What do we mean by that—that he is very political? If it is so obvious, how effective can he be? There is a wonderful story about three mothers who are bragging about their children and one says, "My son is a very famous doctor in New York"; another says, "My son is the most famous lawyer in Los Angeles!" Then the third woman says, "That's nothing. My son is the most famous spy in Europe. Everywhere he goes people say, 'There goes Sammy the spy!' " Such obviousness usually severely limits a planner's ability to maneuver effectively.

The best discussion of the political roles of planners is Guy Benveniste's *The Politics of Expertise.* He outlines a number of ways that planners can acquire power in the political system. I will use "planners" and "experts" interchangeably. Benveniste identifies knowledge as the first source of an expert's power. In discussing knowledge, he says, "Experts deal in a scarce commodity: knowledge, which includes not only the knowledge to which they have access, i.e., their expertise, but, more importantly, the information they obtain and generate." (Benveniste, 1977, p. 145).

Data collection is a method by which knowledge is accumulated, presented, and debated. It becomes an independent source of the planner's power base:

> The ability to acquire, store, handle, and analyze large volumes of data sharply distinguishes the new policy experts from their predecessors and, at the same time, makes the policymaker much more dependent on their services. It is not irrelevant that control of facts can often be translated into social power. (Benveniste, 1977, p. 90)

Furthermore, as DeKema points out, "The act of formulating a technical problem predetermines the direction an answer will take" (DeKema, 1981, p. 543). Even the way the data are collected and processed has political value.

The third way that planners can generate power on their own is by gaining access to those who are powerful. In this sense knowledge becomes a bartering chip. It's something we trade, something we use, something that we accumulate. Benveniste says that "access to the powerful and the political value of information combine to provide another dimension of expert power" (Benveniste, 1977, p. 147). Latest techniques and inside information, for example, are the kinds of entrees planners can use in building a power base.

Fourth, planners can control the flow of information. Since knowledge and access are sources of power, information flows and bottlenecks can create and obstruct. Benveniste indicates that planners become communication filters: "Since they limit participation, they permit information and influence to flow only within a restricted portion of the body politic" (Benveniste, 1977, p. 21).

Fifth, planners can acquire power by changing and directing language. "Planning actions are not only technical, they are also communicative. They shape attention expectations" (Forester, 1980, p. 283). The management of language is a vital tool for the planner to use. Words can be used to convey different meanings and to achieve diverse purposes.

The control of language is a vital tool. How we think about things—the nuances and impressions, the subliminal and overt suggestions—all can be influenced by the choice of words and phrases, and the context in which they are used. The ways that issues are discussed, the terms, the catchwords, and cliches can be as informative and important as the content.

The control and manipulation of language to exercise power raises concerns over which are legitimate means of exercising power and which are not. Zaltman and Duncan outline the following as "onerous" techniques of language control:

(1) Lying. (2) Innuendo—implying an accusation without risking an argument by actually saying it. This technique is often used when an accusation lacks sufficient evidence. The use of innuendos is often more harmful to one's own credibility than to that of its victim. (3) Presenting opinion as fact—this is perhaps the most common of all the questionable techniques of manipulation. Obviously this technique is counterproductive when one talks to those who know that other interpretations exist. (4) Deliberate omission—one particularly dangerous and common form of

deliberate omission is the deliberate refusal to discuss the other side's point of view in a group conflict situation. (5) Implied obviousness—this technique implies that a certain point of view is the only reality and that no further argument or evidence in support of it is needed. (Zaltman and Duncan, 1977, p. 338)

All of these techniques can be used to persuade, twist, and influence. Yet, the same authors say that manipulation as a strategy of persuasion is less onerous when appeals to emotions or attempts to focus attention, for example, are used. Clearly, these authors have prescribed for themselves a set of behaviors that are right and wrong. Each of the techniques that the planner can use to acquire power is laced with similar conflicts. This adds another dimension to the issue of ethics in planning. While planners must formulate a vision of the moral outcomes that are to be achieved, they must also grapple with ethical dilemmas pertaining to how those visions are to be achieved. What are the trade-offs? What are legitimate means to achieve these desirable ends? The guiding norms for these questions are thought to rest in the role of the planner as a professional (see Rein, 1970, pp. 193-199). These answers are often sought through the profession, and this is the topic of the next section.

Professionals have a moral calling, but the guides for behavior are not likely to be found in the profession. The origin of the word *profession* is instructive. The word means to be received formally into a religious community following an acceptance of required vows. It also means to declare openly what those vows will be, as a religious commitment is made to a field. Currently,

the word "profession" has a dual meaning. It is, in the first place, a species of a generic concept, namely, "occupation," and in the second an avowal or promise . . . the second meaning of "profession," however, is of concern to everyone . . . we can always ask whether the avowal or promise has been fulfilled. Does the profession do what it promises to do? Does it accomplish what it professes?" (Freidson, 1970, p. vii)

It is difficult to assess whether the profession does what it is supposed to do, because the "oughts" are usually stated in very general codes of ethics that are more concerned with management of certain career behaviors than with religious commitments. The issues of means and ends are sometimes addressed, but the purposes and visions of the profession are generally left to a few, often vague statements. Marcuse notes that professional ethics do not provide answers to ethical dilemmas, even for day-to-day problems:

> Professional ethics, in that view, might indeed have the potential to emphasize the utopian, the historically progressive, elements in planning. Realistically, however, professional ethics are likely simply to render more efficient the services provided by planners to those presently with the power to use them. Professional ethics are likely to be system maintaining rather than system challenging. The movement to reshape them in a different direction is likely to be a long and an uphill one. (Marcuse, 1976, p. 273)

Marcuse also states:

> Professional issues thus are of minor importance. This is not to say that planners are freed from ethical obligations: it is only to say that there are other and higher obligations towards which planning activities should be oriented. And in some cases, as in guild obligations or prescriptions of allegiance, professional ethics may run counter to higher obligations. (Marcuse, 1976, p. 271)

It is these higher obligations that create the conflict within the individual and between the individual and the institutions that are to be served.

Clearly, the planning profession cannot provide ethical instruction. Martin Buber supports this sentiment in his discussions of ethics:

> But if I am concerned with the education of character, everything becomes problematic. I try to explain to my pupils that envy is despicable, and at once I feel the secret resistance of those who are poorer than their comrades. I try to explain that it is wicked to bully the weak, and at once I see a suppressed smile on the lips of the strong. I try to explain that lying destroys life, and something frightening happens: the worst habitual liar in the class produces a brilliant essay on the destructive power of lying. I have made the fatal mistake of *giving instruction* in ethics. (Buber, 1965)

The instruction of ethics, the instilling of moral character, cannot be derived from the profession alone, and the models for proper behavior will not be found from codes of ethics that are profession protecting. The individual must make serious attempts to view the role of a professional as a calling, a religious obligation as opposed to merely an occupation. Such a view will enable the planner to evaluate decisions, to understand when the demands of the occupation run counter to his professional obligations and when the profession itself has moved away from its religious or moral obligations. As Bolan states, the professional must be an agent both of change and of moral purpose:

> In the final analysis, the professional can be seen as a *moral* agent—not a purely instrumental problem-solver. If professionalism is to be rehabilitated, it must lessen its over-dependence on technique and science and reassert both its humanistic ideals and its own wholly human character. (Bolan, 1980, p. 273)

This is, of course, a difficult command. How is it to be achieved?

Ethical issues must be discussed as such. Moral discussion should take a number of directions. First, an ethical individual must be continually grappling with his or her own value systems, defining, redefining, and weighing personal beliefs. As Gouldner points out:

> It is no easy thing to know what our own value commitments are. In an effort to seem frank and open, we all too easily pawn off a merely glib statement about our values without making any effort to be sure that these are the values to which we are actually committed. (Gouldner, 1968, p. 113)

Glib statements, platitudes, or absolute statements cannot illuminate the complex set of issues with which planners must deal. Constant reappraisal and, in some sense, soul-searching are required. In addition, since a planner's tasks are moral in character and purpose, issues, whenever possible, should be discussed as moral or ethical problems. But as one analyst points out, such discussions are difficult to maintain or initiate:

> The sad truth is that we are unaccustomed to serious moral discussion. We prefer to take our morals in small doses of slogans, epithets, and invectives. When Machiavelli told us to look at the way things are and not as they ought to be, he made us modern men; but in so doing he bequeathed us a sorry legacy of trained incapacity for sound moral debate. (Rohr, 1978, p. 3)

The rhetoric of moral absolutism, particularly in the context of single-issue interest groups, should not be mistaken for sound moral discussion. As Boulding points out:

A person who is ethically mature will constantly be weighing subordinate goals against each other and making decisions about how far to pursue each one.

Even though ethical theory does not come out with any single formula for relating subordinate goals to ultimate goals, it can state with a high degree of certainty that given the complexity of the human organism, no single value index can ever serve without question as a measure of the ultimate goal. That is, in pursuing any particular subordinate goal, we must always get to the point at which we must ask ourselves, "is a little more of this worth what we have to sacrifice in order to get it?" Obsession by single subordinate goals, whether this is money or sex or eating or even stamp-collecting, is a sign of mental or at least ethical ill health. (Boulding, 1966, p. B-165)

Ethical ill health characterizes most of the moral debate in the political arena. This is most easily understood by examining the narrow purposes and activities of single-issue interest groups. These groups are filled with invective, and there is no sense of weighing alternatives or balancing ethical dilemmas. Indeed, debate about moral issues in the political arena is as likely to lead to anti-ethical ends as having no debate at all, since this arena is not conducive to compromise, evaluation, and reason.

There is also some risk of ethical grandstanding, which can lead to two unwanted results. The first is the grand display of moral outrage, which can result in quitting a position or in some other act that removes the individual from a conflict arena. Often, we are forced to stay in unpleasant situations because leaving the scene is a moral abdication. The following anecdote illustrates this point:

The second reason for deemphasizing resignation in protest is a bit more complicated. A brief quotation from George Bernard Shaw might shed some light on the problem. Shaw, who was actively involved in the British Labour party, was annoyed to hear that a Labour candidate named Joseph Burgess had refused to compromise on an issue and had thereby lost his seat in Parliament. Shaw had this to say:

When I think of my own unfortunate character, smirched with compromise, rotted with opportunism, mildewed by expediency, dragged through the mud of borough council and Battersea elections, stretched out of shape with wire-pulling, putrefied by permeating, worn out by twenty-five years pushing to gain an inch here, or straining to stem a backrush, I do think Joe might have put up with just a speck or two on those white robes of his for the sake of the millions of poor devils who cannot afford any character at all because they have no friend in parliament. Oh, these moral dandies, these spiritual toffs, these superior persons. Who is Joe, anyhow, that he should not risk his soul occasionally like the rest of us? (Rohr, 1978, pp. 8-9)

Rohr follows with this analysis:

There are several points in Shaw's comment that are worthy of our attention. The first is the simple fact that all forms of organizational life demand compromises of values one holds dear. The person who is unwilling to "risk his soul occasionally like the rest of us" cannot contribute constructively to any organization. The significant ethical question is not *whether* one should compromise but *when* one should do so—that is, how important are the values at stake? Indeed, compromise is itself one of the most important values of any organization that is effective and enduring. It is the catalyst that makes possible the realization of other values. (Rohr, 1978, pp. 8-9)

Obviously, the role of the moral agent sometimes requires extraordinary action and ability, the willingness to profess and to lead, and at times to compromise, the bane of the ethically immature.

Second, moral discussions, if they are pursued in an antagonistic or absolutist language, may achieve the opposite results. As with "Sammy the Spy," it is difficult to be "Martin the Moralist" and achieve much in the political arena. Most people find it difficult to be preached at, especially by someone who assumes a sanctimonious position about right and wrong. Discussion of moral issues and debates of ethical concerns may often have to take place without being identified as such. It is possible to have moral discussions without making pronouncements, and to speak in "moral language" without declaring it so. But to do so, sound moral discussion must be based in some system of ideas and beliefs that allows for both challenge and order. A hierarchy of goals must be conceptualized, the ability to rank as well as declare. Individual planners are limited by time, resources, and knowledge. While a utopian vision must guide action, if action is to be taken, it must be broken into some smaller components. Sound moral debate, then, must first focus upon the whole and then upon the actions, strategies, and rightness of pursuing its components. If the planner is forced to identify the "good life" in more specific terms, perhaps some progress can be made toward that end.

But such progress is impossible if the language of planning is restricted to matters of efficiency, or if the language of business invades the planning profession and the institutions responsible for human service delivery. Some precepts and processes can be borrowed from the private sector, but others, especially if they are mimicked and lose their contextual underpinnings, can be dangerous. One extreme example is the concept of efficiency as a singular goal. Boulding refers to the "production manager who said that all he wanted to do was to minimize costs, until it was pointed out that the easiest way to do this would be to shut down operations altogether, in which case the costs would be reduced to zero" (Boulding, 1966, p. B-165).

The goal of efficiency is advocated more and more as resources become scarce. "Scarce resources" is, of course, another manipulation of language that can hide real purpose and intent. Often "scarce resources" means that these resources are allocated elsewhere, or not at all, or that the commitment to certain goals has shifted.

Two other phrases worthy of our attention are "quick and dirty" and "the bottom line." "Quick and dirty" implies the need for rapid resolution, and it implies that means and quality are not necessarily important. "Bottom line" is the most dangerous phrase of all in the service professions, particularly the planning professions. The bottom line is void of moral content. Why do we come to the conclusions that we have reached? How does cost measure against our ethical commitments and moral duty? What was considered in reaching the bottom line? How does one conclusion compare to another? As scarce resources become more scarce—that is, as the national commitment to certain social goods becomes less important—to avoid looking first at the bottom line becomes more critical. The line is at the bottom for a reason: it is the conclusion. Few of us read the last line of a novel first, or watch the last frames of a movie first, or begin medical study without basic anatomy. The prevailing logic of how we look at things necessitates that our moral framework come first, then the analysis, and then the bottom line.

Accounting as a planning paradigm is inappropriate. Boulding notes,

> With the development of accounting, the measurement of profit became much more exact, but as a result also, certain other elements of the total value situation became less prominent and, therefore, neglected, such things for instance as morale, loyalty, legitimacy, and intimacy and complexity of personal relations. (Boulding, 1966, p. B-165)

Each of these is important as we analyze and plan for human service delivery. Why is loyalty less important than efficiency? How do we measure it or weigh it? The language of the bottom line cannot account for these aspects of a decision matrix.

If the language of business is inappropriate, so is the language of social work, sociology, and other social sciences. If planners must speak in moral language but must not preach ethics, what language can they use? For the voluntary sector, neither the language of the private sector nor that of the public sector is appropriate.

The ethical issues that planners face in the voluntary sector are quite different from those that are faced in the public sector, and indeed they are radically different from those of the private sector. There is an even greater difference for those working in religious institutions. Therefore, the language must be different. What should be the language for those in the voluntary sector service professions?

The language and therefore the actions of planners in the voluntary sector must be formulated and based within the pluralistic tradition of American planning, calling upon the distinct customs, traditions, and laws of different religions and other active groups. First, individuals in the voluntary sector are torn between their occupational goals and their professional calling as religious workers, in the traditional sense of "professional." This is further complicated by dual or multiple allegiances to trade associations, political parties, unions, school organizations, or other groups and institutions that do not operate in the sphere in which a planner may work. Often there are conflicts between aspirations and goals of the individual as a United Way worker, where there wouldn't be for a member of the Republican Party, for example.

Second, other individuals have rejected religious or humanist law or ethics as unsuitable for their tasks. The language of business or social work—or no particular language framework at all—may guide some planners in the field as a deliberate move away from what they consider to be inadequate, irrelevant, or outdated religious or humanist ethics or norms.

Third, by no means are religious ethics and laws monolithic in their history, construction, or interpretation, within any church or philosophy. Much disagreement exists within a community as to how certain laws are to be implemented, what their purposes might be, who the judges are to be, and so on.

Fourth, as with planners throughout most fields, many individuals simply are unable to discuss moral issues in the ethical terms that relate to some religious or other base, because they either do not know how to do so or they are embarrassed to do so. The serious moral debates are the most difficult ones and require the greatest knowledge and intellectual challenge.

Even as this is written, I can imagine the response that dealing with issues in this way does not deal with political reality. Such a response reinforces my contention that many of us simply cannot deal with moral issues in the face of what is viewed as political reality. We cannot, of course, stop with "What should we do?" Soon, a discussion of *how* to accomplish it best must also occur, since planning is action-oriented. The planner, however, has a serious obligation first to revive the language of morality in voluntary sector work. This requires a number of activities:

1. Ethical discussions and forums must be part of all conferences and professional meetings.

2. As indicated, many voluntary planners must be educated or reeducated in religious or humanist ethics and law. Given the pluralistic nature of our society, each religious or other group must look to both the universalistic and particularistic components. All healthy ethical constructs have both inward- and outward-looking aspects.

3. Whenever possible, issues should be brought back to their ethical roots.

4. Religious institutions that are no longer responsive to ethical constraints should be challenged from within and from without their structures. There is nothing sacrosanct about existing voluntary institutions if they have no relationship to their ethical foundations and origins.

I will end this essay with a final illustration. Elie Wiesel begins his book *The Gates of the Forest* with the following fable:

When the great Rabbi Israel Baal Shem-Tov saw misfortune threatening the Jews it was his custom to go into a certain part of the forest to meditate. There he would light a fire, say a special prayer, and the miracle would be accomplished and the misfortune averted.

Later when his disciple, the celebrated Magid of Mezritch, had occasion, for the same reason, to intercede with heaven, he would go to the same place in the forest and say: "Master of the Universe, listen! I do not know how to light the fire, but I am still able to say the prayer." And again the miracle would be accomplished.

Still later, Rabbi Moshe-Leib of Sasov, in order to save his people once more, would go into the forest and say: "I do not know how to light the fire, I do not know the prayer, but I know the place and this must be sufficient." It was sufficient and the miracle was accomplished.

Then it fell to Rabbi Israel of Rizhyn to overcome misfortune. Sitting in his armchair, his head in his hands, he spoke to God. "I am unable to light the fire and I do not know the prayer; I cannot even find the place in the forest. All I can do is to tell the story, and this must be sufficient." And it was sufficient.

God made man because he loves stories. (Wiesel, English translation, 1966, pp. 6-10)

Let us take the fable one step further. What if the story itself is lost? The lessons cannot be retold or remembered if no one has the story to tell. Planners, who ought to be visionaries, must be the storytellers. (For a discussion of the planner's role as a storyteller, see Rein, *Social Science and Public Policy*, 1976, pp. 249-268.) The planner may hold a professional title that so designates him or her, or may be a volunteer on a committee or a lay leader in an organization. However the role is assumed, each individual must rediscover or assert the knowledge of his or her ethical roots, or the story may indeed be lost, and with it the hope for progress through planning in the voluntary sector.

9

Defining Needs Identification for the Voluntary Sector

RUSSY D. SUMARIWALLA

This chapter discusses techniques used to identify human needs in the voluntary sector. It is designed as a comprehensive analysis of the processes of systematically identifying and determining human care needs of communities and the potential beneficiaries of these services. While the term "Needs Assessment" is commonly used both in literature as well as in practice, this writer prefers "Needs Identification" or "Needs Delineation." It is clear that identification and determination must precede assessment. The term "assessment" connotes valuation of something in relation to other things. Assessing human needs is admittedly a burdensome and ambitious undertaking. Other terms used include the following: needs description, needs analysis, needs estimation, needs measurement, needs appraisal, needs evaluation, and needs determination.

The 1960s and 1970s witnessed a spurt of activity in the needs assessment field, particularly in health and human services at state and community levels. This development was brought about largely by the convergence of three powerful factors: growing federal influence, demands for efficiency and accountability in resource allocation, and the consumer movement.

Push from Washington

With the massive influx of federal dollars to health and human service programs in the mid-1960s came a regulatory push for needs assessment. According to a 1977 U.S. Department of Health, Education and Welfare (HEW) study, a needs assessment (or evidence that one was conducted) is often required as part of a planning process, a component of a plan, or a precondition for grant support.[1] Notable among numerous federal programs requiring needs assessment in one form or another are Title XX of the Social Security Act, Aging Programs, Vocational Education, Health Planning and Resources Development, and Community Mental Health Centers (Public Law 94-63). Another HEW study focused on HEW programs and regulations incorporating needs assessment requirements.[2] The study reached the following interesting conclusions:

NA (Needs Assessment) is required in 28 of the largest HEW grant-in-aid programs. Several programs fund projects whose main purpose is to conduct NA.

In about half the cases, the law clearly requires NA; in the other cases the regulation, by HEW discretion only, mandates the requirement.

The results of the NA are almost always part of the material submitted to Federal officials as a precondition for obtaining a grant, usually in the State plan (for formula grant programs) or application (for project grant programs). Thus NA is viewed by the writers of legislation and regulations as an integral part of the planning process, certainly of sufficient importance to be reviewed at the Federal level prior to awarding program funds.

The responsibility for conducting NA falls on the direct recipient of Federal funds: in formula programs the State usually conducts NA; in project programs the applicant, often either a local or State government agency, does the assessment.[3]

Call for Efficiency and Accountability

Besides federal requirements for needs assessment there was a clarion call from the private sector for economy, efficiency, and accountability. It is not that government requirements for needs assessment were not rationalized on those grounds. But in the absence of any legal mandate to require and conduct needs assessment, the private sector has had to lean heavily on philosophical concepts such as stewardship responsibility for voluntarily contributed dollars, accountability to the donor, and responsibility for the well-being of the whole community. In some instances, concern for efficient and effecive allocation of resources has led to experimentation with the Planning-Programming-Budgeting Systems (PPBS) and Zero-Base Budgeting.[4]

Impetus from the Consumer Movement

Finally, the consumer movement of the past two decades added further impetus to the spread of needs assessment efforts. Aggressive consumer advocates such as Ralph Nader, slogans such as "maximum feasible participation" and "participatory democracy," and demand for citizen participation in policy decisions all coalesced to strengthen the case for formal needs determination endeavors. This consumer impetus has prompted greater use of one particular needs research methodology: namely, going directly to the people to learn their needs.

To conclude this brief discussion of impetus behind contemporary formal needs assessment efforts, it can be said that the political climate and social conditions of the mid-1960s and the 1970s that resulted in massive social legislation and unprecedented growth in social programs made it imperative for social scientists and social workers alike to look for new planning tools. Planning in the voluntary sector has become more sophisticated and now requires more sophisticated data collection and analysis. Needs assessment is part of the growing attempt to make voluntary sector planning more scientific. Needs delineation seems to have come as an answer.

The Planning Context

Although some have gone so far as to claim that needs identification is an end in itself, it is distinctly a part of the broader planning process. Planning is generally understood to be a rational process of decision making in which means and ends are counterposed in a way which results in optimal cost-benefits.

Planning has been defined as

A systematic, deliberative process of determining and laying out a course of action (including the devising of procedures) to achieve a stated goal based on a rational examination of all available pertinent data, for implementation in some future time frame.

The broad concept of "planning" encompasses the following five inter-related and interdependent elements: 1) definition of goals; 2) determination of a course of action to achieve the goals; 3) laying out or detailing the course of action; 4) development and use of needed information; and 5) specification of time period.[5]

In the planning context, one often hears of needs assessment as a natural first step. If you do not know what the needs of the community are, how can you plan for services? Thus, a community-wide needs determination is invariably linked with a comprehensive community-wide planning endeavor:

Comprehensive human services planning has emerged as a major element of the mission to organize and manage human services at the local level. It has gained popularity with elected public officials, administrators, policy analysts, and special interest groups as a means for rationalizing and in some sense controlling the development and delivery of a wide spectrum of services aimed at improving the general social welfare.

The appeal that comprehensive planning has for local officials is based on the possibility that it can help develop a collective definition of the public interest and reconcile diverse views of priorities in an age of increasing political fragmentation and diffusion. Its appeal for administrators derives from its potential for developing interagency collaboration on points of policy and programming and for reducing service delivery costs spawned by redundancy and competition. Its appeal for planners and policy analysts rests in its potential for synopsis and the promise it holds for anticipating the system-wide effects of particular policy choices. *Its appeal for citizens and clients of human services rests on its potential for improving the responsiveness of services to needs and for clarifying the purposes of policy choices in order to advance the accountability of decisionmakers to constituent groups. In an age of increasing confusion and conflicts in the deliberation over human needs and the delivery of human services, comprehensive human services planning seems to offer the best hope for simplification and manageability.*[6] (Emphasis mine)

The broader planning context provides perhaps the strongest rationale for conducting needs determination, as it represents an essential element in the planning process.

Limitations of Needs Assessment

Needs identification is often thought to be a panacea by the client. But the problems in identifying human needs that will have an impact on service planning and resource allocation are numerous. Exaggerated claims of the efficiency and utility of needs research have been known to result in unrealistic and unrealized expectations.

The key factors in the success or failure of a needs determination effort are these:

Sponsorship—under whose direction or auspices is it conducted?

Execution—who is asked to do it, what is the capacity and credibility of the group assigned the "research" work?

Meaning—what do you have in mind, what is your understanding of the venture, and what are your expectations?

Method—what methodology or combination of methodologies are to be employed?

Scope—what areas does it cover and is it comprehensive or selective?

Cost—how much will it cost and are there hidden costs or a probability of cost overrun?

Time—how long before you have usable information, and will the information be stale or obsolete?

Interpretation and Implementation Strategy—have you made plans for a utilization strategy?

Neglect of any one or a combination of the above factors can doom even the most sincere and well-intentioned needs assessment.

Finally, it is axiomatic to say that resource allocation is a political process. Even the most reliable and technically valid needs assessment does not assure its eventual use in service planning and resource allocation. However, what is more sobering is that needs assessment itself is not immune to politics.

To compound the problem, needs identification is sometimes linked with the process of determining and ranking priorities. The two are separate and distinct processes. A valid needs determination is, of course, an indispensable tool for rating priorities. But all priority determinations are finally colored by value judgements.

ABOUT NEED AND NEEDS ASSESSMENT

Definition of Need

It would hardly be an exaggeration to say that the concept of need is vague and elusive and means different things to different people. Let us examine a few definitions.

Webster defines "need" as:

1: necessity; compulsion; obligation; as, there is no *need* to worry now. **2**: a lack of something useful, required, or desired; a call or demand for the presence, possession, etc., of something; as, I feel the *need* of a long rest. **3**: something useful, required, or desired that is lacking; want; requirement; as, what are his daily *needs*? **4**: (a) a condition in which there is a deficiency of something; a time or situation of difficulty; a condition requiring relief or supply; as, a friend in *need*; (b) a condition of poverty; state of extreme want; *if need be*, if it is required; if the occasion demands; *to have need to*, to be compelled or required to; must. Syn.—exigency, emergency, strait, extremity, necessity, distress, destitution, poverty, indigence, penury.[7]

A 1975 report funded by the U.S. Department of Health, Education and Welfare defines "need" in a manner consistent with the open-ended character of the dictionary meaning of the term.

A human need is any identifiable condition which limits a person as an individual or a family member in meeting his or her full potential. Human needs are usually expressed in social, economic or health related terms and are frequently qualitative statements. Needs of individuals may be aggregated to express similar needs in quantified terms. Needs may also be identified in terms of sub-areas of a state.[8]

Expressing the frustration shared by many students of needs assessment, one analyst observes:

However common it may be the concept "needs" is more troublesome. A large share of the literature does not even bother to discuss or attempt to define the word. The meaning is assumed to be clear and obvious. After all, we all have needs.

Unfortunately, "need" is a word with variable meaning because it does not have a specific referent. It does not refer to something in particular but rather to *something which does not exist.* . . .

In short, *"need" is basically an empty term, one without conceptual boundaries. If the term is to have operational meaning it must be defined in a specific context, usually by the use of absolute or relative (comparative) criteria or standards.* . . .

When we speak of need(s) in a human resources context we often think of basic human needs, subsistence needs, survival needs. The word rapidly becomes suffused with emotion, feeling, urgency and passion. It also becomes loaded with cultural, normative, philosophical and political overtones. Because it is both emotion-laden and value-loaded, "need" is subject to many shades of meaning, intent and interpretation. The emotive and mercurial attributes of the word "need" follow the term into activities called "needs assessment."[9]

Need is essentially a normative concept which invariably involves value judgements and is greatly influenced by the social, political, and economic conditions of the times. Moroney identifies three key factors that influence the definition of "need": standard of living, the sociopolitical environment, and the availability of resources and technology.[10]

Definition of Needs Assessment

In the above discussion, we focussed on the elusive concept of need. Earlier in this chapter, we spoke of limitations of needs assessment. We now turn to the widely different views and definitions of the needs assessment process itself. The following sampling of the literature will at once make it clear that a universally accepted definition of "needs assessment" does not exist.

1. Wayne A. Kimmel: "Act of estimating, evaluating or appraising a condition in which something necessary or desirable is required or wanted."[11]

2. Human Services Institute: "Needs assessment is closely related to goal and objective setting in that needs data provides a measure of demand for services against which the service goals and objectives should be set. . . . Needs assessment is also related to resource allocation in that the identified needs become one of the primary considerations upon which to develop . . . staff recommendations on resource allocations. . . ."[12]

3. Center for Social Research and Development: "Needs assessment deals with the attempt to define what is required to insure that a population is able to function at an acceptable level in various domains of living."[13]

4. Warheit, Bell and Schwab: "A needs assessment program can most simply be defined as an attempt to enumerate the needs of a population living in a community." And also a working definition: "A needs assessment program is a research and planning activity designed to

determine a community's mental health services needs and utilization patterns."[14]

5. Minnesota State Planning Agency: "Needs assessment is the process of identifying the incidence, prevalence and nature of certain conditions within a community or target group. The ultimate purpose is to assess the adequacy of existing services and resources in addressing those conditions. The extent to which those conditions are not adequately addressed denotes a need for new or different services or resources."[15]

Contrast the above sample of needs assessment definitions with the one proposed by United Way of America with respect to the provision of health and human services in a given community:

Needs assessment is a systematic process of data collection and analysis as inputs into resource allocation decisions with a view to discovering and identifying goods and services the community is lacking in relation to the generally accepted standards, and for which there exists some consensus as to the community's responsibility for their provision.[16]

The above definition deliberately constricts the meaning of "need." It rejects the broad, open-ended interpretation of the term, and it does not encompass all social needs—only those for which there is some consensus as to the community's responsibility. Thus, this definition of needs assessment is made up of many elements. First, it is a systematic data collection and analysis process, regardless of the methodology employed. Second, it has two purposes: (1) discovery and identification of goods and services the community is lacking in relation to some generally accepted standards, and (2) the transmittal of that information to those who make resource allocation decisions. Third, it does not investigate every type of good or service lacking in the community, but only those for which the community feels a social obligation or for which the community has expressed its will through legislation and the democratic process.

We have seen how meaning can be brought to the difficult and confusing concept of needs assessment by providing a specific context (community health and human services in the above instance) and by providing explicit criteria to constrict the otherwise variable and broad concept of need.

Level and Scope of Needs Identification

Both "level" and "scope" pertain to the dimensions of a needs assessment. "Level" primarily refers to a geographical boundary, although it can also refer to other limitations. For example, a single agency (say, a children's home) might undertake a needs assessment for both the services it is chartered to provide and new services it might add depending on the findings. Or a United Way organization might conduct a needs assessment limited to those services within its domain of funding responsibility. However, the level of the undertaking normally tells us whether the needs assessment is for a village, a county, a multi-county area, a state, a nation, or even a group of nations. For example, many public international institutions—such as the United Nations Development Program, UNESCO, UNICEF, and the World Bank—routinely undertake large-scale needs assessments across many national boundaries.

The "scope" of a needs assessment is generally determined by the needs of a specific population for some specific service(s). For example, are we assessing the needs of the total population of a given area or those of a select group, such as children, the elderly, women, the disadvantaged minority, the handicapped, the developmentally disabled, and so on? On the other hand, we must also know whether the needs assessment is concerned with *all* services, only health and human care services, or one or more specified health or human care services, such as mental health or day care. Both level and scope need to be clearly understood and specified prior to the decision making in a needs determination.

APPROACHES TO NEEDS IDENTIFICATION

In a recent publication on needs determination, seventeen different approaches to conducting needs research are discussed. They are divided into two groups: those using primary data and those using secondary data.[17] The seventeen approaches are listed here:

Use of Primary Data

1. General Population Survey
2. Survey of Subpopulation(s)

3. Survey of Key Informants
4. Survey of Service Providers
5. Survey of Service Recipients
6. Organized Public Meetings
7. Group-Think
8. Teledemocracy
9. Needs Assessment Week (NAW)
10. Donor Plebiscite

Use of Secondary Data

11. Epidemiological Studies
12. Service Statistics
13. Social Indicators
14. Projections of Economic-Demographic Data
15. Inventory of Resources
16. Needs Data Identified by Other Planning Systems
17. Review of Budgets

We shall now describe some of the approaches.

General Population and Subpopulation Survey

Many researchers consider the general population survey one of the best approaches to needs identification because it yields the most reliable and valid data about the needs of the geographical area covered. Three commonly used techniques are personal interviews, telephone surveys, and mailed surveys. Each of these survey methods has its advantages and disadvantages.

Personal Interviews. This technique has a number of advantages over telephone surveys and mailed surveys. First, the generally better response rate makes for greater reliability and scientific validity of the data. Second, this technique allows for better coverage of a more representative sample of the general population. Individuals can be reached who are not able to be reached through telephone or mail. Third, there is ample opportunity to explain and probe, if necessary. The interviewer can ensure that the respondent fully understands the questions and the reasons for the survey.

Cost is among the greatest disadvantages of face-to-face interviews. Recruiting, training, transporting, and supervising the field staff is expensive and time-consuming. To reduce these costs, survey managers have successfully used unpaid volunteers to conduct the interviews, although this alternative carries with it its own liabilities.

Telephone Surveys. The main advantage of the telephone survey is its relatively low cost compared with the face-to-face interview. Also, follow-up with non-respondents is much easier and less costly than in the personal interview approach.

There are several disadvantages to telephone surveys. First, not everyone has a telephone. Second, a number of potential respondents have unlisted telephone numbers. However, this can be mitigated by the use of the random digit dialing system. Another disadvantage is the limited amount of time one can retain an interviewee on the phone. Then there are uncontrollable interruptions and the possibility of having to end the interview before the survey is completed. Also, some interviewees may be less than cooperative because of a suspicion, based on the extensive use of the telephone for marketing purposes, that the caller may be trying to sell something. This difficulty can be averted by mailing a letter to the prospective interviewee alerting him or her about the telephone survey and requesting cooperation. Regardless of these problems, telephone surveys can be used to obtain valid and useful information.

Mailed Surveys. The chief advantage of the mailed survey is its relatively low cost. Second, safety of the interviewer is not an issue since all work is done in the office. For those who decide to participate in the survey, privacy and convenience are added advantages. In addition, since the interviewer is not physically present, there is no opportunity for him or her to influence the respondent in any way.

The biggest disadvantage of a mailed survey is the low rate of response, which usually throws doubt on the validity of the findings. Repeated reminders to complete and return the questionnaire improve the response rate, but the overall rate remains low— somewhere in the 25 to 35 percent range. A second problem is the lack of opportunity for interpretation of complex questions and abstract issues. Many respondents are unable to answer these types of questions without assistance.

Regardless of the technique employed, a survey of the general population is among the most common and reliable methods of obtaining usable data for a needs assessment. The keys to its success are a technically sound, bias-free survey instrument and the selection of a random sample that is statistically representative of the population whose needs are being surveyed.

Survey of Key Informants

Key informants include experts, political and community leaders, and key decision makers. They are people not directly engaged in the provision of services but who, by virtue of their positions, are excellent sources of information about the needs of their communities. Expert judgment can be obtained from specialists in such areas as aging, low-income populations, and minorities. Their advice and viewpoints can be invaluable as to the prevalence of certain social needs and tried responses to those needs.

Political and community leaders and others who regularly influence resource allocation decisions are also important key informants for needs assessment studies. This group includes both elected and appointed public officials; leaders of advocacy organizations; religious and organized labor leaders; chief executive officers of major corporations; eminent leaders of the professions such as law, medicine, and science; philanthropists; and other highly respected members of the community.

A significant advantage of this approach is that it is politically sensitive research. Since resource allocation is fundamentally a political process, it is important to know what the leadership is thinking and what is politically possible. Another advantage is that it is relatively inexpensive. Any one or a combination of the three survey techniques discussed above can be used. The major disadvantage of this approach is the high probability of intended or unintended bias.

In sum, a survey of key informants is a limited, though valuable, tool for needs assessment. Used in combination with other approaches, it can be very effective in contributing to an understanding of social needs.

Survey of Service Providers

As the name suggests, a survey of service providers is a method of needs assessment which seeks information about community needs from those in day-to-day contact with the service recipients or with those who plan or manage service programs. Executives of health and human services agencies and their key program staff may be surveyed using one of the three techniques discussed earlier. Provided it is used as a supplementary method, such a survey can be very helpful.

The main advantage is the likelihood of obtaining an accurate picture of certain social problems that are socially distasteful to discuss or admit. For example, there is a natural tendency to shy away from talking about problems such as child abuse, illiteracy, drug abuse, or spouse abuse. That is a weakness of a general population or target population survey.

The major disadvantages are twofold. First, responses of service providers have greater probability of cultural and class bias, as well as a bias in favor of the need for the specific service(s) provided by their respective agencies. Second, since service providers are more familiar with the needs of the service population than the needs of the non-service population, they may not adequately reflect the needs of those who are not at a given time beneficiaries of services.

Organized Public Meetings

Public hearings, town meetings, and community forums are another approach to needs identification. The general public is invited to attend an open public meeting at which individuals and representatives of various groups present testimony on community needs and problems. This approach is attractive because of its community relations benefits and because of the democratic tradition of open discussion.

The main disadvantage of some organized public meetings is that neither the people nor their duly elected representatives are the ones who speak. The speakers are mostly self-selected or appointed and do not represent the population. There is a danger that such meetings will be dominated by the most vocal, articulate, and self-serving individuals and groups.

Teledemocracy

Teledemocracy is an approach to needs identification which uses the modern communications (telephone and television) technologies to gain direct participation of the mass population in determining community needs.[18]

Early experiments in teledemocracy took place in the 1970s among apartment complexes and housing communities linked by a communications system. Among the most well known systems is the QUBE interactive cable TV system in Columbus, Ohio. In brief, the system provides each subscribing household with a small black box with five buttons connected to its TV set. The subscriber pushes these buttons in response to questions posed about programs.

The use of teledemocracy has probably been severely limited in connection with needs assessment. However, there is no technical reason why something like QUBE could not be adapted for a needs assessment program. With the spread of cable and other forms of advanced and specialized broadcasting and "narrow-casting" systems, it is quite conceivable that teledemocracy will become the methodology of choice for needs assessments in the mid-1980s and 1990s.

Needs Assessment Week (NAW)

Another novel approach is the idea of a Needs Assessment Week (NAW). This approach to needs identification involves the following elements: a proclamation by community leaders of a needs assessment week; cooperation of major employers—both for-profit and non-profit, including government; and cooperation of the mass media, including network television, public broadcasting, and daily newspapers.

Here is a rough sketch of this unique approach to needs assessment. First, in consultation with community leadership, the appropriate authority (e.g., mayor of a city) would proclaim a certain week as "Needs Assessment Week" or "Human Needs Week." This would be accompanied by wide publicity, including posters, editorial support in the media, and other typical fanfare. The publicity would urge the public to participate in the needs identification survey at work, through a survey printed in the local newspaper, or through a telethon.

The survey itself would take the form of a small printed card listing selected problems/needs on one side and allowing space on the reverse side for responses. Respondents would be asked to write, in the blank space provided, three choices from the list and put them in priority order in two categories. The first category would be the respondent's own perception of the most important problems/needs of the community. The second category would be the problems/needs personally confronted by the respondent. An optional feature of the survey would be a list of key demographic characteristics for the respondent to check off. Blank space on the survey card would allow the respondent to add problems and needs not listed on the card. The survey cards could be distributed by employers among employee groups during the NAW and collected in boxes at central work locations.

For those not in the work force, there would be two other ways to participate in NAW. Surveys published by local newspapers could be clipped, filled out, and mailed to the NAW Survey Research Center. The second approach would be to publicize a central telephone number which anyone could call to participate in the survey. The number could be promoted through a local television station telethon. The list of problems and needs could be flashed on the TV screen and the respondents would write their responses on a piece of paper and then call the central telephone number. If a telethon were not feasible, a bank of telephones could be set up to receive responses to the community needs survey. A maximum of two or three minutes per call would prevent the survey from becoming a counselling session. To reduce costs, volunteers could be trained to answer the telephones. Perhaps the telephone company could be persuaded to donate telephone lines for Needs Assessment Week.

This method of needs assessment does not pretend to be scientific. It is in no way comparable to a random sample survey of the general population, nor will it yield detailed information on attitudes and behavior. However, on the plus side, such a survey might reveal the public's perceptions of the major problems confronting the community and themselves. Second, a Needs Assessment Week approach as described above could serve as a valuable public education tool concerning community problems and needs. If planned and executed properly, it could generate enthusiasm and a greater sense of community involvement in identifying human needs and social problems. Lastly, it could generate public appreciation and support for the community's health and human services system. And it could, to some degree, influence the resource allocation process.

Donor Opinion Survey

In this method, a specific donor group—those who contribute money, property, or personal services—would be asked how they wanted their donations to be used. Conceptually, this method can be applied to any consumer-related issue. For example, donors to a symphony orchestra may be polled to learn their musical preferences. Contributors to a public television station may be polled to learn their program preferences. Our comments are limited to the use of the donor survey as it applies to assessing health and human services needs.

In a donor opinion survey approach, a simple printed card may be distributed to donors, requesting them to complete and return the card along with their contribution or pledge. A number of United Ways have experimented with this method and the response seems to have been favorable.[19]

The donor opinion survey approach to needs identification has a number of advantages and disadvantages. Its greatest merit is that it gives prospective donors some influence over resource allocation and a seemingly more direct role in ameliorating community social problems. Second, it may be among the least costly methods of needs assessment. Third, it does not consume an inordinate amount of time. The entire survey can be planned, conducted, and the results analyzed within a period of two or three months. Last, but not least, a donor survey can effectively improve giving performance. It may induce the non-giver to donate and the giver to give more. This feature is important because identified needs invariably demand increased resources for funding new and expanded programs.

On the other hand, the donor survey approach to needs assessment may have serious disadvantages. Perhaps the most important drawback is that donors, who do not necessarily represent the whole community, are the only ones surveyed. We cannot say with certainty that the views of donors represent the views of nondonors. Second, some may argue that donors may not be knowledgeable about community needs and problems. The characteristics of the donor population may be significantly different from those of the non-donor population, thus throwing the validity and reliability of the findings into question.

Notwithstanding the above problems, the donor survey can be an effective tool for needs identification when used in conjunction with other approaches. If this approach is used, the design of the survey card is critical. The survey should attempt to uncover the donor's perceptions of community problems and needs and *not* the donor's preference as to how his or her gift is to be distributed. The two may not coincide and the survey may produce different answers. For example, if a donor is asked, "For which type of service or program would you like your donation to be used?" the answer may be "youth recreational program." If the same donor is asked, "What are some of the most serious social problems or needs of our community?," the answer may be "fear of crime," "services for the mentally ill," or "insufficient day-care services."

While costs vary among the individual methods described above, as a general rule, collection of primary or original data for needs assessment is more costly than the use of secondary data, to which we now turn.

Service Statistics

Service statistics have been used in needs assessments ever since agencies started collecting data on recipients. Such information is generally used by agencies for program expansion or reduction, depending upon the utilization experience. This approach is also called the Management Information System (MIS) approach to needs assessment.

The more formal use of service statistics for community-wide needs identification—sometimes also referred to as the rates-under-treatment approach—involves the systematic collection and analysis of service statistics reported by health and human service agencies in the community. Such analysis may provide useful information on trends, and it may provide researchers with valuable comparative data. In the voluntary sector, many organizations have routinely used service statistics analysis as a substitute for a more rigorous needs identification in their allocations processes.

Also, local Information and Referral (I & R) agencies maintain and provide a wealth of statistical data that can be profitably employed for needs determination.

The merits of the service statistics approach to needs assessment are its simplicity and relatively low cost, as long as no special surveys have to be conducted and the data already produced by agencies are used.

The major disadvantage of this approach is that service statistics say nothing about unmet needs or the needs of the non-service population. Generally speaking, service statistics are more useful to agency managers and program planners in learning about the characteristics of their respective service recipients and their utilization patterns than to those who are concerned with generalized human needs assessment.

Inventory of Resources

Resource inventories play an essential role in any serious needs identification effort. Quite simply, inventories provide a description of "who is doing what for whom." The inventory complements other needs assessment approaches such as the use of service statistics, surveys of service providers, and surveys of service recipients. A needs assessment would be incomplete without a systematic resource inventory. A good inventory will cover all agencies— public as well as voluntary—and the various services or programs they provide. These program categories must be identified and defined on a uniform basis across agency lines. To avoid duplication and overlap in program identification, each program category should be exclusive of all others. Agencies providing a certain program should then be listed under each program category. For example, program categories such as "Day Care" will list all agencies that offer day-care service. The ideal resource inventory has additional data within it, such as client characteristics and service statistics.

While essential, resource inventories are not adequate to determine social needs by themselves. A description of available community services might indirectly indicate what is not available, but it would not reveal the unmet needs in the community. Thus, other approaches are essential to complete the needs assessment picture. Nonetheless, the resource inventory is an important tool in program planning and service delivery. It can answer questions about under- and over-utilization of services, unnecessary duplication and overlap of such services, and the need for improved access and coordination.

The readers of the various approaches to needs identification described above will reach one conclusion: there is no single approach; there is no best method; there is no best combination of methods. The selection of the particular combination of approaches will be circumscribed by three key factors: level and scope, cost, and time frame.

Finally, there are three general shortcomings of the needs identification approaches described above. First, because they are fundamentally data collection, all approaches face the thorny problem of scientific validity and reliability. Techniques to check validity and reliability exist. However, they can be quite costly. How far one needs to go to satisfy the validity-reliability requirements finally becomes a political question. What is the trade-off?

Second, the approaches that employ secondary data may appear to be low-cost. However, even the use of secondary data can turn out to be expensive. Data collection itself is not necessarily costly, but to put it all together in a meaningful way and to relate data—especially those from outside the community—to the local social problems and needs can prove to be a difficult and time-consuming task requiring highly skilled professional analysts.

Third, none of the approaches shows how to synthesize data from various sources. Data collection mechanisms do not automatically result in data synthesis, which is essential in needs assessment, particularly when different collection approaches are used.

THE PROCESS OF NEEDS ASSESSMENT

This section is not intended to be a nuts-and-bolts or "how to" description of the needs assessment process. However, the ideas, thoughts, and clues presented here should be useful to those charged with conducting a needs determination. The managers of each effort will have to customize the process according to their particular sets of circumstances and constraints.

The needs assessment process can be divided into five main phases:

1. Initiation—The Preassessment Planning Process
2. Data Collection and Analysis
3. Data Interpretation—Transmittal of Findings
4. Implementation—Dissemination
5. Evaluation—Was It Worth Doing?

Initiation—Preassessment Planning

This phase is key to a successful needs assessment. During this phase a number of important decisions will be made that govern the entire process. The phase is composed of the following: initiation, auspices, exploratory consideration and decision making, funding, and assignment of responsibility for data collection.

Initiation. An individual or group must initiate the exploratory process. The initiator can be any important public official or a leader of private citizens or a group—for example, a city mayor, a county commissioner, the chairperson of the county board of supervisors, the volunteer president of the local Health and Welfare Planning Council, or the president of a major community foundation. Any one or a combination of the above can take the initiative and call a meeting of key community leaders to explore the need and feasibility of conducting a needs determination.

Auspices. If the initiator is successful in the early exploratory stage and sufficient interest is demonstrated, the next step is to organize a committee to steer or oversee the process. In the case of a community-wide health and human services needs study, a partnership venture between the public and private sectors is the preferred approach. A "blue-ribbon" committee, preferably identified in its title as a needs identification committee (NIC), should be appointed. Representation from major community segments is essential: service providers, consumer advocates, corporate community, foundations and the philanthropic establishment, organized labor, research and educational institutions, professions, and religious institutions. Fair distribution of men and women, and an appropriate ethnic mix, will add to the credibility of committee deliberations.

Exploratory Considerations and Decision-Making. The committee's first order of business is to conduct a formal exploration, or assessment, of (1) what is actually involved in conducting a needs assessment, (2) why they should do it, (3) what the lesser alternatives are, (4) who will actually do the research, (5) whether resources are available, (6) how much time should be allowed, and (7) whether there is a commitment to use findings, and so on.

Funding. If the exploratory considerations are positive, a funding decision must be made. This aspect of the preassessment planning is closely related to deciding who will do the research.

Research Responsibility. The final key step in the preassessment process is to assign responsibility for the data collection and analysis (research) phase of needs assessment. If the sponsoring organization lacks the capacity to execute the assignment, a number of options are available. Examples are local institutions of higher education and research, private for-profit and non-profit consulting organizations, local United Way organizations (planning departments), and local health and welfare planning councils. Others may also be found.

The sponsor may also consider putting out a "request for proposal" (RFP). If outside assistance is sought, the reputation, expertise, and past effectiveness of such assistance become critical selection criteria. A detailed research plan, guaranteed fee levels, and a specific time frame in which to complete the assignment should be required before the final go-ahead is given.

Data Collection and Analysis

Most communities have local access to a variety of data sources. To the lay supervisor of the data collection and analysis phase, four issues are of paramount importance: sampling techniques, statistical techniques, age of the data, and validity and reliability.

First, in surveys of general or target populations, regardless of the method used (i.e., personal interview, mail, or telephone), proper sampling procedures are imperative if a truly representative sample of the population is to be attained. Second, in data analysis various statistical techniques are available—from the simplest to the most sophisticated—using advanced computer programming. The choice of the appropriate technique for the analytical task thus becomes important. Third, the age of data can prove to be a critical factor in data collection and analysis. Obsolete data can only result in obsolete findings. This is usually an easy and convenient target for the critic of needs research, and it detracts greatly from credibility. Fourth, and perhaps the most difficult and general problem in data collection and analysis, is the problem of validity and reliability. As mentioned earlier, ensuring validity and reliability can be a costly proposition. To the extent that resources permit, the researcher must make every effort to obtain the highest possible level of validity and reliability.

Data Interpretation—Transmittal of Findings

This is the next logical stage in the needs identification process. Data have been collected and analyzed, and a report has been prepared. The findings, including all supporting data, are now transmitted to the sponsor of the needs research. Some general observations are in order here.

First, care should be taken that the main report is written in lay language. Technical data, such as sampling procedures and statistical techniques, should be exhibited in an appendix. An executive summary is always helpful. Second, whenever possible, a draft report should be presented prior to the final report so that the steering committee has an opportunity for input. Ideally, and resources permitting, progress reports should be planned to give the committee a sense of participation in the process. This could also serve as a useful check on the direction of the project. If it is determined that the project is not proceeding in the intended direction, midterm corrections may become necessary and should be instituted. Third, a verbal presentation by the researcher (the principal investigator and his or her representative) is recommended, preferably with visual aids such as color slides, maps, charts. The basic point is the effective communication of the findings and stimulation of the customer's interest and enthusiasm for the product. In this phase, revisions or additional work may have to be done to satisfy the customer.

Implementation—Dissemination

Now that the study is complete and the report transmitted, what should be done with the study? And how should the community implement the findings? The best and the most valid needs study is worth little if it never leaves the shelf. Unfortunately, a number of studies have met that fate. We shall discuss this important topic in the next section.

However, a word about dissemination is in order. The needs findings, once adopted by the community, should receive optimal exposure in the community. Appropriate dissemination strategies should be planned. A special subcommittee of the steering committee may be charged with this important task. Cooperation of the major local media should be sought. Health and human service agencies can play a leading role in the dissemination process.

Evaluation

Strictly speaking, a needs assessment ends with the delivery of the report to the customer. However, we have incorporated two follow-up phases, implementation and evaluation.

The basic goal of evaluation is to answer a deceptively simple question: What good did the needs assessment do? Did it accomplish its objectives? Since the major objective of most, if not all, needs assessments is to have some impact on resource allocation, the evaluation should establish whether or not this happened and to what extent allocations were influenced. However, it would be unwise to neglect several unintended consequences and some subtle and intangible benefits of the needs assessment. One such indirect benefit may be an enhanced awareness in the community for human needs and social problems. This could lead to future public support for an improved and expanded service delivery system.

Evaluation can result in several benefits. First, it will demonstrate that the sponsor is both serious and sincere with respect to needs identification. This is important at a time when one confronts a great deal of cynicism about this type of effort. Second, the evaluation can reveal two conditions: that the entire effort was unproductive and therefore should not be attempted again; or that although not completely successful, it was a worthwhile undertaking, and next time a few procedures may be altered for better results. Third, if the evaluation is reasonably successful, the community can rightly feel satisfaction and pride in their accomplishment and provide a model for others to emulate.

The process of needs assessment is at best a difficult art. Despite quantum leaps in survey technology and research methodology, it remains an art. Even the advent of advanced computer and communications technologies has not altered this. Not only is resource allocation a political process (no value judgment implied), but needs identification itself must unavoidably occur in a political context. This is not to denigrate all attempts at needs identification. A properly conducted needs determination can prove to be a worthwhile and rewarding experience to its sponsors.

THE USES OF NEEDS ASSESSMENT

There are ten specific uses of needs research:

1. Priorities Ranking
2. Resource Allocation
3. Program Planning and Development
4. Fund Raising
5. Service Delivery Structures and Mechanisms
6. Legislation
7. Information and Referral
8. Data Base Development
9. Community Education
10. Future Research Applications

Priorities Ranking

Many see needs assessment and priorities determination as a single undifferentiated process. However, that is not the case. The two are separate processes. Needs assessment is generally considered "grist for the mill" in priority ranking.

Priorities determination is not a scientific process. It is the ultimate value judgment. The word "priorities" implies values—"x" is better, superior, or more important than "y." Without getting into a tortuous discussion of the merits and demerits of priority determination, we can assert that needs research is essential to even a judgmental process such as priorities planning. A sound needs assessment can go a long way toward improving the priorities determination process.

Many organizations have used the priority ranking process when allocating funds—some with more success than others.[20] All decisions, however, finally involve the setting of priorities. A formal priority ranking based on needs assessment can add rationality to the decision-making process.

Resource Allocation

Resource allocation is probably the single most important goal of needs identification—if not its sole raison d'être. Quite simply, the implication is that needs assessment will (or should) bring about significant shifts in resource allocations patterns.

Some resource allocation decisions are more difficult to influence than others. For example, is it better to reduce funds to some programs in order to expand existing programs or start new ones, or would it be easier to find new sources of funding? The point remains that, if needs assessment fails to influence resource allocation, the disappointment will be great and will cast serious doubt on the value of the entire undertaking.

Program Planning and Development

This important use of needs assessment has been frequently underrated in the literature. If significant shifts in actual dollar allocations by the funding bodies do not occur, then the next best use for the findings can be in the area of program planning and development.

What does program planning and development mean? There are a number of ways to interpret this important activity. First, it can mean expansion of current programs as indicated by the demand-supply analysis in the needs research. If the research indicates substantial demand for existing services in relation to available community resources, program expansion will be indicated.

Program modification is another approach to program planning. The needs research may indicate that certain programs, while needed and used, can serve the community better if modified. Another approach to program modification may relate to the perceived need for new programs. The question to be asked is, Instead of starting a whole new program, how would it be if we were to modify program "x"?

A third approach to program planning involves the creation and institution of an entirely new program. This would occur if a service did not exist in the community but the needs assessment findings indicated a high degree of need for that service.

A fourth option in program planning involves the termination of given services. This is probably one of the most difficult applications of needs assessment. Since program termination is a painful and serious undertaking, the validity and reliability of the needs assessment become critical.

A fifth approach to program planning entails having agency managers use the data to justify existing programs at current levels. This is important to service providers. The research may indicate that certain programs are serving the needs of the community well without any need for expansion or modification. Thus, the continuation of funding at current levels would be justified.

Needs identification can be used in other ways to foster program planning and development. First, private funding groups, such as community foundations and corporate contributions committees, may take the initiative and provide funding for a new program indicated by the needs research. Some may even put out "requests for proposals" for new and innovative approaches to the unmet needs identified by the research. Second, citizen groups may get together to start a new program if research findings strongly indicate the need for one. Entire new citizen groups may organize in response to identified unmet needs and thus engage in program planning and development. Third, public advocates and advocacy groups may use the needs assessment to influence a community's ranking of priorities, and thus affect program planning and development.

Fund Raising

The fund-raising implications of needs assessment were alluded to in the above discussion of program planning and development. However, needs assessment can be used to raise funds more effectively. Many agencies develop campaign (fund-raising) case statements that highlight community needs. Some organizations have directly used formal needs assessment in their fund-raising efforts.[21]

Service Delivery Structures and Mechanisms

Needs assessment can also change the way services are delivered. Depending upon the type of needs assessment conducted, the data may indicate the need for significant changes in the organization and location of services. Mergers of independent agencies may be one result. Reorganization of departments within agencies may be another. Improved coordination, cooperation, and collaboration among agencies may be a third result. New coalitions or coordinating bodies may be set up as a direct result of a needs assessment. Agencies may be relocated to improve client access. It should be clear from the above examples that there are many ways in which a needs assessment can influence the organization of service delivery systems.

Legislation

Needs assessment could also affect legislation. In fact, most social legislation is based on some form of formal or informal needs assessment. The potential is the greatest at the state and national levels, although it is also possible to use the data at the community level.

A needs study may indicate that present laws or regulations are major obstacles to the provision of certain services. For instance, a simple change in zoning laws could lead to improved delivery of services. A needs study can also highlight the problem of outdated laws that hinder service delivery.

Information and Referral (I & R)

Information and referral is yet another use for needs assessment. First, in communities where there are no organized information and referral agencies, needs data can indicate the need for an I & R service. Second, in communities having more than one I & R agency or program, the needs research may suggest the need for a networking approach or some coordinating mechanism. Third, and perhaps most important, existing I & R agencies or programs can use the information generated by the needs study to improve service.

Data Base Development

Needs assessment is fundamentally a data collection and analysis activity that generates primary data and uses secondary data. It also produces information in a form that probably never before existed in the community. Depending upon the quality of the data and how they are presented, the community may use them for a variety of planning purposes. A properly conducted needs study can produce important baseline data for future uses.

Community Education

Community education is presented here as a formal and specific channel for needs assessment data. First, community and neighborhood organizations can use data on unmet or undermet needs for advocacy. Formal and informal workshops and seminars, using the data, can make the community aware of social problems and needs. Second, a needs assessment can serve as a "social report" or a "state-of-the-community" report. It can point out the community's strengths and weaknesses. And third, if the data are properly disseminated, they can help build community spirit. If citizens know that the community cares about human needs, they will often unite to build a more effective and responsive human service system.

Future Research Applications

Needs studies can help refine and improve needs research technologies and methodologies. There are lessons to be learned from each experience, from each study conducted. Also, different approaches provide different models for others who are considering undertaking a needs assessment. For the scholar, the researcher, or the social scientist, the greater the number and variety of experiences with needs identification, the better. By improving our knowledge of the methodologies and technologies for studying human behavior and social needs, we can better meet human needs and enhance social well-being.

We have attempted here to identify several ways for using needs research. Some are more direct and formal than others. But it is clear that, beyond its impact on resource allocation, needs assessment has many important uses.

Two major obstacles confront the use of needs assessment: political conflict and cost. Of the two, political problems are more formidable and intractable. They involve impediments posed by the bureaucracy as well as issues of turf. Problems of cost often are reduced to political conflict as well. For this reason, prior commitment of potential users and their extensive involvement in the needs identification process from its inception are keys to utilization. With respect to the costs involved in utilization, it should be pointed out that the social costs of *not* implementing should be considered along with the costs of utilization. Implementation should be looked upon as a preventive measure or as a social investment in the community.

THE NEED FOR NEEDS DELINEATION

Is there a need for needs delineation? The answer depends upon one's conception of that activity. If needs delineation means answering, at a minimum, the basic questions of who is in need and what is needed, then our answer will have to be yes.

Needs assessment is not a panacea and is certainly not a science. However, conceding its many weaknesses does not minimize its importance in social planning. Even in incremental social change and resource allocation, one must have some basic facts and estimates.

Further, we must examine the need for needs delineation in the current sociopolitical context. There is now an undeniable shift in decision-making powers from the federal to state and local jurisdictions. Regardless of the final shape of the so-called "New Federalism"—which, incidentally, is not that new—the trend toward decentralization seems irreversible. More and more decisions will be made at the state and municipal levels than in the past, regardless of the party in power. As resource allocation decisions for health and human services are made at the local level, the demand for accountability and responsiveness to human needs and social problems will multiply. Can community leaders afford to ignore this call? What are some of the tools for meeting this demand? Can needs delineation technologies be refined to provide at least part of the answer? What are the alternatives to needs delineation?

And finally, the shift from the central to the local presents opportunities for voluntary and private sector initiatives unmatched in modern American history. Grand opportunities present themselves for the public, private, and voluntary sectors to come together and form creative coalitions and partnerships to ameliorate social problems and satisfy human needs.

10

Strategic Planning in the Voluntary Sector

GEORGE W. WILKINSON

Organizations in the voluntary sector have developed many systematic responses to changing environmental conditions. These management systems, as they are now called, were invented to cope with imperfectly understood problems. As is typical with inventions, technical or otherwise, each appeared to be independent of the preceding one. Enthusiastic adherents of the latest system claimed that it replaced and made obsolete all of the preceding ones.

Some of these systems have been known by acronyms such as PPBS, ZBB, PERT, and MBO. In addition, we have clearly identified that two other complementary systems have been built one upon the other. The first emerged in the 1950s and 1960s, and was called long-range planning. In the 1970s, strategic planning began to grow and is now fairly widespread throughout business, and is growing in the voluntary sector and in government.

The basis for long-range planning was primarily the effort of organizations to operationalize steps for the future. These efforts often produced what could be considered a master plan, a document that was followed no matter what the consequences. As organizations implemented these long-range plans, they often found that the environment they had forecast was not a reality, and that unexpected changes had created new dimensions not planned for. Strategic planners, on the other hand, began to recognize this environmental change and its rapidity. They embraced the notion of projecting current programs and current issues into the future, and focussed as well on the changing environment and issues that would be faced in the future. They called for organizational repositioning in the future so that there would be a better fit to the future environment.

This chapter presents a framework for strategic planning that has emerged in the non-profit sector over the past five years.

THE STRATEGIC PLANNING PROCESS

Strategic planning is often done in non-profit voluntary organizations largely on the basis of intuition. These organizations shy away from structured programs of planning on the premise that they are not in business and that they are not concerned with making a profit. Thus, processes that have evolved from the business sector are often avoided by the non-profit sector.

However, more and more non-profit voluntary organizations have come to recognize that intuitive planning is not enough, and that some business practices do indeed provide a framework for adaptation to the non-profit world. The strategic process is comprised of six building blocks, as shown in the process model in Figure 10-1.

1. *The analysis of external environment.* This is the principal area traditionally associated with foresight. It involves judgement concerning alternative outcomes of existing trends as well as speculation about emerging developments. Specifically, it focuses on threats and opportunities.

2. *Analysis of the internal environment.* This involves self-assessment in which the organization evaluates its human, financial, technological, structural, and informational capacities and potentials. It focusses on the organization's strengths and weaknesses.

3. *Direction setting.* The strategic process is usually contained in the vision that guides the organization. Direction setting renders this vision in concrete terms by defining operational mission, goals, and objectives.

4. *Definition and selection of base and contingency plans.* This part of the process focusses the identification of alternative courses of action with alternative futures.

5. *Implementation.* This activity involves accountability and execution of work programs throughout the organization.

6. *Performance evaluation.* This involves comparison of actual

Figure 10–1. The Strategic Process

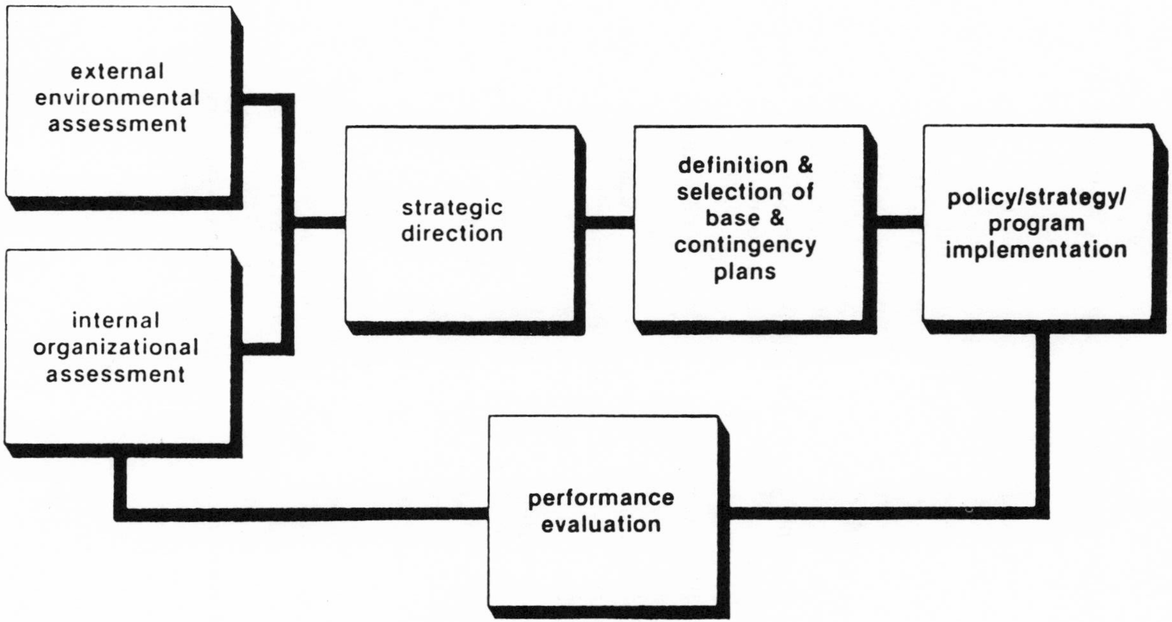

and expected results and identification of the reasons for the magnitude of the differences.

PREREQUISITES FOR SUCCESSFUL STRATEGIC PLANNING

Deciding what data to use and in what form is crucial in the strategic effort. It is important to resist the temptation to overload the process with data. Identifying and generating the right data are far more important than finding all of the data. Because people involved in the process are limited in the amount of data they can digest, determining with them what they need to know to make a decision can be a useful technique both for identifying data needs and for helping people clarify their thinking on an issue. Many organizations form environmental scanning committees to assist in this endeavor. The committee membership is drawn from corporations, universities, governmental and community planning bodies, and others who use and have access to data.

Environmental scanning involves the macro environment, the industrial environment, and the competitive environment. The importance of environmental scanning for voluntary organizations in the environment of the mid-1980s can be seen from several perspectives. First, the changing value system that continues to emphasize people over institutions, individualism over conformity, and participation over authority, will mean for voluntary agencies a greater demand for their volunteers in agency activities, and the participation of staff in decisions that will affect them. In addition, the organizational structures that are typically hierarchial will become more like networks, with decisions moving not from the top down, but coming up and down as well as across the organization. It means that organizational structure will change and that the 1980s may well be a time of worker rights. Voluntary organizations can expect an increasing move to organize both support and professional staff.

From an economic standpoint, because of the decline of federal as well as state funds for voluntary agencies at a time when special interests are continuing to spawn more agencies, the 1980s will be a time of intense competition within the voluntary sector. This competition will be not only for resources but for volunteers, as more and more women stream into the work force.

Demographic changes, the population getting older, the decreasing percentage of youths, and changing racial composition will continue to create havoc for organizations that do not plan. For example, many churches that built magnificent edifices and had large congregations in the early part of this decade found themselves by mid-decade with a shrunken congregation or a congregation of a different racial mix. Often as not, they found that older, wealthier patrons moved away and that the younger people were not interested in joining the church. Some churches, because of the changing racial mixes of their communities in the 1960s, found themselves attacked by minority groups for being insensitive to the new racial groups in their neighborhoods and were confronted by sidewalk demonstrations by human rights groups. Shortage of funds led to the continued cutting of programs, particularly those for youths, and as a result, young families never came for second visits. In the 1970s, many of these churches closed their doors, victims of changing neighborhood and social environments. Changes of this nature will continue in religious, educational, and recreational institutions.

Advances in technology, particularly in the health field, could dramatically alter our health care system, as well as our social care system. Breakthroughs in genetic engineering and cures for diseases like cancer could come at any moment. These changes could easily extend life expectancy by the year 2000 (for those born at that time) to beyond 100 years, as opposed to current projections of 80 years. The implications of this change are enormous.

The decline of "smokestack industries" will have another important impact on the voluntary system. From a fund-raising perspective, agencies and organizations that have been existing on gifts from large corporations will now find these gifts static or perhaps even reduced as certain industries continue to shrink. The heavy impact of the dislocation of the people who work for these industries and who cannot be retrained to work in new industries will place an increasing burden on the voluntary services system.

The 1980s will be a time of turbulence. To ignore that turbulence and plan on business as usual is unrealistic. Every organization needs to develop a capacity to scan its operating environment and to identify the issues, the threats, and the opportunities. This requires strategic planning.

Analysis of the Internal Environment

A key to understanding an organization's future will be an assessment of current strengths and weaknesses. This self-assessment which evaluates human, financial, technological, structural, and informational capacities can be undertaken in many ways. An organization may look at previously identified goals to ascertain its success in accomplishing them; it may compare itself with similar organizations on the basis of structure, finance, and programs. It may test perceptions toward the organization through market research.

Through market research, we may want to examine the perceptions of the organization held by people who are deeply involved in its operation, its professional staff and volunteers. We may also seek the views of clients of the system and see how they perceive the services that are delivered, and we may seek the views of community leaders and the general public. Different techniques may be used: survey research, interviews, and focus groups. Each of these endeavors can help evaluate how well programs and services are being delivered and what programs and services should be delivered that are not being offered. In addition, attitudes about the organization's meeting of community needs can be assessed.

Strategic Direction Setting

The strategic process provides a vision that defines an operational mission and goals for the organization. The first step in setting strategic direction is clear identification of the reason for the organization's existence. Generally, this is a mission statement for the whole organization. It may be found in the corporate formation papers—the charter, articles of incorporation, or bylaws. In rare circumstances, it may not exist.

As a major step in the strategic process, the establishment or revitalization of the organization's mission can prove to be a very difficult hurdle. Several problems can hinder this effort.

1. *The notion that the organization's purpose is self-evident.* Many volunteers and professionals believe that people associated with the organization, particularly those involved on the board or on long-range strategic planning committees, have a clear picture of

the reason for the organization's existence and its purpose in the community. They believe its purpose to be so obvious that examining it would be a waste of time.

2. *The belief that an existing charter, set of bylaws, or mission statement will automatically suffice.* This view is based on the belief that a sense of purpose, once it has been established, will serve the organization indefinitely. Therefore, where there is a mission statement, or its rough equivalent, there is no reason to develop another one.

3. *The feeling that while spending time on the relatively philo-sophical task of constructing a mission statement is important, it is taking time away from the strategic planning committee's main job, the construction of an action-oriented strategic plan.*

Each of these views can create significant problems in motivating the committee to construct a mission statement. If one or more of these views cause the committee to bypass the deliberation of the organization's mission, there can be significant problems later in the process.

The first meeting of a strategic planning committee should include a review of the historical perspective. The written reason for the formation of the organization should be explored. Secondly, how the organization has carried out this mission since its inception should be analyzed, along with current activities and purposes of the organization. This later may be an amendment to the constitution and bylaws of the organization or by a vote of the board.

Information gathered in the analyses of the internal and external environments should be considered. The question should then be posed: If this is what the organization is, and this is what the environment will be, then what should the organization be?

A short case history of such a process, in which an organization's mission changed, concerns the National Foundation for Infantile Paralysis. President Franklin D. Roosevelt founded the organization in 1938 to raise money for research, education, and patient care in connection with the dreaded disease of infantile paralysis. The March of Dimes was created to support the cause. The public responded generously, and the funds eventually helped lead to a solution in the form of the Salk vaccine in 1955, and shortly thereafter the oral Sabine vaccine. Within a short time, the disease was virtually eliminated, and so was the need for the National Foundation for Infantile Paralysis.

When an organization loses its mission, it is on the road to extinction. The National Foundation for Infantile Paralysis, however, decided not to give up, believing that it could be of value to society by using its volunteers to raise money for some other cause. The foundation identified a number of health causes that needed financial support, and chose one, birth defects, that was consistent with its reputation for serving children who were victims of ill health. In 1958, it changed its name to the National Foundation and became a major charitable organization, supporting research, education, and patient care for children with birth defects. Trends and events thus affected the organization and its mission. It strategically viewed the future, repositioned itself with a new mission, and continued forward.

In a similar vein, many United Way organizations that were originally formed to raise money for a select group of agencies have paused to reflect on changing times and have recast their purposes. Many now have as their mission statement the following: to enhance the organized capacity of people to care for one another. With this mission statement, they have moved to develop a variety of programs to carry out this mission. These programs include government relations, year-round education, volunteer recruitment and training, management assistance to other agencies, information and referral, community needs assessment and allocations, donor option, and other forms of resource deployment, such as venture, emergency, and transition funding. Thus, they have become much more than just fund-raising organizations.

Once the mission is stated, it must be examined in light of environmental change and internal capabilities, so that strategic issues can be defined. As we describe it, a strategic issue is a new development, either inside or outside the organization. An issue may be an opportunity to be grasped in the environment, or an internal strength to be used. It can also be an external threat or an internal weakness, both of which imperil the continued success and even the survival of the enterprise. Frequently, external threats, because they signal significant continuities in the environment, can be converted into opportunities by aggressive and entrepreneurial management. Indeed, such ability to convert threats into opportunities has been one of the characteristics of the private sector that can be emulated by the voluntary sector.

When deciding if a strategic issue is important for the organization, it must be considered whether the issue is important enough to warrant a commitment of the organization's resources, and it must also be determined whether the organization may reasonably expect to exert some influence on the issue. If the answer to these two questions is yes, and the issue can have an impact on the organization's performance, then a strategic issue has been stated, and it should be considered for further study.

The link between environmental scanning and issues identification is critical to the strategic process, since there are life cycles to these issues (see Figure 10-2). The issues have a curve very much like the product life cycle curve, which has two dimensions: (1) a time dimension depicting the narrowing of options and the expansion of organizational liability, and (2) a public attention dimension.

Issues and issues management are like products, industries, and even whole societies. Issues are subject to life cycle principles moving through emerging, developing, maturing, and declining stages.

A variety of techniques help us identify and examine strategic issues to determine their impact on the organization, and to determine which are the most critical for organizational focus in the strategic process. One useful technique for exploring the implications of an issue, a trend, or an event was developed by Joel Barker at the University of Massachusetts. It has been used extensively by a number of corporations and United Way organizations over the last few years, and is called the "Implications Wheel." The exercise begins by placing an issue, event, or trend being examined in the center of a wheel (see Figure 10-3, for example).[1] Implications are spun off until the study group runs out of ideas, which usually occurs in 20 to 30 minutes.

In this process, no censoring is allowed; every implication goes up no matter how seemingly ridiculous. The study group quickly builds implications from implications, sometimes out to third- and fourth-order implications that otherwise would not have surfaced. At the end of the session each "bubble," or group of implications, is labeled as an opportunity and a challenge.

Once a list of potential issues is developed from the implications wheel exercise, a further refinement may be made by submitting the

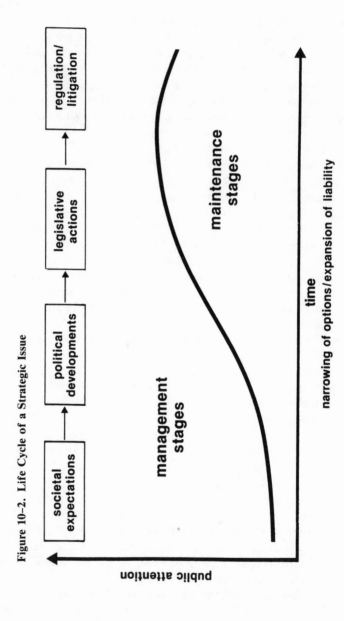

Figure 10-2. Life Cycle of a Strategic Issue

societal expectations → political developments → legislative actions → regulation/litigation

management stages

maintenance stages

public attention

time
narrowing of options/expansion of liability

198

Figure 10-3. Implications Wheel Exercise

The above exercise was run by the Long Range Planning Committee of the United Way of Essex and West Hudson, Newark, New Jersey. Only partial results have shown.

issues to a three-way test (see Figure 10-4).[2] This three-way test encompasses (1) testing for the probability of the issue to become a major issue for the organization, (2) the amount of impact that it would have on the organization should it become a major issue, and (3) when it may become a major issue. These tests can be done on a zero-to-ten scale and then plotted in a nine-cell matrix, such as the one shown below.

The value that this approach has over a simple rank ordering is that it provides a multi-dimensional analysis. Magnitude of impact on the organization and probability of occurring are the first two sorts (see Figure 10-5). After the time dimension is added, those issues that fall in the high-priority areas can be sorted into near-, medium-, and long-term matrix. Thus immediate attention for action can be focussed on the short-term issues while the organization can establish a monitoring procedure for the long-term ones.

The group then selects those issues that have high impact and high probability as critical issues for further strategic study. Seven to nine such issues are about the maximum that any organization can usually handle.

The strategic issues brief is a paper on each major issue and provides a summary of the conclusions reached in the environmental analysis, as well as in the implications wheel exercises.[3] These papers should contain the following segments:

1. Title of the issue—a succinct, one-sentence statement of the issue from the point of view of organizational strategy
2. Strategic significance—identification of threats and opportunities for the organization posed by the issue
3. Background and driving influences—the key environmental forces, now and in the future, that make this an issue
4. Prospects—potential outcomes under alternative scenarios
5. Effect on the organization—quantitative measures of the potential impact of the issues on the organization under the alternative scenarios
6. Planning challenges—require two statements that set out the overall actions required to maximize opportunities and minimize threats.

An example of this issue brief, in outline form, is shown below.

Figure 10-4. Exploring Issues Exercises

ISSUES PROBABILITY EXERCISE

■ What is the probability that this will develop into a major issue?

  (As measured by extent of, e.g., interest group activity,
  media attention, legislation, regulation, litigation, etc.)

0	1	2	3	4	5	6	7	8	9	10
highly improbable					unlikely		as likely as not		more likely than not	highly probable

■ In assessing probability consider:
  —Pressure of trends (net: reinforcing trends less inhibiting trends)
  —Pressure of interest groups/constituencies (net: support less opposition)

Issue:_____

0	1	2	3	4	5	6	7	8	9	10
highly Improbable		unlikely		as likely as not			more likely than not			highly probable

ISSUES IMPACT EXERCISE

■ Assuming that this does become a major issue, how great would its eventual impact be on the United Way?

  (As measured by extent of its effects on, e.g., costs, fund raising, allocations, management organization/policies/practices, "image"/reputation, etc.)

0	1	2	3	4	5	6	7	8	9	10
negligible Impact			incremental change			substantial change			major structural change	

■ In assessing impact consider:
  —Opportunities as well as threats/problems
  —Longer term as well as immediate impact

Issue:_____

0	1	2	3	4	5	6	7	8	9	10
negligible impact			incremental change			substantial change			major structural change	

ISSUES MATURITY EXERCISE

■ In what time-frame will the issue mature sufficiently to require significant resources for its analysis/management?
  —Near-term: this year-next year, e.g., 1980-81
  —Medium-term: the following three years, e.g., 1982-84
  —Long-term: the five years after, e.g., 1985-90

Issue:_____   1980-81   1982-84   1985-90

Can Also Be Done This Way:

Issue:_____   1980 1 2 3 4 5 6 7 8 9 1990

Figure 10-5. Issues Priority Matrix

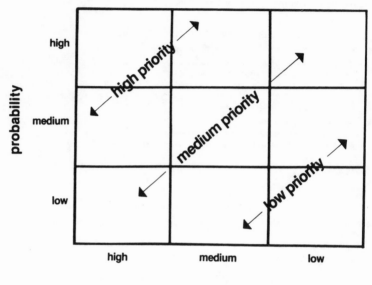

impact

Segments

1. Title of Issue

2. Strategic Significance
   (Challenges/Opportunities)

3. Background
   (Driving Influences)

Example

1. Mounting competition for
   work place solicitation.

2. Challenge: Multiple campaigns at the
   work place would significantly erode
   organization fund-raising capacity
   and foster popularity contests.
   Opportunity: Organization could
   capitalize on demand for access to
   become more inclusive and guarantee legitimacy of participants.

3. High Inflation
   Changing Values
   Rise of Special Interest Groups
   Reduction in Government Funding
   for Social Services
   Changing Work Environment

Segments	Example
4. Prospects	4. Worst Case: Work place solicitation becomes total popularity contest run by payroll departments. Organization Fund-Raising/Allocations functions become defunct. Current Path: Continued inroads are made for multiple in-plant solicitations and designation campaigns. Best Case: Organization becomes "all-inclusive," balances donor interest in selection with citizen review process.

5. Effect on Organization (Quantitative Measures over Three Time Periods in $ of Campaign Production and Market Position)

5.

Current Path	$ Raised (millions)	Market Share	(Health/ Welfare)
1981	1.5	60%	
1984	1.7	45%	
1990	1.9	30%	

Segments	Example
6. Planning Challenges ("Need to" Statements)	6. Need to develop new approaches to inclusiveness that will avoid campaign "popularity contest." Need to introduce motivational techniques compatible with new work environment to build organizational acceptance.

Once we have developed the strategic issue briefs, we move on to our next building block: definition and selection of base and contingency plans.

Definition and Selection of Base and Contingency Plans

In this phase of strategic planning, the organization begins to develop a strategy or series of strategies to reach its mission objectives, carry out a program that will take advantage of the issues' opportunities, and reduce the threats posed by the issues to the organization. In seeking feasible strategies, the organization may employ several techniques to generate the ideas that can form the basis of strategies. One technique is known as a "nominal group process," while the other is called "synectics."

The nominal group technique is useful when working with both large and small groups to brainstorm means of dealing with the stated issue. In normal process, the issue brief is reviewed and then individual members are requested to write down lists of potential strategies to deal with the issue. After each member has recorded his or her ideas, a facilitator asks each member to list one idea. Each idea is then recorded on a flip chart. This process is continued until all ideas have been recorded. The facilitator then reviews the ideas as listed, seeks clarification from the group as necessary, and combines ideas that are similar. After this clarification and compression has occurred, the facilitator will ask the group to select those five ideas that they believe are the most feasible for dealing with the issue. By either written or hand vote, each item is voted on and a numerical value given to it equaling the number of people who have selected that item. At the end of the voting, those items that won the most votes are selected as potential strategies for dealing with the issue.

Another means for more of a freewheeling brainstorming approach to find ways of dealing with the issue is synectics. Synectics is a process designed by a group of the same name located in Cambridge, Massachusetts. The process works in the following way: a one-sentence headline of the problem or issue being studied is recorded; a client is selected who has responsibility for the issue, and this person gives a brief background on the issue—why it is an issue, what may have already been thought of or tried. Then the group begins to speculate on how to solve the problem, converting facts, opinions, feelings, and concerns into action-oriented statements beginning with "how to" or "I wish." From this list of statements, the client selects an idea to pursue or a direction that needs an idea for its accomplishment. The next step is to evaluate the idea, when it has been selected, by identifying at least three useful aspects or advantages of the idea, as well as the concerns that the client would have in terms of how to carry out the idea. The group then begins to build on or modify an idea to overcome the concerns.

A list of alternative strategies is generated through these processes. The organization must then examine each strategy in terms of its feasibility. The resources required (fiscal and human) must be determined in order to learn whether the organization can carry out the process unilaterally or through some coalition, what the process means to organizational structure, and how it would change current operations. Once an analysis has been performed, the strategies are selected.

The next phase is to examine the selected strategies and assess alternative scenarios. If other possibilities would not alter action, the decision is probably sound. If other scenarios would alter the strategy, then alternative courses of action should be outlined in case such changes in the environment do occur. These alternative courses form the basis of a contingency plan for dealing with the issue.

Preferred strategies help frame a strategic plan. Generally speaking, the plan consists of several major parts. First, there is an introduction that states why the process was undertaken, identifies the methodologies used, and reports the time it took to accomplish the planning process. The second section normally identifies the people who are involved in the process. The third section states the organization's mission and the mission objectives that have been set for the planning period. (This planning period normally ranges from three to five years.) The fourth section typically identifies the issues and the conditions that made the issues critical. The fifth section of the plan lays out the strategies and sets forth a rationale for their selection; it also identifies the resources needed, the time frame for accomplishment, and the responsible operating division or divisions.

Implementation

Implementation occurs once the basic guidelines and strategies have been developed from a corporate standpoint. Operational divisions receive direction and have been allocated the necessary resources. Often in this process, management by objectives (MBO) as an organizational tool is used to link the organization's divisional objectives to departmental objectives and to individual objectives. All are tied to the strategic plan. The aggregate of these plans is then moved forward for executive approval as well as board approval in the annual budget cycle.

Performance Evaluation

Performance evaluation, which compares expected results with actual results and identifies the differences, is a critical juncture in keeping strategic planning vibrant. It is critical because it is the necessary link between the first effort and all subsequent efforts. If strategic planning is not an ongoing management function that is continually renewed, then it will have a short life and will disappear from the scene.

When the results of the evaluation are in, recognition and rewards should flow to those individuals, departments, divisions, and groups with high performance. Such reinforcement supports the second phase of strategic planning, which is the renewal activity of examining the changes in the environment, accomplishments, and failures. This allows for refinement and for addition of new strategies. The turbulence within the operational environment will determine the scope of the changes made to the first plan.

Strategic planning is hardly a new discovery. It is the latest step in an evolutionary process of organizations attempting to find better ways to manage in times of turbulent environmental change. In simple terms, strategic planning is the process of exploring

1. Where you need to go—and when
2. Whether you are prepared for the trip
3. What kind of trip it probably will be
4. Whether there will be suitable rewards when you arrive.

The process need not be overly sophisticated and should be designed to fit the culture, the structure, and the size of the organization. It should be an integral, ongoing function that drives the entire enterprise to do better.

The goal of strategic planning is strategic management. It must tie together planning and management in an ongoing system that is responsive to the organization's changing operational environment. It must set clear and specific objectives, and strategies to reach them. It is a process of management development and education, one that must accommodate all of the key constituent groups involved or concerned with the organization. Its strength must lie in accommodating diversity, rather than in attempting to impose uniformity.

Organizations of the voluntary sector are still in the embryonic state of this new management form. They will continue to learn from business and from their own experience, building on that experience to bring strategic thinking to their everyday activity. Thus, those who engage in the process will take a firm step toward better planning and management.

11

The Planning Structure of Voluntary Organizations: The Relationship of Professional Staff to Lay Leaders

JOHN FORESTER

This chapter considers a case of a human service volunteer organization, and it focusses upon several pressing practical issues. The scope of staff activity is constrained not only by client needs, but by anticipated funder satisfaction or dissatisfaction. Staff relations with lay volunteers are influenced by the limited time budgets of the volunteers, and by their corresponding information-handling limits. Expectations of staff and volunteers alike may be tempered by the lack of client participation in agency processes. And the management of attention and status—looking good and reducing uncertainty—may be as important as any technical-professional competence of staff or volunteers. These and related issues are important for prospective voluntary agency staff and volunteers alike to know about, for they directly shape the actual performance of voluntary human service agencies. By considering the perspectives of funders, staff, volunteers, and clients, this chapter seeks to contribute to a clear and sensitive understanding of voluntary human service programs, and in particular of the prospects of staff-lay leader working relations in such programs. Although the discussion here begins with one case, the problem of conflict between social service goals and funder requirements seems to be a widespread concern of human service organizations.

Let us take a specific example. In one northeastern U.S. community, the county legislators have for many years contracted with a local voluntary organization, the Social Services Coalition (SSC), for advice about the priorities that they should observe when reviewing the funding requests of human service programs. Though not providing direct social services, the SSC does provide coordination, referral, evaluation, and information services to local governments and human service organizations alike. The SSC is staffed by a small number of professionals, but it consists largely of community volunteers and representatives from various social service agencies throughout the community.[1] The review committee, which we consider here, evaluates the requests of those human service agencies applying to the county (among other sources) for funding. To avoid conflicts of interest in the review committee, recipient agencies are not represented; concerned citizens with varied human services or local government experience serve instead. The committee meets with agency staff and a board member and provides a forum for agency staff to present, explain, defend, or otherwise clarify their budget requests. The professional staff of the SSC meets with agency staff before and after the review committee's session to prepare and then to follow-up with the agencies' budget requests. By considering first the various actors involved in the review process, we can infer from their behavior lessons for voluntary organizations.

THE ACTORS

The county legislators. These elected officials provide the mandate and the funds for the SSC and the review committee specifically. The county legislators could create another process to take its place. Thus, the SSC both serves and depends for its very existence upon the county legislators. Furthermore, the county legislators have expectations. They expect that the review process will allow the budget requests of the various human service agencies to be scrutinized well before the county's final budgeting takes place. That not only allows a range of problems to be ironed out before it might be too late to deal with them, but it also provides a forum (the SSC) in which problems and needs can be discussed and examined. At the same time, of course, the structure of this process means that this very forum for the discussion of human service needs *will not be the public forum* of the county legislators' own committee meetings. We return to the implications of this fact below.

The clients of the agencies. The clients of the agencies have relatively little to say in front of the review committee. Once in a while, the agency staff presenting a budget will bring along an agency client to testify to the importance, the smooth operation, the genuine service delivered, and the satisfaction of clients with a program in the proposed budget. Yet the review committee is hardly a forum for clients—time is too short—and clients for all practical purposes have little voice there. Whatever consideration of clients there may be comes with the particular knowledge of the review committee members themselves. Often clients are knowledgeable about other programs, and it is common for clients of one program to be clients of another. Client satisfaction here is a matter of reputation, not one of participation, analysis, or voice.

Yet such indirectness does not reflect the wishes of the review committee, its formal intent, or even the sentiment of many of its members. The review committee is staffed by volunteers, and the time of volunteers is limited. Time limits mean that procedures must be streamlined and efficient. No one wants to waste time, and few volunteers will commit themselves to a process which threatens to demand unlimited time. Substantive issues are inevitably affected as well. This fact in no way distinguishes this county; clients are generally the very people for whom public participation in an uncertain and long budget process would be most costly. For middle-class people, the review process may provide a certain status; certainly this is one of the benefits of being a committee member. For poorer people, though, such status is likely to mean little when far more basic needs—health, shelter, counsel, legal aid—are lacking.

The staffs of the agencies. The staffs of the agencies requesting funds may be quite ambivalent about the review process. On the one hand, they may get valuable assistance from the SSC staff in preparing their budgets; this will be especially true for smaller programs and agencies which are severely understaffed. On the other hand, agency staff are likely to feel vulnerable, dependent, and at the mercy of the review committee when they may have only one hour (or less) in front of the review committee to present their entire county budget request for the year (which may run from several thousand dollars to perhaps $100,000). Facing the review committee, the staff must appear competent and careful, having considered all budgetary alternatives, being closely attuned to the needs of their clients and the efficacy of their agency's services, recognizing last year's problems and failings without being stigmatized or taken to task for them, and promising realistic benefits from services to be rendered in the coming year. At the same time, these agency professionals must open their budgets and hold their performances up for the scrutiny of the review committee, a largely non-professional, volunteer committee operating under clear time constraints. A resource for the committee members' reputation may be a threat for the agency staff: reputation and rumor may be difficult to distinguish. Furthermore, the agency staff has little sense of the context in which its proposals are being reviewed. Each agency comes in separately, and the review committee ranks the merits of all the progams that come before it. Thus, an agency staff is in the somewhat perverse situation of having to compete effectively against all other human service agencies for funds, even when that same staff might feel very strongly about the need for other programs in the county to receive adequate funding for their services.

The professional staff of the SSC. The staff of the SSC walks a tightrope. It must help the agencies make the best possible case for their programs. It must provide review committee members with the best information about the programs, so they can ask pointed and probing questions to provide the basis for the committee's priority rankings. The staff must help agency personnel anticipate the concerns of the review committee's members. In the closed portion of the review committee's meetings, the SSC staff must help the committee members focus upon what seem to be the major problems of the various agencies' performances. In each case, an appeal to professionalism justifies the discretion used by SSC staff to speak to the issues at hand. If the staff were to make ad hominen arguments, it might be seen as subjective, biased, arbitrary, or lacking in sound judgment. Yet, if statements about personality are couched in program performance terms—"he's not always reliable; he'll promise you information but then not have it three weeks later, a week after you were supposed to get it—and it's his budget we're talking about!"—then such a judgment will be recognized as considered professional advice.

But this is not the only tightrope the SSC staff walks. It must serve the county legislators when those officials request information; yet, it must also be seen as trustworthy by agency staff, or its credibility and respect as a group of human service professionals will suffer. Seeking to defend valuable social services, the SSC staff must provide information carefully to the elected officials; for in serving the legislators during budget deliberations, especially in a time of austerity, the staff cannot be seen by those officeholders as advocating those social services. Advocacy for services would be seen by the legislators as lobbying, and such lobbying could lead to spending more county dollars. This, of course, is something that every elected official is reluctant to do and something that a conservative county board is doubly unwilling to do during a national recession. Thus, the SSC staff is caught in a dilemma: wishing to serve social service needs and assure funding for deserving programs, it cannot—due to the very structure of the review committee process—serve as an advocate for those programs. Almost the contrary, in fact: since it is perceived by the agency staff as presenting one of the hurdles on the way to eventual funding, the SSC staff may be viewed suspiciously by the very staff whom it would most like to support. And as we shall see, the volunteer members of the review committee may find themselves in the same position.

The professional staff in such circumstances may find that it has a somewhat thankless job, and this will be all the more frustrating to the degree that it attempts to serve social service needs. Yet its organizational position—mediating between county legislators and the agencies needing funds—means that it may be viewed suspiciously by both sides, distrusted by both, who feel that for their good works they have precious little support from anyone. That such a position may lead to problems of morale should not be surprising. Still, these frustrations may be limited, and the staff has various strategies for overcoming them.

While many variations exist, one overall strategy seems most appropriate: if there is a professionally open, well-informed, neutral review procedure that can be publicized and followed, suspicions from both the county legislators and local agency staff may be minimized. For the procedure effectively becomes a statement to legislators and staff alike that the SSC staff is not acting arbitrarily or with bias; that it is not an advocate for particular agencies, and it is not threatening others or demanding more funding for all the agencies. A public and open procedure may take some of the heat off the SSC's staff, but the same tensions remain as particular projects become the focus of work. Furthermore, there is no truly open and neutral procedure for reviewing progam budgets, however better attempts in this direction are than the backroom machinations that are possible when program needs, budgets, recommendations, and decisions are hidden from public view. We return to the problem of professional neutrality below.

Volunteer members of the review committee. The members of the review committee share some of the SSC staff's dilemmas. Serving on a committee charged with the fair review of all requests for funding which come before it, members obviously cannot overtly advocate the cause of any one agency independently of the details of the agency's budget requests, program capacity, and client needs. Yet, the particular sentiments of the members cannot but come out. Some members may feel particularly strongly about legal services, programs for the handicapped, the elderly, youths, and so on. The structure of the committee, though, serves *in part* to balance such biases; the number of biases is itself one limited check upon such bias adversely affecting fair consideration of projects. But other biases may be more subtle.

Biases of Class, Status, and Stigma

While the largely middle-class backgrounds of the committee members may be adequate for the judgment of many administrative and budgetary concerns, that background indicates a gulf between the everyday worlds of the committee members and the everyday lives of many program clients. Not only is client participation in the review process difficult, but client participation on the review committee itself is also discouraged by the same economics of time that affects membership. Another influence may come into play as well. If review committee members are selected by the SSC volunteer board with an eye to their good standing in the eyes of the county legislators, then members will be sought who have experience in administering programs, teaching others about such programs, working for such programs, serving on city or county legislative committees, and so on: in effect having, by reputation at least, the knowledge of the "hard realities" of administering such programs. If such criteria for selection are used—and there is pressure to use them precisely to the extent that SSC's own funding from the county is vulnerable—then participation on the committee by clients in need may be discouraged precisely because of such need, because the clients are somehow not fully autonomous, self-supporting people.

There is a perversity here, of course. Democratic participation in public decisions is a commonplace value in the United States. This value is invoked daily by national leaders, for example, in discussions of Poland, Central America, Cuba, and the Middle East. Yet in cases at home, things are not so straightforward. In the local case, the very fact of being a client of a social service agency may become a stigma that works against the democratic reality of participation in decisions affecting one's life.

Notice that this result requires no ill will on the part of the professional staff or the broader governing board of the SSC; in trying to maximize the strength of the SSC review committee in the eyes of the legislators, they may search for experienced and accomplished persons, even if in so doing agency clients (also experienced and accomplished!) are subtly excluded from committee membership. Worse, a further reason for such subtle exclusion may be surmised: surely the clients of particular agencies could not be selected to serve on that basis, for then many agencies without client representatives would feel that the review committee held a built-in bias against them. One way to handle this problem would be to find people who were simultaneously clients of several agencies, but then for all the reasons mentioned above—from the costliness of participation to the stigma of being recognized as in need—participation by such clients would be the most unlikely of all.

Thus, the middle-class character of the review committee is reasonably assured. The impact of socioeconomic class differences is likely to be indirect. Because direct knowledge of client needs and, therefore, empathy with clients will be reduced the more that class differences exist, the SSC review committee members may be less likely to advocate specific programs or the pool of social service agencies in general. This experiential distance from the clients and familiarity with program administration and funding may predispose committee members to scrutinize administrative issues to the neglect of issues of client need. Such generalizations are difficult to verify, though, and almost impossible to use to predict behavior as committee members face any given project. Yet as a matter of predisposition and indeed competence in understanding the experiences of others, socioeconomic class may be important in assessing the overall performance of volunteers and voluntary agencies.

The Presentation of Self and Impression Management: Neutrality or Advocacy

Still, the economics of participation do not render the review committee ineffective. Members of the committee are often quite knowledgeable about social service delivery, and their questions to applicants are often pointed, insightful, and helpful. Applicants may learn how better to present a budget request as a result of the review committee's questioning, and stronger agency performance before county legislators and other funding sources is only to the agency's benefit.

Like SSC staff, review committee members can be in conflicting positions, but they live with the contradictions and frustrations for a far shorter time. Committee members, too, must be concerned with the "presentation of face," with "looking good" to the county legislators, or they will imperil the whole review process. Yet while "looking good" (fair, considered, impartial, neutral, and non-advocating) to the county is important, many members of the review committee feel that the agencies coming before them are often sorely strapped for funds, often already unable to serve more than a fraction of the existing need for services by their clients.

As a result, committee members are caught in a bind. While they value services for those in need, they cannot help but anticipate in their committee meetings what the board of representatives (the legislators) will think. If the committee members give the impression of lobbying for more funds from the county, they are likely—so the common argument runs—to undermine their own standing with the county. They would become not trusted counsel, but only another special interest group vying for favors, another self-interested advocate to be expected to exaggerate needs and crises and emergencies, and to minimize problems, inefficiencies, and program failures. Beyond reviewing budget requests, then, the review committee must protect its credibility with the county as an impartial, professional, responsible body. This threat of losing credibility shows up most explicitly in the bounds of committee discussion; statements that might be taken to advocate a program's cause rather than dissect its budget request are discouraged before ever being drafted. The result is frustration: the integrity of the review process (seen as mandated by county legislators) seems to contradict what the integrity of professionals who review understaffed programs might seem to require—advocating increased funding for those programs. And yet there are strategies for handling this contradiction too. Recommendations for increased funding for certain programs may indeed be made, supported by conventional, objective assessments of program strength and need, and there need be no appearance of advocacy. Program requests may indeed be supported, and agency staff may at rare times even be informally encouraged to apply for more funding, but there are political and organizational constraints on the review process.

Constraints of Time and Information

Review committee members also work under severe time constraints. They depend heavily upon SSC staff for the information available to them, though they supplement that with their own knowledge of local programs and their own networks of human services contacts in the community. Still, their reviews are necessarily circumscribed. Rarely is time available for site visits, for example. Client participation is welcomed, but more so in theory than in practice. The amount of work to be done, the number of budget requests to be considered, dictates—within the constraints of volunteer time available to members who are already generally quite busy—that budget presentations be tailored: trim, specific, precise, to the point of detailed budgetary items that are new and changing, set in the context of the agency as a whole and perhaps in the context of the social service community as well. Such budget presentations can best be done, of course, by agency staff, those most familiar not only with specific programs, but with the details of the budgets, with the details of the six or seven other funding sources to whom the agency may also be applying for partial funds, and with the administrative history of the particular programs.

Client participation and presentation would take—should take, some would argue—much more time. If provision for it were made in a systematic way, the entire review process would need to be restructured, and the feasibility of a volunteer review committee would certainly be put in doubt. Would a *professional* review committee hearing clients' views be better than a *volunteer* committee whose time constraints severely limited client participation? Volunteer review committee members are hardly in a position to ask, much less answer, such a question. Members volunteer, and they understand themselves to provide a community service; they provide a forum for the review of agency budgets in a way that may shield agencies and their clients from arbitrary political pressures that they might otherwise face, were there no review committee. Yet this good intention has its costs, as argued above: the de facto discouragement—without words ever being spoken to this effect!—of client participation in the review process. This good intention has its benefits too: the creation of a forum in which budget requests can be prepared, discussed, revised, and supported by a combination of professional and volunteer effort, with a degree of insulation from arbitrary political disruptions.

Again, however, the review committee members work under severe informational constraints. Sent a stack of budget requests one week before the meeting in which they may be considered, members have limited time to pursue their questions. The narratives that accompany the budget requests are often very general, and specific questions must wait for the review committee meeting. In the meeting, specific questions may be asked and answered; more general questions about relations with other programs or the effectiveness of particular subprograms may be very difficult to answer. It is a good deal easier to be precise about an increase in clients seen last year by the Battered Women's Program than it is to be precise about the need for transportation services for the elderly. Review committee members may feel, then, that the pressures of time and the search for objectivity compound the problem of a lack of information; this seems universally to characterize such human service review processes.

Having considered some of the organizational dynamics of the SSC review committee, let us now summarize several of the more interesting, if necessarily tentative, findings. In each case, relations between professional staff and volunteers are affected.

IMPLICATIONS: INFERENCES TOWARD LESSONS

First, the professional-voluntary provision of a forum for budgetary review may represent a displacement of social service issues from a political to a voluntary-administrative arena. Agency and client needs can be institutionally redefined from issues of a public, political character to issues of a professional, relatively more administrative sort. While the necessity for expertise and professional judgment may not be contested here for the moment, this potential depoliticization of social service needs should not go unnoticed. Furthermore, to the extent that legislators politically equate agency participation in the review process with evidence of fair hearings, and thus with legitimate outcomes, the professional-voluntary review process may unwittingly undercut possible broader political support very much deserved by agencies whose funding is in jeopardy.

For professionals and volunteers alike—though in different ways—the very organization of the review process circumscribes their attempts to assure that people in need will receive needed services. What may appear to the staff and volunteers as a careful, considered, reasoned process may be used by legislators for quite different purposes, purposes independent of those held by the volunitary agency's board and committee members. In a time of fiscal austerity and pressure to reduce government spending, legislators may use the review process as a means to avoid tough questions themselves. They may use the formal process simply to show concern for social welfare, even if they ignore such concern once budget decisions must be made. They may, then, use the review process not for its results (e.g., a rank ordering of projects) but simply for its formal and symbolic message; for the process appears to be fair, neutral, open, considered—who can complain? Should legislators be taken to task for neglecting human services needs, they can point to the review process, whether they have honored its recommendations or not, and they can claim that any deviations from its recommendations were the result of the inevitable "hard choices" that had to be made at the time of final budget adoption.

There is no telling in which localities such a process will be used for these ulterior purposes by local legislators and in which localities the ostensible purpose of the review process will be honored. For our purposes here, it is important that such an apparently benign and well-intentioned review process may be used for quite different political purposes, and that the best intentions of professional staff and volunteers alike may be manipulated for the political ends of others. In each locality an open question remains: Does a local review process like the one described here represent a careful and considered evaluation resulting in effective recommendations for local funding sources? Or, does the review process instead represent, *against all good intentions of its participants*, a means for local politicians to avoid debate, to minimize their accountability regarding human service programs, to appeal to the legitimacy of an open review process while they neglect the very needs that so often are being poignantly articulated in that process?

Second, the mixed professional-volunteer nature of project review in this case illuminates organizational problems faced by much larger and even more professionally expert organizations. In particular, concerns with routine items will drive out concerns with the non-routine. In an environment in which time, information, and expertise are scarce, in which statements of client needs and professional response are ambiguous (the need for, or provision of, various types of counselling, for example), the project reviewers will likely focus upon what they can readily monitor or document. While the number of clients seen is known and will get attention, the ambiguous quality of care delivered is difficult to assess.

Quality of care in human services is notoriously difficult to define, measure, and monitor, and these difficulties have practical consequences in the review process: the ambiguities of assessing quality of care will be avoided in favor of more readily presentable data and numbers, which will be almost independent of whatever true outputs these figures describe. The attention of the committee is a scarce good and it must be conserved. Project reviewers thus need to pay attention to problems and issues for which they can get answers in the time available, or the review process will soon be in shambles. This economics of attention (and the necessarily simultaneous neglect) deserves much more attention itself than it has received (Forester, 1982a). Interesting and related accounts may be found in Aaron Wildavsky's now classic *Politics of the Budgetary Process*, Charles Lindblom's work on disjointed incrementalism, and the work of James March and Herbert Simon, from their *Organizations* to March's more recent essays on organizational change, decision making, and ambiguity. Suggestive as it is, however, even this work has often ignored the normative, ethical, and value implications of the processes described (Forester, 1984a, 1984b).

The purging of the non-routine has important political and ethical consequences. When attention is scarce and uncertainty and ambiguity abound, when clear-cut solutions are almost never achieved and seem always a distant second to organizational compromises, attention will be paid to the interests of those who already have the power, status, access, organization, and skills to shape the agendas of review processes (Forester, 1982b). Unorganized groups, however, may be treated as if they have no needs deserving of consideration. Project reviewers may often passively accept requests for project reviews but hardly encourage the organized or unorganized (and if the latter the question arises of how) to attend to or serve what seem to be neglected needs.[2]

Social and political-economic inequalities mean that the processes are more open to the already organized, to those with well-developed social service networks, to those already familiar with the world of governmental and social service funding and program development. Unless specific professional, volunteer, and community-based efforts are made to counteract this effect, the scarcities of time, information, and staff (professional and volunteer) will mean that a formally neutral review process will in fact favor the more organized over the less organized, the more powerful over the less powerful, the more affluent—even among low-income people—over the less affluent.

This is an ironic consequence of the doctrine of equality of opportunity so popular in this country. For in a race—a competition open to all, in which the entrants bring to the starting line all of their inequalities of health, training, and resources—is it a surprise to anyone that the odds favor those who are already healthy, well

trained, and relatively more "resource-full"? If professional and
volunteer-staffed human service agencies are to work to correct
inequality instead of reproducing inequality, they must focus
efforts on those needs that are not already well articulated by an
organized constituency—or be certain that no important needs of
that type exist.

Third, in this case the very name Social Services *Coalition* represents a perplexing problem. Remember that the review process
brings individual agencies before the review committee for the
purpose of budget and administrative review. Ordinarily this
process takes many months. Budget requests are submitted, presented, discussed, taken back for revision, often altered, and resub-
mitted. The SSC staff and the review committee become a node
from which individual relations with the agencies requesting funds
emanate. But little happens in this process to facilitate or encourage
actual coalition formation. While an SSC planning committee is
charged with coordination, here too the avoidance of the advocacy
posture is important. Opportunities for coordination are sought,
but cooperation for the purpose of presenting a more compelling
case for increased funding is necessarily (as discussed above) discouraged. As a result, the word "coalition" in the SSC's title may
mask an ironic effect of the attention provided by the review committee: the Social Services Coalition, and similar agencies, may
continue social services' *fragmentation* as much as foster any real
coalition of social service agencies.

Project reviews may not actively prevent agency coalition formation, but they may well not encourage it either. Were the review
agency to hire not a community organizer but an interagency
organizer to remedy this situation, the legislators of course could be
expected to complain that the agency was biting the hand that fed
it. Thus, the dependency of this voluntary organization upon legislators' funding creates a situation in which volunteers' hopes for
the strongest possible articulation of social service needs are systematically frustrated. Perhaps other organizational and organizing
strategies are possible. At the very least, though, human service
professionals and volunteers alike should be aware of such per-
verse organizational results when they join or work for such
organizations.

Finally, this discussion bears witness to the wisdom of E. E.

Schattschneider's dictum to the effect that any organization represents a "mobilization of bias." Schattschneider was not imputing evil, bad faith, mischief, greed, or political manipulation to anyone and everyone; he was remarking upon what we have here referred to as the economics of attention. Professional and volunteer attention is scarce, and any organization of professionals and volunteers (or one or the other) will inevitably be able to attend to just so much. The definition, purpose, mandate, and indeed personnel policies and job descriptions of any organization will indicate the types of issues and concerns to which it will pay attention, and thus the types of issues and concerns that it will probably effectively neglect as well.

In the theoretical world of market economics, neglect is not an issue, for some other entrepreneur can be expected (*in theory*) to enter the market to respond to any effective demand that exists for a good or service. But the world of human services is not quite the world of the perfect economic market characterized by perfect information, effectively dispersed buying power, and so on. Neglect in the world of human services is a major issue, precisely because no systematic mechanism exists to assure attention to pressing social needs, particularly if those in need are, first, already quite dependent on services that do exist and, second, are thus less likely to organize for fear of losing what modicum of benefits they do have. In the non-market world, we must examine how it is that need is articulated and defined; we must recognize that unlike the theoretical case of the economic market, the articulation of and attention to social needs reflect political and economic inequalities, that behind the present articulated needs may lie others equally pressing and perhaps even more opportune to be addressed. The argument here does not begin with Schattschneider's notion of organizational limits and biases to turn against him and suggest that organizations ought to pay attention to what, by their own definitions, they cannot pay attention to; that, of course, would be absurd. Yet the contrast with the perfectly operating market is instructive. If such a resource allocation mechanism existed, the *theory* tells us, the organizational bias would be automatically counteracted by entrepreneurship and innovation. Human services, however, ought not to be understood as markets (for many reasons that cannot be argued here). As a result, lacking the corrective assurances of free market theory, human services professionals and volunteers must be constantly vigilant for pressing needs that lack organized articulation—needs of those least able to participate in a political system in which participation is hardly as costless as the mythology that says everyone is equal because they have one vote every four years might suggest.

Consider once more the organizational posture of working to provide equal opportunity for all, whether to students applying to schools or to human service organizations applying for funds. Voluntary organizations that do this will, ironically, participate in a process that sets up a race among those who are unequal, assuring not that no one will place first, second, or third, but perhaps that those most in need, those least able to run, may not place at all. This problem, surely, deserves the attention of all those working to meet human services needs.

12

Volunteerism: Attracting Volunteers and Staffing Shrinking Programs

DAVID HORTON SMITH

My approach to understanding volunteer recruitment and placement starts with the general and proceeds to the specific, taking the foreword of this volume as a base. The aim is to mention the major issues and findings, listing briefly where possible the detailed results of research.

GOVERNMENT RELATIONSHIPS TO VOLUNTEERING

Volunteering is a special topic politically in that it has an attraction for both liberals and conservatives, depending on the aspects of volunteering that are emphasized. For instance, liberals are likely to be attracted to the notions of decentralization and participatory democracy as these relate to volunteering. Conservatives are likely to be attracted to the notions of self-help and independence of government as these relate to volunteering. It should come as no surprise that volunteer work is highly relevant to ideologies anywhere along the political spectrum, any more than it should come as a surprise that paid work has its relevance across the entire spectrum. What varies according to political ideology is favor toward certain kinds of volunteering and towards certain structures and contexts of volunteering, as is correspondingly true of paid work.

The implication of the foregoing for volunteer recruitment and retention is that these processes should take into account the currently dominant political ideologies and frame appeals and approaches accordingly, insofar as this does not cause significant deviation from long-term group or program goals. Such framing is best seen as adaptation to changing political climates so as to survive and continue to be effective, rather than as a "blowing with the wind" of political ideology. For some groups or programs, no such adaptation will be possible, given the political ideology underlying their goals and activities. So be it. For other groups and programs, perhaps the majority, such adaptation will be possible and essentially cosmetic, given a lack of strong underlying political ideology. And if certain leaders are too scrupulous to accept relevant cosmetic changes because of their "marketability" in a given political climate, then let them march to their own drummer knowing that, to a significant extent, their recruitment and retention are likely to be adversely affected. The relationships here are often complex, so that refusal to yield to the prevailing political climate may indeed serve as a special attraction to some potential recruits while at the same time alienating others. The net result in terms of volunteer recruitment and retention could go either way for a particular group or program. Finally, groups and programs that spend too much of their time trying to adapt to changing political climates can easily fail their primary mission, whatever that may be. Hence, changing one's volunteer recruitment and retention approaches should always be secondary to one's primary goals.

Naturally, the more attractive one can make a volunteer group or program appear to the current government, the greater is the likelihood of gaining support from the government, other things being equal. But support from government is a sharp, two-edged sword here, especially in the United States, where changes in the political coloration of the presidency have been frequent for the past several decades. The closer a volunteer group frames its appeal to current ideology, the more difficulty it will encounter at the next shift in the political winds. The conclusions to be drawn are perhaps as follows: If a volunteer group has a strong underlying political ideology, then it should probably not do much to adapt to changing political climates beyond accentuating its similarities or differences, as the case may be. If a volunteer group or program does *not* have a strong underlying political ideology, then it should probably make some attempt to frame itself, at least cosmetically, so as to be most attractive in terms of the current political climate; however, it should not go so far in this adaptation as to significantly hinder its fundamental service delivery or to appear to be merely blowing in the shifting winds of politics without roots of its own in *some* values.

Federal government support for volunteers in the United States in the past two decades has been often more harmful than helpful. Federal agencies such as ACTION have been more interested generally in competing with the voluntary sector than in supporting it. Specifically, ACTION and other federal agencies have been principally concerned with having their own volunteer programs, managed and funded by the government, rather than facilitating existing or new volunteer groups or programs as independent entities of the voluntary sector. This folly has been as true under Democratic administrations as under the current Republican one, espoused ideologies to the contrary notwithstanding. A similar shortsightedness tends to be present at state levels of government as well.

What is needed, in my view, is a thorough restructuring of the relationships of government to volunteering, so that government facilitates performance of needed services by groups or programs using volunteers that are in (or wish to be in) the independent, voluntary sector of society. The proprietary volunteer programs that governments own or manage should generally be phased out, and the funds used for facilitation of the relevant services by independent groups. If the service is deemed too important to be left to an independent group, then probably the time has come to make delivery of that service a responsibility of paid government workers. With the exception of tax collection, virtually all government services accepted today as proper for government to perform were initiated by the voluntary sector. This process will no doubt continue.

The mechanism for most appropriately supporting needed voluntary sector groups and programs is a matter for serious thought and discussion. My own preference is for a National Foundation for Volunteerism, structured along the lines of the National Science Foundation or the National Endowment for the Arts and Humanities (see my unpublished paper on this topic, commissioned by the Alliance for Volunteerism). Such a foundation would be set up as a quasi-independent, non-partisan, government agency whose grants to voluntary sector groups would be a result of intensive, non-partisan peer review using funds from the government. State governments with foresight might set up statewide foundations of this sort in advance of a federal move in this direction. It is unlikely that the ACTION Agency or its state-level offices can effectively function as part of the proposed National Foundation for Volunteerism, given this agency's history of ineffectiveness, competition with the voluntary sector, and drastic political shifts.

Finally, there must be a long, serious, wide-ranging discussion (at all levels, including the federal) of the role of volunteerism in America today and in the future. As we move more and more toward an economy of scarcity rather than abundance, and an economy of service delivery rather than manufacturing or extraction, the role of volunteerism will loom ever larger in importance. In not many years, we may find the imputed (estimated) value of volunteer service work included in our gross national product. Valuable work done is valuable work done, whether the person doing that work is paid or not. We need to seek the best way of structuring our society so that we have a synergistic partnership of paid and volunteer work, not cutthroat competition between the two. And similarly, we need to sort out the best roles for the government, commercial (profit-seeking), non-profit, and family (household) sectors of society. When we have accomplished the restructuring needed to meet these goals, we will have a "voluntary society," which is something to be fervently wished for.

VOLUNTEER UTILIZATION ISSUES

There is a series of issues I shall cluster under the rubric "volunteer utilization," or alternatively, "*resistances* to volunteer utilization." Too often the matter of volunteer recruitment and placement is treated solely at a micro level without taking the macro level context of the work setting into account. It is taken for granted that volunteers are genuinely wanted and that they will be treated as serious workers. But beneath the surface is the smoldering resistance to the use of volunteers in the first place, let alone to treating them as serious workers once recruited.

Resistance to the use of volunteers in the voluntary sector may seem paradoxical to the outsider, but not to the insider. This barrier to effective recruitment and placement of human service volunteers is most prevalent in voluntary organizations that depend primarily upon paid staff for service delivery, although it also surfaces to a lesser extent in voluntary associations where volunteers are the primary mode of service delivery.

A recent statement of the most important kinds of resistance to volunteer utilization came out of the 1980 National Forum on Volunteerism as conclusions emerging from the in-depth discussions of a distinguished panel of experts who had experience with volunteerism. The fourth conclusion speaks directly to our present concern: "Institutional barriers to effective volunteer involvement exist. Such barriers may reflect an inherent conflict in the concept of unpaid work in partnership with paid workers and/or reflect an unwillingness on the part of those in power to allow citizens to assume full responsibilty for the control over their lives" (National Forum on Volunteerism, 1980, p. 29).

Participants in the forum discussed three main barriers to effective involvement—namely, "the resistance of paid helping professionals to volunteers, the concern of organized labor with the role of volunteers, and institutional barriers within the volunteer community itself" (National Forum on Volunteerism, 1980, p. 31). These barriers or resistance sources are explored in more depth in the forum report (sponsored by VOLUNTEER: The National Center for Citizen Involvement and the Aid Association for Lutherans), a summary of which is given in the source just cited. Briefly, paid staff in volunteer work settings are worried about volunteer utilization in these settings for various reasons, such as concern for quality of services and fear of displacement by volunteers. Similarly, organized labor tends to see volunteers in any work setting as a threat to paid workers, viewing volunteers either as "underpaid" workers who will bring downward pressure on wage rates or as "do-gooders" whose unpaid work will result in the loss of jobs for union workers in the same work setting. Neither of these types of resistance is easily overcome, because there is some validity to both of these claims as well as to the counterclaims of the volunteer community that it has an inherent right in a free society to do volunteer service work freely and thereby give of itself for the general welfare. Specific non-displacement compromises need to be worked out in each volunteer work setting between volunteers and paid professionals and union workers if these forms of resistance are to be ameliorated. And work quality standards for volunteers need to be upheld to meet the criticism of paid professionals (see Wilson, 1981); this will require proper selection, training, placement, supervision, motivation, and evaluation of volunteers—matters that have in the past been too often neglected or dealt with cavalierly.

The third type of resistance to volunteers identified (not for the first time) by the forum participants is more subtle: institutional barriers. In this case the very structure of contemporary volunteerism is the barrier. The emergence of volunteer administration as a profession and the development of various standards for volunteers to meet may be hindering the very volunteering these developments seek to foster. Clearly, there is a need for those in volunteer organizations to reexamine their recent strides toward professionalism to make sure that such strides have not been taken at the expense of "the creative energies of citizens who wish to volunteer" (National Forum on Volunteerism, 1980, p. 32).

Still another major form of resistance to the utilization of volunteers, one that the forum gave relatively little attention to, is the contemporary feminist movement. Over a dozen years ago the National Organization for Women issued its well-known statement "Volunteerism and the Status of Women" (see Loeser, 1974, Chapter 5). Crucial to that statement was the point that women should be more involved in volunteerism for social change (advocacy volunteerism) than in human service volunteerism, since in the latter work contexts women were mainly being exploited—taken for granted, unrecognized, kept in subordinate positions, working for free when they could have been part of the paid labor force, and so on. In the interim there has been a heated exchange between the feminists and the representatives of the established volunteer service organizations involving women. Out of this exchange has come, gradually, a rapprochement of the two positions, so that Betty Friedan, founder of NOW, was recently able to declare publicly that the earlier distinctions between advocacy and service volunteers "have been transcended by the necessities of these times" (Voluntary Action Leadership, 1981, p. 21; see also the related articles in this magazine issue). The necessities referred to were inflation and other economic problems. Yet the issue continues to smolder and could flare up again because economic conditions have improved. Resolving this resistance involves recognition by the feminists that volunteer service work with suitable recognition, treatment, and advancement opportunities can be good for women and good for the general welfare. On the other side, resolution also involves recognition by established volunteer service organizations involving women that neither the reality nor even the appearance of exploitation can be allowed to continue.

Related to this latter point is a series of obstacles to optimum volunteerism that the National Forum on Volunteerism (1980, p. 32) further identified:

. . . questions of liability, insurance, inability to provide reimbursement for out-of-pocket expenses, confidentiality, and accountability; demands for credentials to perform certain functions; limits to the types and levels of jobs available to volunteers; a lack of recognition of the capabilities and experiences volunteers may bring to the job.

STAFF SHRINKAGE IN HUMAN SERVICE PROGRAMS

In recent years there have been two separate types of reductions in human service programs and human service organization budgets. One type has been the result of economic recession, as America has passed through what is sometimes characterized as the worst recession since the Great Depression of the 1930s. Comparisons aside, the recession that ended roughly at the end of 1982 has had a marked effect on the economics of human service organizations. This recession was accompanied, for most of its duration, by high inflation and interest rates, which exacerbated the budget squeeze on such organizations. Unemployment rates rose nationally by several percentage points to post-World War II highs, and human service organizations endured more than their share of staff shrinkage with regard to paid employees. Human service delivery programs were also cut significantly.

However, a second type of shrinkage has had far more drastic effects—namely, that resulting from President Reagan's federal economic policies, the first three years of which have at this writing already become history. Reagan came into office committed to a program of tax cuts, human service program cuts, and defense program increases. For the first two full fiscal years of his administration (1981-1983) he has been able to obtain from Congress enactment of the great majority of his economic policy requests. A recent report by Salamon (1982), part of a larger project, begins to spell out in detail the full implications of the Reagan Economic Recovery Plan for non-profit organizations. The report points out, first of all, that private, non-profit organizations in fiscal year 1981 (October 1980 to September 1981) received more than one and one-half times as much of their total funding from federal government programs as they did from all private charity in this period ($40.4 billion versus $25.5 billion).

But Reagan budget proposals call for 27 percent less real dollar federal support in 1985 than in 1980 for non-profit organizations; and as noted above, the first two years of this plan have already been implemented essentially. The situation becomes far more severe when specific categories of non-profits are considered: *Human service non-profits, in particular, can expect a real dollar decline in federal support of 64 percent from 1980 to 1985.* This translates into an overall budget shrinkage of about one-quarter for such organizations during this period—unless the income is some-how made up from other sources. And because of the huge pro-jected budget deficits, along with the largest *actual* budget deficits in history for the past two federal fiscal years (FY, 1982; FY, 1983), even further human service budget cuts may well be forthcoming.

Not surprisingly, these actual and projected cuts in human service organization budgets have stimulated ever greater attention to the "volunteer alternative" and to new initiatives from the inde-pendent, voluntary sector in general to deal with the problems of declining federal support for human service (and other) programs directed toward the public good. President Reagan has attempted to stimulate such activity through his 1982 "President's Task Force on Private Sector Initiatives." Allen (1983, p. 23) assesses some of the results of this task force's activities that have had an impact directly on volunteering, and concludes that "there can be little doubt that there has been a renewal of citizen involvement nation-wide. . ." (Allen, 1983, p. 24). However, Allen goes on to point out that the essence of this renewal is enhanced commitment rather than major increases in volunteer activity (1983, p. 25).

Other observers, both in the United States and abroad (e.g., Leissner, 1983), have taken sharp issue with volunteerism and human service delivery by voluntary organizations as an easy way for national governments to evade their very real responsibilities for the general welfare of the people. Leissner (1983) is very articulate on this matter, pointing out that it has been a long political struggle to get national governments to accept the notion of the welfare state, in which governments are *obligated* to provide for the general welfare of their citizens. He refers to this as the institutional conception of social welfare and the welfare state, a very basic attitude toward social justice and social responsibility. By contrast, the earlier "residual" conception of social welfare "sees welfare as a combination of temporary emergency measures and a minimum of subsistence maintenance" (Leissner, 1983, p. 16). Leissner, like many others, decries the attempts by national government to revert to the residual from the institutional conception of social welfare and human service delivery. The clash between these two perspectives is an ongoing one not only in the United States and the United Kingdom, but in other advanced (developed) nations of the Western world. The currently prevailing perspective will have an important impact on volunteer recruitment and placement in these nations. And there is an important place for human service volunteers in either case—a place perceived in relation to the national government: Human service volunteers are more central to the general welfare when the residual conception of social welfare prevails, and more secondary and supplemental when the institutional conception prevails.

SOME GENERAL VOLUNTEER RECRUITMENT MODES

Let us now turn to a narrower discussion of the strategy and tactics of recruitment. The term "recruitment" itself I have defined elsewhere:

The term "recruitment" is likely to call to mind a very narrow range of activities or phenomena for most people in the field of voluntary action. Therefore, it is important to make clear the broad sense in which this term is used here. In its narrowest sense, recruitment might be viewed solely as the set of activities by a FVG (formal voluntary group) that are officially and consciously intended by the group to attract new members or participants in its activities. In the present document, the term "recruitment" is used in its broadest sense to include all those events, circumstances, and factors that affect whether or not a particular individual joins or becomes actively involved in a FVG. The difference between the two definitions is that the broader one involves examination of "self-recruitment" and "*un*intended FVG recruitment" as well as intended recruitment by a FVG. Thus, we are concerned here most basically with who participates in or joins a FVG and why they do it, not simply FVG recruitment practices and methods. (Smith, 1973, pp. 4-5)

The broad strategy of human service volunteer recruitment should be as inclusive as possible, and consistent with the volunteer needs of a given work setting. A mix of general recruitment modes is called for, and this mix may well be different for different organizations or work settings. The most appropriate mix may be estimated by careful analysis of recruitment needs; but in the end, trial and error with careful monitoring of relative cost-effectiveness of different modes is likely to yield the optimum mix for a given organization or work setting. To be most useful, such monitoring should avoid "playing the numbers game," reporting sheer numbers of people expressing interest in volunteer human service work. Such people include, usually, many "nominal" (in name only) volunteers. Instead, the monitoring process should focus on those recruitment modes that provide actual or contributing volunteers —people who do more than express interest, who go on to engage in actual volunteer work on a regular basis.

The most common general mode of volunteer recruitment is linked recruitment, or what is commonly called "word-of-mouth" recruitment. People who belong to an existing volunteer group informally recruit relatives, friends, neighbors, co-workers, acquaintances and others with whom they come in contact on a daily basis. Most often an unofficial, informal process carried out on a haphazard basis, this approach can be used consciously and intentionally as an official recruitment mode by a group, since it is quite effective according to research. A small percentage of volunteer groups already do this, terming the process "each one reach one" or "each one bring one," for example.

The second most common mode of recruitment of human service volunteers is by means of the mass media, one aspect of a more general mode I shall call "general public recruitment." As such, this kind of recruitment is always a conscious and intended process.

At the local level, radio public service announcements and newspaper stories, announcements, or advertisements are most frequent, coupled with the use of signs, posters, and banners announcing events and meetings. At state and national levels, television public service (or paid) advertisements, and direct mail to selected mailing lists (often purchased for use from list brokers) are most frequent, along with some magazine, newsletter, and journal advertisements. These methods are generally more costly than linked recruitment, and their percentage "payoff" (recruited volunteers per 1,000 people contacted) is far lower. However, in starting an organization or expanding a small organization, and in reaching special populations of volunteers (e.g., people with a certain disease), public recruitment methods may be indispensable. They are certainly worth trying if a volunteer group has the resources *and* if they are done with proper care and attention to detail. A poorly planned or implemented general public recruitment campaign can backfire by giving a negative image to a group; it does not guarantee success.

A third fairly common general recruitment mode is canvassing, either in person or by telephone. "Canvassing" as used here refers to the practice of contacting strangers (mainly) on a house-to-house basis or geographic area basis in order to recruit volunteers. The method is a familiar one in fund raising for voluntary groups, but is seldom used so far in seeking volunteers, in spite of research indicating its probable effectiveness (less effective than linked recruitment, but far more effective in percentage payoff than general public recruitment). Political parties and advocacy groups, and to a lesser extent some religious volunteer groups (especially new or revitalized sects and cults), have used this technique with success. Human service volunteer groups should give it more serious consideration as an approach. Humans are social animals, and as such are generally quite responsive to well-presented personal appeals for help. Recall the great reservoir of potential volunteers for community and neighborhood service that surveys have shown to be present.

Related to the above-noted recruitment modes is the use of organizational open house evenings and days—and expanding this concept, volunteer fairs as a recruitment mode. The notion here is to invite the public, whether by mass media or linked recruitment, to attend either a single organization's "show-and-tell" session at its headquarters or to attend a multi-organizational set of simultaneous sessions (usually with booths, displays, slide shows, organizational representatives, publications, and so on) held in some large hall or exhibition-type building. This gives potential volunteers the opportunity to find out more about one or more volunteer work settings in an efficient, low-risk manner. People can get a feel for the nature of the organization, its most common activities, its membership, its structure, and so on, without having to commit themselves in advance.

The reverse of open houses and volunteer fairs, where the public comes to the organization, is to take the organization to the public —specifically, to make presentations regarding the organization before public groups in one or another context. Common examples are presentations to high school audiences in assemblies, to high school or college human service groups, to adult human service groups, to members of a business firm or government agency, and to people at a center for the aged. Such presentations, where they can be arranged, usually seek volunteers for a specific project or program of general relevance to the larger community or nation. To be successful, the presentation usually needs a dynamic speaker who is a volunteer group participant (paid or volunteer) and who can make an attractive multi-media approach to the audience. When a carefully designed mix of audiovisual aids is combined with a rousing talk and thoughtful question and answer session, both short-term (immediate) and long-term (delayed) recruitment can be substantial. This can be helped along still further by arranging in advance for a few previously committed potential volunteers to speak up from the audience about getting involved and having them stay after the presentation to sign up. These will serve as public role models for others who are hesitant to be the first ones, thus breaking the ice and realizing the fullest possible volunteer potential from the audience.

The final general recruitment mode is the use of a volunteer register or skillsbank. The most common and probably earliest form of such volunteer registers is the Volunteer Bureau, which was invented more than 50 years ago in Boston. Volunteer Bureaus, now found in several nations, serve to recruit *potential* volunteers from the general public, using methods such as those discussed briefly above. At the same time, volunteer work settings and organizations are also recruited as potential work sites for these volunteers, and an attempt is made to match potential volunteers to appropriate work settings in terms of the needs and preferences of both the volunteer and the work setting. In the past decade or so, many U.S. Volunteer Bureaus have changed their names to Voluntary Action Centers, and new volunteer registers use the name Voluntary Action Center. At the same time, the past ten to fifteen years witnessed the rise in numbers of related types of potential volunteer registers in specialized settings, particularly in colleges and universities, high schools, and corporations. Where the latter are called Corporate Volunteer Programs (volunteers from a usually large corporation are recruited by an in-house office and placed in one of several selected work settings in the community external to the corporation), the former are called, respectively, College Volunteer Programs and High School Volunteer Programs, and operate in a manner similar to the Corporate Volunteer Programs.

In the last several years particularly, a number of the foregoing kinds of volunteer registers have begun to use the technology and name of Skillsbank to refer to a more detailed process of matching potential volunteers with very specific skills to work settings needing those specific skills. This represents a change, because in their earliest forms volunteer registers focussed more on matching a person with a volunteer work setting than on matching a person with a special skill with a work setting (see Saccomandi, 1981). Finally, there are specialized volunteer registers, in existence for many years, that are in effect Skillsbanks even though they don't use the name (for example, Volunteers in Technical Assistance/VITA; Senior Corps of Retired Executives/SCORE; Active Corps of Executives/ACE). Detailed information on all of these kinds of volunteer registers and skillsbanks can be obtained from VOLUNTEER: The National Center for Citizen Involvement, now headquartered in Arlington, Virginia (1111 North 19th Street, Room 500, Arlington, Virginia 22209).

KEY FACTORS IN RECRUITMENT TACTICS

The tactical elements of recruitment to be considered here are drawn from a base of over 1,000 pieces of research and some practical manuals drawing on accumulated practitioner experience (see Smith et al., 1972, Part Two; Smith, 1975; Smith, 1979). I mention this research base not only to lead the interested reader to the primary sources involved, but also to point out that many important factors in recruitment are subtle and hard to discern, showing up often only in carefully performed research. The crude attempts to understand volunteer motivation and recruitment represented by such studies as *Americans Volunteer—1974* (ACTION, 1974) barely scratch the surface in attempting to understand volunteer motivation; they pose simplistic questions about why people began, continue, or have ceased to do volunteer work. The wealth of knowledge we have about who participates and why they do it demands a highly complex model containing a variety of variables in order to make sense of these complex phenomena (see Smith et al., 1980, Parts One and Five; Smith, 1975; Smith et al., 1972, Part Two). The material presented in this section is organized in terms of one such model that I have developed and presented in the sources just cited.

Contextual Variables

There are various aspects of a work setting for volunteers that can affect recruitment. One such aspect is the cultural context, including cultural values, ideologies, and customs. Research suggests that volunteering and volunteer groups are more common where cultural values emphasize one or more of the following (Smith, 1979, pp. 8-9):

- concern for individuals and groups external to one's own family;
- altruistic orientations toward helping those less fortunate;
- trusting and friendly relationships with individuals external to one's family, even with individuals external to one's circle of close friends;
- pluralism and the acceptance of varieties of different viewpoints, perspectives, beliefs, and values as legitimate in their own terms;
- civil libertarianism and concern for the preservation of freedoms of speech, the press, the broadcast media, assembly, association, peaceful dissent, etc.;
- democracy and individual participation in decision making regarding public policy;

- efficacy, mastery, and accomplishment in the secular world, rather than submission to a pre-ordained destiny or fate;
- rationality and efficiency in accomplishment of tasks;
- "organizationalism" or the utility and fruitfulness of formal organizations as means of accomplishing desired ends, in contrast with informal relations, individualism, or kinship emphasis;
- egalitarianism and the diminution of socioeconomic differentials in access to resources, services, participation, and satisfactions.

An international organization can use such information in choosing potential sites for new national associations, and national organizations similarly can use it to select states or smaller subareas as potential sites for organizing new local or higher-level units. As for the local volunteer organization, the most practical task it can set itself in view of these findings on cultural context and recruitment is to try to foster local or national cultural change that will favor volunteer service work. And in its recruiting, it can emphasize, where appropriate, elements of the cultural values and ideologies that tend to foster volunteering and volunteer groups. However, the cultural factors most likely to foster more volunteer human service work "can be most effectively and significantly changed intentionally by either concentrated efforts of the national government or by the major voluntary organizations forming a broad social movement cooperating toward this end" (Smith, 1979, p. 11). INDEPENDENT SECTOR and VOLUNTEER are two very important organizations in the United States working along these lines.

A second aspect of the work setting affecting volunteer work and recruitment is social structural factors. Again, literature reviews suggest that volunteer work and recruitment are likely to be greater where there is one or more of the following (Smith, 1979, pp. 13-14):

- less government suppression of FVGs [formal volunteer groups] generally, or of specific kinds of FVGs and VW [volunteer work];
- more government facilitation (through funding, technical assistance, etc.) of FVGs and VW;
- more government (usually political and financial) pressure for individuals to engage in VW, including government employees;

- more social pressure from corporate employers for VW (as in most large U.S. firms, for instance);

- inability of statutory [government] agencies to deal with the complexity of the societal problems recognized as needing solutions;

- insufficient public tax revenues, because of economic cycle or longer term economic problems, to permit statutory agencies to deal with the socially recognized problems adequately;

- greater industrialization and modernization level of society, including higher literacy rate, wider prevalence of mass media, etc.;

- higher socio-economic level of town or neighborhood;

- a local wage/salary structure and individual tax rates structure that makes VW with statutory agencies locally likely to save individuals money (i.e., by paying lower local tax rates);

- greater homogeneity of local neighborhoods in terms of socio-economic status;

- less distance to sites of VW generally, or to a specific VW site;

- greater level of organizational prevalence of all kinds—statutory [government] agencies, businesses, banks, shops, etc.;

- greater distance from the nearest large town or city (50,000 or larger population);

- more pages of local newspaper(s) published per week, and usually a daily rather than a weekly local newspaper;

- smaller town (i.e., under 50,000 population, and especially under 10,000 population);

- suburban rather than inner-city area, if in a large urban area;

- greater variety of local businesses and industries (rather than a "one industry town" or city);

- greater prevalence of interpersonal informal relationships among the people in the community;

- shortage of professionals to fill paid jobs in agencies and organizations where volunteer workers can do various tasks (such a shortage being a result of maldistribution of professionals or not enough professionals being trained, rather than economic constraints, which have already been mentioned earlier);

- greater responsiveness of local authorities to the pressures and demands of citizen groups for changes and improved services, etc.;

- less opposition of labor unions, associations of businessmen or manufacturers, professional associations, and similar occupation-related groups to VW and non-occupation-related FVGs;

- more residential stability (average length of residence in the community) rather than a high transiency rate;

- better and more developed local or regional public transportation system and communication system (telephones, postal service, public bulletin boards, etc.);

- stronger community norms or social pressure to get involved in VW and FVGs as a part of community commitment and citizen duty;

- greater general acceptance of the use of paraprofessionals (whether paid or unpaid) in the performance of tasks formerly performed only by professionals in agencies and organizations;

- higher levels of expectations of adequate and personalized social services from service organizations for those in need;

- greater role expectations among youth for involvement in the resolution of societal problems and the making of public decisions affecting one's own quality of life;

- greater role expectations among women for involvement in paid or unpaid work outside the home and family context;

- greater perceptions of VW and FVGs as relevant steps toward paid work, fostered by the actual creation of paid jobs for former volunteers in organizations and the acceptance of VW as relevant experience on paid-job application forms;

- greater expectations among adults that work should be meaningful and lead to personal growth and self-actualization, and that one should do paid or unpaid work in order to see such ends;

- greater role expectations among the elderly for involvement in community activities on an on-going basis, rather than being cast aside and considered useless after retirement age;

- greater role expectations among the poor, minority groups, and otherwise disadvantaged that they can and should get involved in VW and FVGs to do something themselves about their problems, either because they can do so better (knowing their special needs and problems "from the inside"), or because they will otherwise never receve the help they need from those more fortunate;

- greater alienation from and distrust of established institutions in the statutory, commercial and even the voluntary sector, leading individuals to attempt to set up new groups and schemes (FVGs and VW) to deal with unmet societal and human needs.

As with cultural factors, the foregoing social structural factors are not easy to change, and changing them takes a concerted effort.

However, such concerted effort can come at any territorial level, from the neighborhood to the national levels, and is likely to bring about significant change that will affect VW recruitment both directly and indirectly (e.g., through increasing FVG prevalence). And as with cultural factors, the concerted effort needed is likely to be either a solid government commitment at a given territorial level or a relevant social movement or social movement organization. Cooperation and networking activities (see, for example, Smith with Judge, 1978) among voluntary groups and other organizations can also play a major part in bringing about the social structural changes that foster volunteering, at any territorial level.

Organizational Variables

The organizational context in which volunteer work is to take place has itself an effect on recruitment as well as on retention and satisfaction of volunteers. The kinds of resistance to volunteers discussed in the earlier section on volunteer utilization lead not only to internal inefficiencies but also to reduced recruitment, as certain organizations that use volunteers get negative reputations for their treatment of the volunteers they do manage to recruit. Clearly, such organizations should attempt to reduce or eliminate such resistance if they are serious about volunteer recruitment. Techniques for doing this include the obvious one of emphasizing to paid staff that volunteers will do only work that supplements the work of paid staff, rather than duplicating or taking over paid staff work—and this needs to be negotiated and carried out in practice. Further, to allay fears of lower work quality by volunteers, "great care must be taken to develop and maintain a really high quality and effective volunteer program that clearly is useful, not an interference with paid workers' activities, and doing much more good than harm, if any" (Smith, 1979, p. 25). In addition, one should "keep the paid workers of the organization in all job categories informed of the impact and effectiveness of the [volunteer program], assuming such can be demonstrated or documented as a result of following the [above] approach . . ." (Smith, 1979, p. 25).

The research literature on recruitment further suggests that recruitment for volunteer work sites is improved where the organization or FVG involved has one or more of the following (Smith, 1979, pp. 26-27):

- utilization of a sponsoring organization or agency for the FVG that will provide leadership and access to other resources including facilities, funds, equipment, and sources of potential volunteers . . . ;
- greater integration and cooperative relationships with other community (or higher territorial level) FVG's in a multi-organizational field with some common purposes and values, thus permitting the FVG to draw on these other organizations as potential resources of volunteers to a greater degree . . . ;
- utilization of the services of a Volunteer Bureau or equivalent organization, such as a school or college volunteer job clearinghouse, etc. . . . ;
- greater use of paraprofessionals in the larger organization, for the case of VP [volunteer program] recruitment . . . since this already legitimates certain kinds of roles and tasks being performed by other than professionals, whether paid or unpaid;
- greater spread of control and greater participatory democracy in the FVG, as contrasted with oligarchy and lack of involvement of lower level (i.e., non-policy-making) volunteers in decisions . . . ;
- more selective incentives provided by the FVG to members and participants that are not available to outsiders . . . ;
- for college or high school students, availability of course credits through VW with the FVG . . . this being one good example of the foregoing general point about selective incentives;
- greater effectiveness of the FVG in achieving its stated aims, goals, and purposes through successful programs and projects . . . ;
- greater prestige, power, and altruism of the FVG . . . ;
- greater satisfactions provided to present volunteers by the FVG, meeting their needs and expectations successfully.

Each of the foregoing factors is to a greater or lesser degree under the control of the organization concerned with volunteer recruitment. If the leaders of the organization give priority to the foregoing and do so with sufficient expertise, perhaps drawing on outside consultants and groups as resources, systemic factors affecting recruitment can be improved. Comparing a given organization with the above-listed characteristics should tell the leaders of that organization what organizational variables affecting recruitment they need to work on most.

Social Background Variables

There is a variety of social background variables that pertain to whether a person will get involved in volunteer work, particularly volunteer service work. Since the list is long and I have dealt with them elsewhere, as have others, I shall not go into them here, instead referring the interested reader to the relevant prior sources (Smith, 1979, pp. 30-32; Smith, 1975; Smith et al., 1972, Chapter 11; Tomeh, 1973; Smith and Freedman, 1972). The general principle underlying these factors is that people with more dominant or high-prestige social positions are more likely to get involved in volunteering (especially human service VW), as are those with volunteering or other socially valued participation experience (see Smith et al., 1980, Part Five, for a full statement of the theory underlying this principle).

The social background and role factors are important mainly as shortcuts to identifying people with psychological characteristics likely to lead them to volunteer. Yet, with the exception of extremely poor health, none of the social background factors need be an ultimate barrier to volunteering—they merely define categories of people with higher and lower probabilities of participating. Therefore, recruitment programs should take account of the research results regarding social background factors, but emphasize overcoming "poor probabilities" by proper attention to other important factors when the full range of popular participation is desired or when a particular group is targeted as desired volunteers.

Psychological Variables

Most recruiters of volunteers give far too little attention to psychological factors and far too much attention to social background factors. In the case of social background factors, there is little chance of change for many characteristics, though this is not always so. For many kinds of psychological variables, however, change is much more feasible as part of a recruitment program. Admittedly, it is not easy to change intellectual capacities and personality traits (though even these can undergo change), but attitudes, information, knowledge, beliefs, and situational factors can be readily manipulated to foster recruitment. Even personality trait results presented below can be used as part of a well-designed recruitment campaign by making a special appeal to potential volunteers with personality traits most likely to lead them to participate. The following are characteristics of a more psychological sort that have been found in the research literature to be associated with a greater tendency toward volunteering (Smith, 1979, pp. 32-35):

- higher *intelligence*, especially verbal and interpersonal skills . . . ; this has been relatively little studied, however;

- higher levels of manifestation of certain personality *traits*, including extroversion, ego-strength (self-confidence), emotional stability, intimacy/ empathy, assertiveness, efficacy or sense of internal control over events, prominence need, practicality, morality/altruism, flexibility, energy/ activation, deliberateness, stimulation/sensation seeking, curiosity, self-actualization need, effective ego-defense, and effective ego-expression . . . ;

- higher levels on certain *general attitudes* dealing with FVGs and the use of leisure time, including general sense of obligation to participate in FVGs; general perception of the effectiveness and utility of FVGs in society; support of civil liberties and human rights; preference for formal groups in order to accomplish desired aims; preference for using leisure time in service to others; preference for using leisure time to accomplish something useful; preference for using leisure time to learn new skills or have new experiences; preference for spending leisure time outside the home and doing something; wide range of social interests; interest in and commitment to local community; sense of political efficacy; obligation to help one's community; cosmopolitan attitudes and interest in national and societal affairs; perceived support by significant others for FVG participation . . . ;

- more positive general attitudes towards the *realm of activity*, general purposes, or types of clients/constituency dealt with by a certain kind of FVG and VW; for instance, more accepting attitudes towards possible suicidal persons . . . ; less fear of the possible dangers of mental patients to society . . . ; more supportive attitudes towards students with problems . . . ; more supportive attitudes towards the social action goals of a type of organization or social movement . . . ;

- more positive *specific attitudes* towards a particular FVG, including attitude toward the effectiveness of the FVG in achieving its goals, felt obligation to participate in the FVG, perceived significant others' positive attitudes towards the FVG and one's participation in it, perceived sense of personal fit with the FVG and its members/participants, felt attractiveness of the FVG, felt commitment to the FVG and its aims and goals, perceived friendliness with one or more persons already in the FVG, perceived relevance of the FVG to one's personal welfare and interests, perceived personal competence to help . . . ;

- more positive *information-knowledge-beliefs* relevant to FVGs or a particular FVG, including awareness of the existence of the FVG . . . ; greater familiarity with the nature of the FVG, and its working on what is perceived to be a real need or problem; greater similarity of own opinions and ideology to the opinions of FVG leaders and the ideology of the FVG . . . ; possession of sufficient information about the FVG to be able to get involved if its nature is attractive to one . . . ;

- greater immediate perception of *situational factors* conducive to participation in a particular FVG, including greater perception of other individuals volunteering in one's presence to get involved in VW, and less perception of others refusing to do so in one's presence . . . ; more exposure to moderately guilt-inducing stimuli relevant to participation; more recent experiencing of a major change in work or school demands, domestic or social obligations, health or residence, any of which may at least temporarily create additional [perception of] free time for the individual . . . ; greater exposure to friends, spouse, or parents who are involved in similar FVGs, even though they do not directly ask the individual to get involved in VW–role model effects . . . ; encounter with a person who encouraged, suggested, or invited the individual to join a particular FVG, especially a friend, acquaintance or person (even a stranger) currently involved in the FVG. . . .

Relative Importance of Recruitment Factors

Clearly not all of the research findings briefly reviewed here (see Smith, 1979, for more detail and for the recent supporting references) have equal solidity, and even if they did, there are some clear differences in strength of various factors. Knowledge of the foregoing generalizations should help one design a recruitment program for a given volunteer service work setting by giving an idea of the general currents or causes. Variation from these trends may occur for specific groups, so that again there will be some trial and error, and there should be careful monitoring of what is most successful in the way of tactics for a given work setting. Beyond this advice, however, it is clear that the motivational factors—personality traits and attitudes—are the keys to successful recruitment tactics. The other types of factors act mainly as barriers or increase conduciveness, particularly information-knowledge-beliefs. Clearly, if a given volunteer work setting never becomes known to any potential volunteers, none will be recruited; this makes formal or informal informational campaigns a necessary part of recruitment. Situational factors are an exception in that they can serve as triggers for participation even when much of the usual motivation is lacking—therefore careful attention must be paid to them in any recruitment.

But the key remains motivation, especially if the recruitment is to be optimally cost-effective. In the voluntary sector, design of recruitment campaigns is perhaps *fifty years behind the times* when compared to motivational and marketing research and their corresponding tactics in the business sector. The gap will remain between current volunteers and people willing to volunteer unless potential volunteers are approached properly by the right organization. There is a "volunteer gap"—not just in terms of volunteers needed, but in terms of use of scientific knowledge to help fill the need for more and better volunteers. And even though there has been a good deal of research on why people volunteer, much more is needed and should be supported by national foundations, relevant government agencies, and national voluntary organizations to help increase our scientific understanding, basic and applied, of why people volunteer. Much current practice in the field of volunteer recruitment is based mainly on unreliable "seat-of-the-pants" experience. There is nothing wrong with learning by experience, of course, but the question to be asked is whether one can generalize from experience at one time and place for a given organization (or type of organization) to other times, places, and organizations. Too often, out of ignorance, practitioners assume that such generalizations can be properly made when this is *not* the case. The result is a situation in which some recruitment efforts are very successful and others fail miserably, without anyone knowing why.

Let me conclude this section with a further citation of my earlier review document on recruitment, since its conclusion still applies:

Some competent volunteerism resource organization of national stature and demonstrated competence should be given the task . . . of (a) collating the full range of VW [volunteer work] recruitment suggestions from the practical literature along with related suggestions for recruitment of paid workers, (b) conducting or commissioning the performance of adequate cost-effectiveness evaluations of the various recruitment methods, (c) encouraging such evaluations by FVGs themselves and by voluntary action researchers even where the resource organization cannot provide funding, (d) encouraging funding sources, both statutory [governmental] and private (i.e., foundations or philanthropists), to support such evaluations, (e) keeping careful track of the results of such evaluations and formulating conclusions periodically, based on existing knowledge, and (f) disseminating these conclusions widely and periodically, both in the form of printed documents, training sessions or seminars with FVG [formal volunteer group] leaders, incorporating into VW recruitment planning and implementation "kits," and by other relevant means so as to reach the largest possible audience of FVG leaders. These activities should focus not only on cost-effectiveness evaluations of FVG and VW recruitment methods in one's own nation but also utilize the results of similar evaluations from other nations of a similar political structure. (Smith, 1979, p. 52)

RETENTION OF VOLUNTEERS

Without adequate recruitment, obviously, there are no volunteers to retain. *With* adequate recruitment, along the lines suggested above, further problems in staffing volunteer programs and groups can still arise, problems that may be clustered under the rubric of retention of volunters. Space limitations prevent full treatment here, but a few generalizations can be made, again based on both research and accumulated practitioner experience.

Training of various kinds is essential to proper staffing of volunteer programs and in the long term to adequate recruitment (since training or lack thereof relates in the long term to volunteer satisfaction, word-of-mouth information about a group, and ultimately attractiveness of the group to potential recruits). Good training of volunteers is multifaceted and essentially continuous. It includes initial training of a general sort that may be termed "orientation" to the group or program and to the role of volunteers therein. It includes intensive formal training in the sense of an attempt to raise the competence levels of volunteers for accomplishing a particular task or role. It includes on-the-job training in the sense of guided and monitored learning-by-doing of the volunteer job or task, under the supervision of someone more skilled who is concerned with helping the volunteer accomplish a given role or task better. It includes refresher training to monitor whether volunteers are maintaining competence levels once they have been attained, and to bring those who have reduced competence levels back up to established standards, And it includes other kinds of incidental training, as when there are major changes in the structure or goals of an organization, when new kinds of clientele are taken on, when new equipment (e.g., computer terminals) changes the work roles significantly, and so on. The more educated and eager the volunteer, the more important do the foregoing kinds of training become for staffing and retention, since such volunteers are particularly sensitive to being underutilized or poorly utilized.

Volunteer placement is an equally important process if a group is to optimize volunteer retention. Placing the wrong person in a given job or task as a volunteer is a gross error that will generally lead both to reduced organizational productivity and reduced volunteer satisfaction, with the long-term result of reduced recruitment —the same result as with poor training. As with paid jobs and tasks, with volunteer jobs and tasks a serious effort should be made to find an appropriate match between the technical and emotional requirements of a role and the technical skills and emotional make-up of the individual. Volunteer satisfaction is likely to be greatly enhanced by such treatment of volunteers as though they really matter—and they do. The recently growing use of volunteer skills-banks (Saccomandi, 1981) is one example of an attempt to take matching seriously.

There are many other facets of personnel practices that also have an important impact on volunteer retention and, in the long run, on recruitment. A few of these are supervision, leadership, communications, morale maintenance, reward systems, openness to feedback, regular evaluation, access to equipment and supplies, expense reimbursement (where relevant), promotion and volunteer career ladders, and paid staff-volunteer relations. The relative importance of these has not been firmly established. Research is therefore necessary. It does seem well established by research that training, placement, and paid staff-volunteer relations are of special importance in volunteer retention. However, other facets that have as yet been little studied, let alone studied in comparison with these facets of personnel practices, may prove to be equally or more important.

Volunteer recruitment and retention are very complex matters. We know far more about the former than the latter, and hence need research effort allocated accordingly. What we do know from research on these topics is greatly underutilized by practitioners. Major national resource organizations for volunteerism and the non-profit sector (e.g., VOLUNTEER and INDEPENDENT SECTOR), and their state and local counterparts, have much to do to increase the use of knowledge here. The Association of Voluntary Action Scholars, the only North American association of researchers who are devoted to the study of volunteering and voluntary action, could greatly aid in this translation and use of knowledge. But whoever is involved in the effort, more and better use of knowledge is necessary if volunteers are to be attracted and staff shrinking alleviated. Volunteer service delivery is needed now more than ever before, and the need can only increase in the long run as more and more social problems and social service delivery needs are recognized and defined by society. Voluntary service delivery programs thus need not shrink, even though their budgets (exclusive of the imputed value of volunteer services and goods) may have shrunk and may continue to shrink. And, as noted earlier in connection with the gross national product, future organizational budgets will routinely include the imputed value of volunteer services and goods (a donation or gift is a "volunteer good"). Hence, even in dollar terms, organizations with volunteer programs can be expected to expand in the future if their budgets are properly computed and if they make effective use of expanding knowledge about volunteer recruitment and retention.

As always, researchers have much to do to increase the scope and precision of our knowledge about voluntary action. The areas most in need of attention can be inferred from the sections of this chapter reporting research results: we have the most to learn where there was the least to report. But more importantly, more research on volunteering must assess the relative powers of various factors that affect the recruitment and especially the retention of volunteers. Disciplinary boundaries continue to restrain the growth of such research and knowledge.

Those who are truly serious about the expanding effectiveness of volunteerism will seek not only to use existing knowledge better, but also to support and generate support for research that will lead to additional knowledge. For example, the National Science Foundation, the National Institutes of Health, and other agencies might be pressed to greater awareness of the need for funding research related to volunteering. Major U.S. foundations might similarly be pressed to support such research, instead of limiting their support mainly to volunteer programs and voluntary organizations. Support a good voluntary organization and you help its service recipients. Support good voluntary action research and you help *all* volunteer service recipients in the long term. Clearly this is not an either-or situation; both are needed. But the balance has for too long been weighted against thoughtful, innovative, interdisciplinary research on voluntary action. Some significant change is needed in this situation.

Notes

CHAPTER 1

1. The English background is provided in Tierney, 1959; de Schweinitz, 1943; and Owen, 1964. Summaries of welfare in colonial America are made in Trattner, 1979 and Jernegan, 1960.

2. The ideology and theology of charity in colonial America are reflected in documents edited by Rothman, 1971. The dominance of public assistance over religious benevolence is documented in articles by Jernegan, 1929; Schneider, 1938; and Parkhurst, 1937.

3. The best book-length synthesis of the revolutionary generation is by Alexander, 1980.

4. Various aspects of the work of benevolent societies, often from a "social control" model of interpretation, are traced in Boyer, 1978; Griffin, 1960; Mohl, 1971; and Smith-Rosenberg, 1971.

5. Sound general analyses, in addition to Trattner's survey, can be found in Rothman, 1971 and Leiby, 1978.

6. Here and below, see, for example, Treudly, 1940; Teeters, 1956; Coll, 1955; Hall, 1974; Heale, 1973; and Wyllie, 1959. An affirming account of evangelical aid to the poor is provided by Smith, 1957.

7. Dolan, 1975. A now outdated but official and still useful account of Catholic charities in the nineteenth century is O'Grady, 1930.

8. The standard work on public outdoor assistance is by Klebaner, 1976. The role of public almshouses is brilliantly analyzed by Katz, 1983.

9. Langsam, 1964.

10. Brace, 1872.

11. Ibid.

12. Ibid.

13. Ibid. The italics are his.

14. Banner, 1973; Becker, 1941; and Melder, 1967.

15. There are many monographs; the best general account is Bremner, 1980.

16. Bremner, 1968; Olds, 1963; Ross, 1978.

17. Scott, 1970.

18. Among many specialized studies of the movement to organize charity, the following general works are among the most useful: Huggins, 1971; Lloyd, 1971; McCarthy, 1982; and Woodroofe, 1962. The classic account by a professional charity leader is Watson, 1922.

19. In addition to the books listed in note 18, the following specialized studies are useful: Becker, 1964; Hall, 1974; Lewis, 1966; Kaplan, 1978; and Siegel, 1956.

20. Davis, 1967 remains the standard account, although Davis stresses political and social actions over the service work of the settlements. Neighborhood work receives attention also by Bremner, 1956; Chambers, 1963; and Trolander, 1975.

21. On settlement history, and indeed for developments in all fields of human services during the first half of the twentieth century, one can consult the journal of social work that was published under various names and in different formats. A historical study of that journal is Chambers, 1971.

22. Jane Addams was a chief articulator of settlement philosophy. On her social theories see Davis, 1973; Levine, 1971; and Chambers, 1979.

23. No single historical account has been published that describes and analyzes these developments. A useful reference work is Romanofsky and Chambers, 1978.

24. Abell, 1960; Gavin, 1962.

25. Freund and Morris, eds., 1966; Goldstein, 1955; Lurie, 1961; Solomon, 1956; and Stein, 1955.

26. The records of the Sheltering Arms, 1882-1982, are located in the Social Welfare Archives, University of Minnesota, Twin Cities Campus.

27. Kurtz, 1979.

28. Many of these national coordinating federations and societies have deposited their official records with the Social Welfare History Archives, University of Minnesota. An inventory of holdings may be obtained by writing to Clarke A. Chambers, Director, Social Welfare History Archives, 614 Social Sciences Building, University of Minnesota, Minneapolis, MN 55455.

29. Of many general works surveying the relationship of government

programs to economic and social developments over the past century or so, see Patterson, 1981.

30. See, for example, Howell, 1975; Collins and Pancoast, 1976; and Froland, 1980.

CHAPTER 2

1. The research on which this article is based was supported by the National Science Foundation, Program in Geography and Regional Science. Baer, Manuel, Castells, Geiger, Reiner, Wolpert, Lim, and Steinberg provided valuable insights, comments, and technical assistance. The author is solely responsible for the chapter's contents, however.

2. These figures are derived from unpublished Internal Revenue Service 990 Reports, 1977; unpublished California Registry of Charitable Trusts CT-2 Reports, 1979; and U.S. Department of Commerce, Bureau of Economic Analysis, *Local Area Personal Income*, 1980.

3. Unpublished California Registry of Charitable Trusts CT-2 Reports, 1979; U.S. Department of Commerce, Bureau of the Census, *Census of Population*, 1983; and Internal Revenue Service Personal Income File, 1976:

CHAPTER 3

1. An excellent description of "private benevolences" is presented by Chambers in Chapter 1 of this volume.

2. Chambers, this volume.

3. Chambers, this volume.

4. Chambers, this volume.

5. A brief historical survey of Catholic, Jewish, and Protestant developments is presented by Chambers in Chapter 1, this volume.

6. Chambers, this volume.

7. *1981 Annual Report* of National Benevolent Association of the Christian Church (Disciples of Christ), p. 11.

8. *1981 Annual Survey* of the National Conference of Catholic Charities, p. 43.

9. The Council on Foundations reported that "American churches and synagogues contributed an estimated $5.6 million to help meet human needs and services in 1982, far exceeding the amount annually contributed by corporations and foundations" (*Newsletter*, 1983).

10. *Biennial Report* (1981-1983)—United Church Board for Homeland Ministries, New York, N.Y.; Health and Welfare Ministries, General Board of Global Ministries, United Methodist Church, New York, N.Y.; *1981 Annual Report*, National Benevolent Association, Christian Church

(Disciples of Christ), St. Louis, Mo.; *1981 Annual Survey*, National Conference of Catholic Charities, New York, N.Y.; *Directory of Lutheran Church Affiliated Social Ministry Organizations*, Lutheran Social Service System, Minneapolis, Minn.

11. The author is indebted to Ms. Kathryn M. Brewer, Executive Associate of LS/3, for assistance in preparing this section and in editing of the entire chapter.

12. Eisenstadt and Kahn, 1983.

13. Ibid., p. 18.

14. Welniak and Fendler, 1983.

15. Moore, 1983.

16. *Memorandum*, August 2, 1983.

17. Urban Institute, *Serving Community Needs: The Non-profit Sector in an Era of Government Retrenchment*, 1983.

18. Chambers, this volume.

CHAPTER 4

1. U.S. Department of Commerce, Bureau of the Census, 1983.

2. Morgan, 1970.

3. See, for example, Rossi, 1977; Ruddick, 1980; Thorne, 1982; Chodorow, 1978.

4. Rossi, 1977, p. 25.

5. Lesch, 1979.

6. Thorne, 1982, p. 20.

7. Belsky and Steinberg, 1978.

8. Kagan, 1978.

9. Stevens, 1982a.

10. Suransky, 1982; Steinfels, 1973.

11. Belsky and Steinberg, 1978, p. 929.

12. Stevens, 1982b.

13. Kagan, 1978, p. 36.

14. I have not seen research comparing children's attachment to their fathers with their attachment to caretakers. It would be interesting indeed.

15. Kagan, 1978, p. 41.

16. Baxandall, 1975.

17. See, e.g., The General Mills American Family Report 1980-81.

18. Suransky, 1982.

19. Ibid., p. 27.

20. Ibid., p. 176.

21. Ibid., p. 51.

22. For a survey of utilization studies, see Hill, 1978.

23. U.S. Department of Commerce, *Trends in Child Care Arrangements*, 1983.

24. Woolsey, 1977.
25. Hill, 1978, p. 533.
26. General Mills, p. 48.
27. Hill, 1978, p. 545.
28. For a full description of these programs and Reagan's proposed modifications of them, see Children's Defense Fund: 1982.
29. Kamerman and Kahn, 1979.
30. Children's Defense Fund, 1982.
31. Suransky, 1982.
32. For more extensive discussions of efforts in this regard, see McCroskey, 1982; Children's Defense Fund, 1982; and U.S. Department of Labor, Women's Bureau, 1982.

CHAPTER 5

1. Schattschneider, 1960.
2. Lipset and Schneider, 1983.
3. Olson, 1970.
4. Lipsky, 1970.
5. Cobb and Elder, 1972.
6. Funkhouser, 1973.
7. Argyris, 1974; Epstein, 1973; Gans, 1979.
8. Rakove, 1975.
9. Lovich and Pierce, 1983.
10. Riker, 1963.
11. Lowi, 1979.
12. Peltason, 1955; Cook, 1980; O'Conner, 1980.
13. Sears and Citrin, 1982.
14. Hayes, 1981.

CHAPTER 6

This research was supported in part by funds granted to the Institute for Research on Poverty by the Department of Health and Human Services pursuant to the Economic Opportunity Act of 1964. It was also partly supported by a grant from the Graduate School of the University of Wisconsin-Madison. My thanks to Suzanne Rinaldo and Irving Piliavin, who commented on earlier drafts of this paper.

1. The names of the counties were confidential because of restrictions of other parts of the study.
2. To achieve the appropriate quality of data, twelve directories were collected, two from each of the six stratifications. The most complete in each cell was coded.

3. The specific items were developed largely from an internal analysis of the directories. Because agencies may have coverage of multiple problems, services, and population groups, lists of these domain elements were developed and the coding scheme recorded whether or not each agency included each problem, service, or client group in its domain. The hypothesis was tested by cross-classifying domain elements with auspice and funding variables included in the coding.

4. The relation is statistically significant at the .05 level.

5. Relations involving day care must be treated with caution because public support for day care may come indirectly, through reimbursement of fees to parents.

6. Here are some examples: unemployment services are correlated to problems of the unemployed; material assistance is correlated to the need for material aid; counseling, which correlates to a statistically significant degree to six problems, is probably more common in public agencies, partly because these agencies tend to deal with more problems than private agencies—1.73 compared to 1.50.

CHAPTER 8

1. Rachels, 1981.
2. Wildavsky, 1979.
3. Rein, 1970.
4. Rein, 1976.

CHAPTER 9

1. Kimmel, 1977.
2. Zangwill, 1977.
3. Ibid., p. 4.
4. For example, see United Way of America, 1972.
5. Ibid., p. 6.
6. Atkins and Delahanty, 1981.
7. *Webster's*, 1976.
8. Human Services Institute for Children and Families: 1975.
9. Kimmel, 1977, pp. 11-13.
10. See Moroney: 1977 for an excellent overview of needs assessment.
11. Kimmel, 1977, p. 12.
12. Human Services Institute for Children and Families, 1975, p. 16.
13. Center for Social Research and Development: 1974.
14. Warheit, Bell, and Schwab, n.d.
15. Minnesota State Planning Agency, 1977; Kimmel, 1977, p. 9.
16. United Way of America, 1972, p. 9.

17. Ibid.

18. Becker, 1981.

19. According to a recent United Way of America study, as of December 1981, 56 United Way organizations were using some form of donor survey approach to resource allocation.

20. For an excellent discussion of this subject, see United Way of America, 1974.

21. A good example of this is the "3 Choices in Meeting Community Needs," an approach developed and installed by the Mile High United Way in 1982.

CHAPTER 10

1. United Way of America, 1980.

2. Ibid.

3. Ibid.

CHAPTER 11

1. These observations have been derived from several years of participation in and observation of the Social Services Coalition in a county in the northeastern United States. Names of organizations have been changed to protect the people involved, and no one has been discussed directly. A more detailed ethnographic account of the actions of specific individuals in this county and in the organizations discussed here is far beyond the purview of this essay and the intentions of this author. Instead, the broader inter- and intra-organizational dynamics of the SSC are discussed here for their suggestiveness about types of practical problems that professional staff, lay leaders, and other volunteers may face as they work together on social services programs. For more analytic treatments of similar problems, see Forester, 1982a, 1982b, cited below.

2. Instead, the SSC has a planning committee with representatives from diverse agencies, and such initiatives might be taken there, eventually to be evaluated by the review committee—but this seems not to have been the case for many reasons similar to those constraining the review committee.

Bibliography

Abell, Aaron. *American Catholicism and Social Action, 1865-1950* (Garden City, N.Y.: Hanover House, 1960).

Ackoff, Russell. *Creating the Corporate Future* (New York: John Wiley and Sons, 1981).

ACTION. *Americans Volunteer* (Washington, D.C.: The ACTION Agency, United States Government, 1974).

Albert, Kenneth J. *The Strategic Management Handbook.* (New York: McGraw-Hill, 1983).

Alexander, John K. *Render Them Submissive: Responses to Poverty in Philadelphia, 1760-1800* (Amherst: University of Massachusetts Press, 1980).

Allen, Kerry Kenn. "Status Report: Volunteering in America, 1982-83," *Voluntary Action Leadership* (Winter 1983), pp. 22-25.

American Association of Fund-Raising Officials. *Giving U.S.A.* (New York, 1980).

Argyris, Chris. *Behind the Front Page* (San Francisco: Jossey-Bass, 1974).

Atkins, G. Lawrence, and Dolores S. Delahanty. *Strategic Local Planning: A Collaborate Model*, Human Services Monograph Series No. 23 (Rockville, Md.: Project SHARE, A National Clearinghouse for Improving the Management of Human Services, July 1981).

Bachman, Theodore E. *Churches and Social Welfare: The Activating Concern.* Volume 1 (New York: National Council of Churches in Christ in the USA, 1955).

Banner, Lois W. "Religious Benevolence as Social Control," *Journal of American History* 60 (June 1973), pp. 23-41.

Baumol, William J. "Enlightened Self-Interest and Corporate Philan-
    thropy," in William J. Baumol, Rensis Likert, Henry C. Wallich,
    and John J. McGowan, eds., A New Rationale for Corporate Social
    Policy, Lexington, Mass.: D. C. Heath (1970).
Baxandall, Rosalyn F. "Who Shall Care for Our Children? The History
    and Development of Day Care in the U.S.," in Jo Freeman, ed.,
    Women: A Feminist Perspective (Palo Alto, Calif.: Mayfield Pub-
    lishing Company, 1975), pp. 88-102.
Becker, Dorothy G. "Exit Lady Bountiful: The Volunteer and the Pro-
    fessional Social Worker," Social Service Review 38 (March 1964),
    pp. 57-72.
_____. "The Visitor to the New York City Poor," Social Service Review
    35 (December 1941), pp. 382-396.
Becker, Gary. "A Theory of Social Interactions," Journal of Political
    Economy 82 (1974), pp. 1063-1083.
Becker, Ted. "Teledemocracy, Bringing Power Back to People," in
    Futurist XV, No. 6 (December 1981), pp. 6-9.
Beckman, Norman. "The Planner as a Bureaucrat," Journal of the Amer-
    can Institute of Planners 30 (1974), pp. 323-327.
Belsky, Jay, and Lawrence Steinberg. "The Effects of Day Care: A Critical
    Review," Child Development 49 (1978), pp. 929-949.
Benveniste, Guy. The Politics of Expertise, 2d ed. (San Francisco: Boyd &
    Fraser Publishing Company, 1977).
Bolan, Richard S. "The Practitioner as Theorist," Journal of the Ameri-
    can Institute of Planners 46, No. 3 (July 1980), pp. 261-274.
Boulding, Kenneth E. "The Ethics of Rational Decision," Management
    Science 12 (February 1966), pp. 161-168.
Boyer, Paul S. Urban Masses and Moral Order in America, 1820-1920
    (Cambridge, Mass.: Harvard University Press, 1978).
Brace, Charles Loring. The Dangerous Classes of New York (New York:
    Wynkoop and Hallenbeck, 1872).
Braybrooke, David, and Charles Lindblom. Strategy for Decision (New
    York: The Free Press, 1963).
Bremner, Robert H. From the Depths: The Discovery of Poverty in Ameri-
    ca (New York: New York University Press, 1956).
_____. "The Prelude: Philanthropic Rivalries in the Civil War," Social
    Casework 49 (February 1968), pp. 77-81.
_____. The Public Good: Welfare in the Civil War Era (New York:
    Knopf, 1980).
Brittain, Jack W., and John Freeman. "Organizational Prolifera-
    tion and Density-Dependent Selection," in John R. Kimberley and
    Robert H. Miles, eds., The Organizational Life Cycle (San Fran-
    cisco: Jossey-Bass, 1980), pp. 291-341.

Buber, Martin. "The Education of Character," in *Between Man and Man* (New York: Macmillan, 1965), pp. 104-117.

Carroll, Jackson, Douglas W. Johnson, and Martin E. Marty. *Religion in America: 1950 to the Present* (San Francisco: Harper & Row, 1979).

Center for Social Research and Development. *Analysis and Synthesis of Needs Assessment Research in the Field of Human Services* (Denver: Denver Research Institute, University of Denver, July 1974).

Chambers, Clarke A. "Jane Addams," in Leonard Unger, ed., *American Writers* (New York: Charles Scribner's Sons, 1979), pp. 1-27.

_____. *Paul V. Kellog and the Survey: Voices for Social Welfare and Social Justice* (Minneapolis: University of Minnesota Press, 1971).

_____. *Seedtime of Reform: American Social Service and Social Action, 1918-1933* (Minneapolis: University of Minnesota Press, 1963), Chapters 5 and 6.

Children's Defense Fund. *A Children's Defense Budget: An Analysis of the President's Budget and Children* (Washington, D.C.: Children's Defense Fund, 1982).

_____. *A Corporate Reader* (Washington, D.C.: Children's Defense Fund, 1982).

Chodorow, Nancy. *The Reproduction of Mothering* (Berkeley: University of California Press, 1978).

Citrin, Jack, and David O. Sears. *Tax Revolt* (Cambridge, Mass.: Harvard University Press, 1982).

Clark, Berton R. "Organizational Adoption and Precarious Values," *American Sociological Review* 21 (1956), pp. 327-336.

Clotefelter, Charles, and Lester Salamon. *The Federal Government and the Nonprofit Sector: The Impact of the 1981 Tax Act on Individual Charitable Giving* (Washington, D.C.: The Urban Institute, 1981).

Cobb, Rober W., and Charles D. Elder. *Participation in American Politics: The Dynamics of Agenda Building* (Boston: Allyn and Bacon, 1972).

Coll, Blanche D. "The Baltimore Society for the Prevention of Pauperism," *American Historical Review* 61 (October 1955), pp. 77-87.

Collins, Alice H., and Diane L. Pancoast. *Natural Helping Networks: A Strategy for Prevention* (Washington, D.C.: National Association of Social Workers, 1976).

Congressional Quarterly, Inc. *Budgeting for America: The Politics and Process of Federal Spending* (Washington, D.C.: 1982).

Cook, Constance Ewing. *Nuclear Power and Legal Advocacy* (Lexington, Mass.: Lexington Books, 1980).

Davis, Allen F. *American Heroine: The Life and Legend of Jane Addams* (New York: Oxford University Press, 1973).

_____. *Spearheads for Reform: The Social Settlements and the Progressive Movement, 1890-1914* (New York: Oxford University Press, 1967).

DeKema, Jan. "Incommensurability and Judgment," *Theory Society* 10 (1981), pp. 521-546.

Dolan, Jay P. *The Immigrant Church: New York's Irish and German Catholics, 1815-1865* (Baltimore: The Johns Hopkins University Press, 1975).

Donzelot, Jacques. *The Policing of Families* (New York: Pantheon Books, 1979).

Dye, Richard. "Contributions of Volunteer Time: Some Evidence on Income Tax Effects," *National Tax Journal* 33 (1980), pp. 89-93.

Eisenstadt, Stuart E., and Paul W. Kahn. "A Rational Federalism," *Public Welfare* 41 (Spring 1983), pp. 16-21.

Epstein, Edward J. *News From Nowhere* (New York: Random House, 1973).

Erikson, Erik H. *Identity, Youth and Crisis* (New York: W. W. Norton, 1968).

Fahey, Liam, William R. King, and Vadake K. Narayanan. "Environmental Scanning and Forecasting in Strategic Planning—The State of the Arts," in *Long Range Planning* 14 (February 1981), pp. 32-39.

Feldman, Martha S., and James March. "Information in Organizations as Signal and Symbol," *Administrative Science Quarterly* 26 (1981), pp. 171-186.

Feldstein, Martin. "The Income Tax and Charitable Contributions," *National Tax Journal* 28 (1974), pp. 81-100.

Forester, John. "Critical Theory and Planning Practice," *Journal of the American Institute of Planners* 46, No. 3 (July 1980), pp. 275-286.

_____. "Understanding Planning Practice: An Empirical, Practical and Ethical Account," *Journal of Planning Education and Research* 6 (1982a), pp. 59-71.

_____. "Critical Reason and Political Power in Project Review Activity: Serving Freedom in Planning and Public Administration, *Policy and Politics* 10 (1982b), pp. 65-84.

_____. "Planning in the Face of Power," *Journal of the American Planning Association* 48, No. 1 (Winter 1982c).

_____. "The Practical Politics of a Rebounded Rationality," *Public Administration Review* 44, No. 1 (January-February, 1984a).

_____. "From Equity and Efficiency to the Practical Analysis of Ambiguity in Planning Practice," to appear as a monograph of the Lincoln Institute of Land Policy and in the *Proceedings* of the Second World Congress on Land Policy. (Lexington, Mass.: Lexington Books, both scheduled to appear in 1984b).

Freidson, Eliot. *Profession of Medicine: A Study of the Sociology of Applied Knowledge* (New York: Dodd, Mead and Company, 1970).

Freund, Michael, and Robert Morris, eds. *Trends and Issues in Jewish Social Welfare in the United States, 1899-1952* (Philadelphia: Jewish Publication Society of America, 1966).

Froland, Charles. "Formal and Informal Care: Discontinuities in a Continuum," *Social Service Review* 54 (December 1980), pp. 572-597.

Funkhouser, G. Ray. "The Issues of the Sixties: An Exploratory Study in the Dynamics of Public Opinion," *Public Opinion Quarterly* 37 (Spring 1973), pp. 62-75.

Gallup, George, Jr. "Volunteerism: America's Best Hope for the Future," *Voluntary Action Leadership* 13, No. 1 (Fall 1980), pp. 24-27.

Gans, Herbert J. *Deciding What's News* (New York: Pantheon Books, 1979).

Gavin, Donald. *The National Conference of Catholic Charities, 1910-1960* (Milwaukee: Catholic Life Publications, 1962).

The General Mills American Family Report 1980-81. "Families at Work" (General Mills, Inc., 9200 Wayzata Boulevard, Minneapolis, MN 55440, 1981).

Gibleman, Margaret. "Are Clients Served Better When Services Are Purchased?" *Public Welfare* 39 (Fall 1981), pp. 27-33.

Gilbert, Neil. *Capitalism and the Welfare State* (New Haven, Conn.: Yale University Press, 1983).

Goldstein, Sidney. *The Synagogue and Social Welfare, 1907-1953* (New York: Hebrew Union College—Jewish Institute of Religion, 1955).

Gouldner, Alvin. "The Sociologist as Partisan: Sociology and the Welfare State," *American Sociologist* 3 (1968), pp. 103-116.

Griffin, Clifford. *Their Brother's Keeper: Moral Stewardship in the United States, 1800-1865* (New Brunswick, N.J.: Rutgers University Press, 1960).

Grønbjerg, Kirsten A. "Private Welfare in the Welfare State: Recent U.S. Patterns," *Social Service Review* 56 (March 1982), pp. 1-26.

Hall, Peter. "The Model of Boston Charity," *Science and Society* 38 (Winter 1974-75), pp. 464-477.

Handler, Joel, and Michael Sosin. *Last Resorts: Emergency Assistance and Special Needs Programs in Public Welfare* (New York: Academic Press, 1983).

Hargreaves, John, and Jan Dauman. *Business Survival and Social Change* (New York: John Wiley and Sons, 1975).

Hayes, Michael T. *Lobbyists and Legislators* (New Brunswick, N.J.: Rutgers University Press, 1981).

Heale, J. M. "Patterns of Benevolence," *Societas* 3 (Autumn 1973), pp. 337-359.

Hill, Russell C. "Private Demand for Child Care: Implications for Public Policy," *Evaluation Quarterly* 2, No. 4 (November 1978), pp. 523-546.

Hochman, Harold, and James Rodgers. "Utility Interdependence and Income Transfers Through Charity," in K. Boulding, M. Plaaff, and A. Plaaff, eds., *Transfers in an Urbanized Economy* (Belmont, Calif.: Wadsworth Press, 1973), pp. 63-77.

Horowitz, Irving L. "Social Planning and Social Science: Historical Continuities and Comparative Discontinuities," in Robert Burchell and George Sternlieb, eds., *Planning Theory in the 1980s* (New Brunswick, N.J.: Rutgers Center for Urban Policy Research, 1978), pp. 41-68.

Howell, Mary C. *Helping Ourselves: Families and the Human Network* (Boston: Beacon Press, 1975).

Huggins, Nathan. *Protestants Against Poverty: Boston's Charities, 1870-1900* (Westport, Conn.: Greenwood Press, 1971).

Human Services Institute for Children and Families, Inc. *Needs Assessment in a Title XX State Social Services Planning System* (n.p., April 1975), pp. 4, 16.

Huntsberger, David. *Elements of Statistical Inference, Second Edition* (Boston: Allyn and Bacon, 1967).

INDEPENDENT SECTOR. "Dollar Value of Volunteer Time," *Voluntary Action Leadership* (Spring 1982), p. 33.

Jacobs, Barry G., Kenneth B. Harney, Charles L. Edson, and Bruce S. Lane. *Guide to Federal Housing Programs* (Washington, D.C.: The Bureau of National Affairs, 1982).

Jernegan, Marcus. *Laboring and Dependent Classes in Colonial America, 1607-1783* (Chicago: University of Chicago Press, 1960).

_____. "The Development of Poor Relief in Colonial Virginia," *Social Service Review* 3 (March 1929), pp. 1-18.

Kagan, Jerome. "The Child in the Family," in Alice Rossi, Jerome Kagan, Tamara Hareven, eds., *The Family* (New York: W. W. Norton, 1978), pp. 35-56.

Kahn, Alfred J. *Social Policy and Social Services* (New York: Random House, 1973).

Kahn, Alfred J., and Sheila B. Kamerman. *Social Services in International Perspective: The Emergence of the Sixth System* (Washington, D.C.: Government Printing Office, 1976).

_____. "The Day-Care Debate: A Wider View," *The Public Interest* 54 (1979), pp. 76-93.

Kaplan, Barry J. "Reformers and Charity," *Social Service Review* 52 (June 1978), pp. 202-214.

Katz, Michael B. *Poverty and Policy in American History* (New York: Academic Press, 1983).

Kelley, Dean M., ed. *Government Intervention in Religious Affairs* (New York: The Pilgrim Press, 1982).

Kimmel, Wayne A. *Needs Assessment: A Critical Perspective* (Washington, D.C.: U.S. Department of Health, Education, and Welfare, December 1977).

Klaassen, L. *Social Amenities in Area Economic Growth* (Paris: O.E.C.D., 1968).

Klebaner, Benjamin. *Public Poor Relief in America, 1790-1860* (New York: Arno Press, 1976; previously unpublished thesis, Columbia University, 1952).

Kramer, Ralph. *Voluntary Agencies in the Welfare State* (Berkeley: University of California Press, 1981).

Kurtz, Ernest. *Not Good—A History of Alcoholics Anonymous* (Center City, Minn.: Hazelden Educational Services, 1979).

Langsam, Miriam. *Children West: A History of the Placing-Out System in the New York Children's Aid Society* (Madison: State Historical Society of Wisconsin, 1964).

Larsen, Donald H. "Health and Healing in the Lutheran Church: Tradition and Practice," in *Health and Healing: Ministry of the Church* (Chicago: Wheat Ridge Foundation, 1980), pp. 43-59.

Leiby, James. *A History of Social Welfare and Social Work in the United States* (New York: Columbia University Press, 1978).

Leissner, Aryeh. "Alternative Perspectives on Statutory Versus Voluntary Provision of Social Services: Community Work and Political Realities," in David Horton Smith, et al., eds., *International Perspectives on Voluntary Action Research* (Washington, D.C.: University Press of America, 1983), pp. 15-18.

Lesch, Christopher. *Haven in a Heartless World* (New York: Basic Books, 1979).

Levine, Daniel. *Jane Addams and the Liberal Tradition* (Madison: State Historical Society of Wisconsin, 1971).

Levine, Sol, and Paul White. "Exchange as Conceptual Framework for Interorganizational Relations," *Administrative Science Quarterly* 5 (September 1961), pp. 583-601.

Lewis, Verl. "Stephen Humphrey Gurteen and the American Origins of Charity Organization," *Social Service Review* 40 (June 1966), pp. 190-201.

Lipset, Seymour Martin, and William Schneider. *The Confidence Gap* (New York: The Free Press, 1983).

Lipsky, Michael. *Protest in City Politics: Rent Strikes, Housing and the Power of the Poor* (Chicago: Rand McNally, 1970).

Lloyd, Gary. *Charities, Settlements, and Social Work, 1890-1915* (New Orleans: Tulane University Press, 1971).

Loeser, Herta. *Women, Work and Volunteering* (Boston: Beacon Press, 1974).

Lovrich, Nicholas P., Jr., and John C. Pierce. "Trust in the Technical Information Provided by Interest Groups: The Views of Legislators, Activists, Experts, and the General Public," *Policy Studies Journal* 11 (June 1983), pp. 626-639.

Lowi, Theodore J. *The End of Liberalism*, 2d ed. (New York: W. W. Norton, 1979).

Lueking, F. Dean. *A Century of Caring: The Welfare Ministry Among Missouri Lutherans, 1868-1968* (St. Louis: LC-MS Board of Social Ministry, 1968).

Lurie, Harry. *A Heritage Affirmed: The Jewish Federation Movement in America* (Philadelphia: Jewish Publication Society of America, 1961).

Lutheran Council in the USA. *The Nature of the Church and its Relationship with Government* (New York: Lutheran Council in the USA, 1979).

McCarthy, Kathleen D. *Noblesse Oblige: Charity and Cultural Philanthropy in Chicago, 1849-1929* (Chicago: University of Chicago Press, 1982).

McCroskey, Jacquelyn. "Work and Families: What is the Employer's Responsibility?" *Personnel Journal* 61 (January 1982), pp. 30-38.

Manser, Gordon, and Rosemary Higgins Cass. *Voluntarism and the Crossroads* (New York: Family Service Association of America, 1976).

March, James. "Footnotes to Organizational Change," *Administrative Science Quarterly* 26 (1981), pp. 563-577.

March, James, and Herbert Simon. *Organizations* (New York: John Wiley and Sons, 1958).

Marcuse, Peter. "Professional Ethics and Beyond: Values in Planning," *Journal of the American Institute of Planners* 42 (July 1976), pp. 264-274.

Maslow, Abraham H. *Motivation and Personality*, 2d ed. (New York: Harper & Row, 1970).

Mason, Richard O., and Ian I. Mitroff. *Challenging Strategic Planning Assumptions* (New York: John Wiley and Sons, 1981).

Melder, Keith. "Ladies Bountiful: Organized Women's Benevolence in Early Nineteenth Century America," *New York History* 48 (July 1967), pp. 231-254.

Mile High United Way. "3 Choices in Meeting Community Needs" (Denver: United Way, 1982).

Miller, Charles. *An Introduction to the Jewish Federation* (New York: Council of Jewish Federations, 1976).

Minnesota State Planning Agency. *Needs Assessment: A Guide for Human Services Agencies* (St. Paul: January 1977), as quoted in Kimmel: 1977, p. 9.

Mohl, Raymond. *Poverty in New York, 1783-1825* (New York: Oxford University Press, 1971).

Moore, Thomas. "Beverly Enterprises: Way Out Front in Nursing Homes," *Fortune*, June 13, 1983, pp. 142-151.

Morgan, Robin, ed. *Sisterhood is Powerful* (New York: Vintage Books, 1970).

Moroney, Robert. "Needs Assessment for Human Services," in Wayne F. Anderson, Bernard J. Frieden, and Michael J. Murphy, eds., *Managing Human Services* (Washington, D.C.: International City Management Association, 1977), pp. 128-154.

Naibitt, John. *Megatrends* (New York: Warner Books, 1982).

Nanus, B. "QUEST—Quick Environmental Scanning Technique," in *Long Range Planning* 15, No. 2 (April 1982), pp. 39-45.

National Association of Area Agencies on Aging. *Community Based Long Term Care* (Washington, D.C.: National Association of Area Agencies on Aging, 1983).

National Benevolent Association of the Christian Church (Disciples of Christ). *1981 Annual Report* (St. Louis: National Benevolent Association, 1982).

National Conference of Catholic Charities. *NCCC Annual Survey, 1981* (Washington, D.C.: National Conference of Catholic Charities, 1982).

National Forum on Volunteerism. "The Shape of Things to Come," *Voluntary Action Leadership* 13, No. 1 (Fall 1980), pp. 28-32.

National Governors Association. *America's Children: Powerless and in Need of Powerful Friends, 1983 Status Report* (Prepared by Michael R. Petit, Commissioner, and Donna Overcash, Special Assistant to the Commissioner, Maine Department of Human Services, Augusta, Maine, 1983).

Netting, Florence W. "The Church Related Social Service Agency and the Meaning of Its Religious Connection" (Ph.D. diss., University of Chicago, 1982).

New York Times. "Private Sector Aid Sought by Reagan," September 27, 1981, column 1, p. 35.

O'Conner, Karen. *Women's Organizations Use of the Courts* (Lexington, Mass.: Lexington Books, 1980).

O'Grady, John. *Catholic Charities in the United States* (Washington, D.C.: National Conference of Catholic Charities, 1930).

Olds, Victoria. "The Freedmen's Bureau," *Social Casework* 44 (May 1963), pp. 247-253.

Olson, Mancur, Jr. *The Logic of Collective Action* (New York: Schooken, 1970).

Owen, David. *English Philanthropy* (Cambridge, Mass.: Harvard University Press, 1964).

Palmer, John L., and Isabel V. Sawhill, eds. *The Reagan Experiment* (Washington, D.C.: The Urban Institute Press, 1982).

Parkhurst, Eleanor. "Poor Relief in a Massachusetts Village in the Eighteenth Century," *Social Service Review* 11 (September 1937), pp. 446-464.

Patterson, Kenneth J. "Emerging Conflicts in Need Assessment: Armchair Electronics Versus Back-to-Basics" (paper presented at the United Way Biennial Staff Conference, Atlanta, Ga., March 1982).

Patterson, James P. *America's Struggle Against Poverty, 1900-1980* (Cambridge, Mass.: Harvard University Press, 1981).

Peltason, Jack. *Federal Courts in the Political Process* (New York: Random House, 1955).

Pennings, Johannas M. "Environmental Influences on the Creation Process," in John R. Kimberly and Robert H. Miles, eds., *The Organizational Life Cycle* (San Francisco: Jossey-Bass, 1980), pp. 134-160.

Pettie, Lisa R. "Politics, Planning, and Categories Bridging the Gap," in Robert Burchell and George Sternlieb, eds., *Planning Theory in the 1980s* (New Brunswick, N.J.: Rutgers Center for Urban Policy Research, 1978), pp. 83-93.

Piven, Frances Fox, and Richard A. Cloward. *The New Class War* (New York: Pantheon Books, 1981).

Ponsioen, J. A. *Social Welfare Policy: Contributions to Theory*, Publications of the Institute of Social Studies, Series Major, Vol. 3 (The Hague: Mouton and Co., 1962).

Rachels, James. "Can Ethics Provide Answers?," in Arthur L. Caplan and Daniel Callahan, eds., *Ethics in Hard Times*, The Hastings Center Series in Ethics (New York: Plenum Press, 1981), pp. 1-30.

Rakove, Milton. *Don't Make No Waves, Don't Back No Losers* (Bloomington, Ind.: Indiana University Press, 1975).

Reece, W. "Charitable Contributions: New Evidence on Household Behavior," *American Economic Review* 69 (1979), pp. 142-151.

Rein, Martin. *Social Policy: Issues of Choice and Change* (New York: Random House, 1970).

_____. *Social Science and Public Policy* (New York: Penguin Books, 1976).

Reiner, Thomas, and Julian Wolpert. "The Nonprofit Sector in the Metropolitan Economy," *Economic Geography* 57 (1981), pp. 23-33.

Richardson, Harry. *Regional Growth Theory.* (London: Macmillan Press, 1973).

Riker, William H. *The Theory of Political Coalitions* (New Haven, Conn.: Yale University Press, 1963).

Rohr, John A. *Ethics for Bureaucrats: An Essay on Law and Values* (New York: Marcel Dekker, 1978).

Romanofsky, Peter, and Clarke A. Chambers (editor-in-chief and advisory editor). *Social Service Organizations.* 2 vols. (Westport, Conn.: Greenwood Press, 1978).

Ross, Edyth L., comp. and ed. *Black Heritage in Social Welfare, 1860-1930* (Metuchen, N.J.: Scarecrow Press, 1978).

Rossi, Alice. "A Biosocial Perspective on Parenting," *Daedulus* 106, No. 2 (Spring 1977), pp. 1-32.

Rothman, David. *The Charitable Impulse in Eighteenth Century America* (New York: Arno Press, 1971).

_____. *The Discovery of the Asylum: Social Order and Disorder in the New Republic* (Boston: Little, Brown and Company, 1971).

Ruddick, Sara. "Maternal Thinking," *Feminist Studies* 6, No. 3 (Summer 1980), pp. 343-367.

Ryan, William. *Blaming the Victim* (New York: Vintage Press, 1976).

Saccomandi, Pat. *The Volunteer Skillsbank* (Boulder, Colo.: VOLUNTEER, 1981).

Salamon, Lester, and Alan Abramson. *The Federal Budget and the Nonprofit Sector* (Washington, D.C.: The Urban Institute, 1982),

Schattschneider, E. E. *The Semisovereign People* (Hinsdale, Ill.: The Dryden Press, 1960).

Schneider, David M. "The Patchwork of Relief in Provincial New York, 1664-1775," *Social Service Review* 12 (September 1938), pp. 464-494.

Schwartz, R. "Personal Philanthropic Contributions," *Journal of Political Economy* 78 (1970), pp. 1264-1291.

de Schweinitz, Karl. *England's Road to Social Security, 1349-1942* (Philadelphia: University of Pennsylvania Press, 1943).

Scott, Anne Firor. *The Southern Lady: From Pedestal to Politics, 1830-1930* (Chicago: University of Chicago Press, 1970), pp. 80-102.

Scott, Richard. "The Factory as a Social Service Organization," *Social Problems* 15 (1967), pp. 110-175.

Selig, Martha. "The Challenge of Public Funds to Voluntary Agencies,"

Journal of Jewish Communal Service 39 (Summer 1963), pp. 368-377.

Selznick, Phillip. TVA and the Grassroots (Berkeley: University of California Press, 1949).

Siegel, Sheldon. "Friendly Visiting and Social Casework," Social Casework 37 (January 1956), pp. 20-25.

Sills, D. "Voluntary Associations: Sociological Aspects," in D. Sills, ed., International Encyclopedia of the Social Sciences, 16 (New York: Macmillan Press, 1968), pp. 362-376.

Smith, Constance, and Anne Freedman. Voluntary Associations (Cambridge, Mass.: Harvard University Press, 1972).

Smith, David Horton. "A Parsimonious Definition of 'Group': Toward Conceptual Clarity and Scientific Utility," Sociological Inquiry 37 (1967), pp. 141-168.

_____. "Altruism, Volunteers, and Volunteerism," in John D. Harman, ed. Volunteerism in the Eighties (Washington, D.C.: University Press of America, 1982), pp. 23-44.

_____. "Interorganizational Networking," Transnational Associations 30 (1978), pp. 429-434, 440.

_____. "Organizational Boundaries and Organizational Affiliates," Sociology and Social Research 56 (1972), pp. 494-512.

_____. Recruitment to Voluntary Action: A Review of Research and Accumulated Practical Experience and Their Implications. (Berkhamsted, England: The Volunteer Centre, 1979).

_____, ed. Voluntary Action Research: 1973. (Lexington, Mass.: D. C. Heath, Lexington Books, 1973).

_____, ed. Voluntary Action Research: 1974 (Lexington, Mass.: D. C. Heath, Lexington Books, 1974).

_____. "Voluntary Action and Voluntary Groups," in Alex Inkeles, et al., eds., Annual Review of Sociology, Volume 1 (Palo Alto, Calif.: Annual Reviews, Inc., 1975), pp. 247-270.

Smith, David Horton, and Burt R. Baldwin. "Voluntary Associations and Volunteering in the United States," in David Horton Smith, ed. Voluntary Action Research: 1974 (Lexington, Mass.: D. C. Heath, Lexington Books, 1974), pp. 277-305.

Smith, David Horton, Burt R. Baldwin, and William Chittick. "U.S. National Voluntary Organizations, Transnational Orientations, and Development," International Journal of Comparative Sociology 21 (1980), pp. 10-25.

Smith, David Horton, Burt R. Baldwin, and Eugene D. White. "The Nonprofit Sector," in Tracy Connors, ed. The Nonprofit Organization Handbook (New York: McGraw-Hill, 1980), pp. 1-15.

Smith, David Horton, and Frederick Elkin. *Volunteers, Voluntary Associations, and Development* (Leiden, Holland: E. J. Brill, 1981).

Smith, David Horton, Jacqueline Macauley, et al. *Participation in Social and Political Activities* (San Francisco: Jossey-Bass, 1980).

Smith, David Horton, Richard D. Reddy, and Burt R. Baldwin. *Voluntary Action Research: 1972* (Lexington, Mass.: D. C. Heath, Lexington Books, 1972).

Smith, David Horton, Mary Seguin, and Marjorie Collins. "Dimensions and Categories of Voluntary Organizatons/NGOs," *Journal of Voluntary Action Research* 2 (1973), pp. 116-120.

Smith, David Horton, Jon Van Til, Dan Bernfeld, Victor Pestoff, and David Zeldin, eds. *International Perspectives on Voluntary Action Research.* (Washington, D.C.: University Press of America, 1983).

Smith, Timothy L. *Revivalism and Social Reform in Mid-Nineteenth Century America* (New York: Abingdon Press, 1957).

Smith-Rosenberg, Carroll. *Religion and the Rise of the American City: The New York City Mission Movement, 1812-1870* (Ithaca, N.Y.: Cornell University Press, 1971).

Solomon, Barbara. *Pioneers in Service: The History of the Associated Jewish Philanthropies in Boston* (Boston: Associated Jewish Philanthropies, 1956).

Starling, Grover. *The Changing Environment of Business* (Boston, Mass.: Kent Publishing, 1980).

Stedman-Jones, Gareth. *Outcast London* (London: Oxford University Press, 1971).

Stein, Herman. "Jewish Social Work in the United States, 1654-1954," *American Jewish Yearbook* 57 (1955), pp. 3-93.

Steiner, George A. *Strategic Planning* (New York: The Free Press, 1979).

Steinfels, Margaret O'Brien. *Who's Minding the Children?* (New York: Simon and Schuster, 1973).

Stevens, Joseph H., Jr. "The National Day Care Home Study: Family Day Care in the United States," *Young Children* 37 (May 1982), pp. 59-62.

―――. "The New York City Infant Day Care Study," *Young Children* 37 (January 1982), pp. 47-53.

Stinchcombe, Arthur L. "Social Structure and Organization," in James March, ed., *Handbook of Organizations* (Chicago: Rand McNally, 1965), pp. 142-193.

Suransky, Valerie Polakow. *The Erosion of Childhood* (Chicago: The University of Chicago Press, 1982).

Szalai, Alexander, et al. *The Use of Time* (The Hague: Mouton, 1972).

Teeters, Negley K. "The Early Days of the Magdalen Society of Philadelphia," *Social Science Review* 30 (June 1956), pp. 158-167.

Terrell, Paul. "Private Alternatives to Public Human Services Administration," *Social Service Review* 53 (March 1979), pp. 56-74.

Thompson, James D. *Organizations in Action* (New York: McGraw-Hill, 1967).

Thorne, Barrie. "Feminist Rethinking of the Family: An Overview," in Thorne and Yalom, eds., *Rethinking the Family* (New York: Longman, 1982), pp. 1-24.

Tiebout, Charles. "A Pure Theory of Local Public Expenditures," *Journal of Political Economy* 64 (1956), pp. 416-424.

Tierney, Brian. *Medieval Poor Law* (Berkeley: University of California Press, 1959).

Tomeh, Aida. "Formal Voluntary Organizations: Participation, Correlates and Interrelationships," *Sociological Inquiry* 43 (1973), pp. 89-122.

Tourangeau, Kevin W. *Strategy Management* (New York: McGraw-Hill, 1981).

Trattner, Walter. *From Poor Law to Welfare State* (New York: The Free Press, 1979).

Tregoe, Benjamin, and John W. Zimmerman. *Top Management Strategy* (New York: Simon and Schuster, 1980).

Treudly, Mary B. "The 'Benevolent Fair,' " *Social Science Review* 14 (September 1940), pp. 509-522.

Trolander, Judith. *Settlement Houses and the Great Depression* (Detroit: Wayne State University Press, 1975).

United Church Board for Homeland Ministries. *Were You There? The Biennial Report, 1981-83* (New York: United Church Board, 1983).

United States Catholic Conference. *Political Responsibility: Choices for the 1980s* (Washington, D.C.: USCC Publication Office, 1980).

U.S. Department of Commerce, Bureau of Census. *Trends in Child Care Arrangements of Working Mothers* (Washington, D.C.: Government Printing Office, 1983).

U.S. Department of Labor, Women's Bureau. *Employers and Child Care: Establishing Services Through the Workplace*, Women's Bureau Pamphlet 23 (Washington, D.C., August 1982).

U.S. Department of Treasury. *Research Papers*, Commission on Private Philanthropy and Public Needs, Chairman, J. H. Filer (Washington, D.C., 1977).

United Way of America. *A "PDBS" Approach to Budgeting Human Service Programs for United Ways* (Alexandria, Va.: United Way of America, December 1972).

_____. *The Painful Necessity of Choice, An Analysis of Priorities, Plans and Policies in the United Way Movement* (Alexandria, Va.: United Way of America, May 1974).

_____. *Environmental Scanning* (Alexandria, Va.: United Way of America, December 1980).

_____. *Needs Assessment, The State of the Art, A Guide for Planners, Managers, and Funders of Health and Human Care Services* (Alexandria, Va.: The United Way of America, November 1982).

Varencus, Kristina. *Needs Assessment: An Exploratory Critique*, HEW Publication No. 05-77-007 (Washington, D.C.: Office of Assistant Secretary for Planning and Evaluation, U.S. Department of Health, Education and Welfare, May 1977).

Voluntary Action Leadership. "Women in Volunteering: Ten Years Later," *Voluntary Action Leadership* 14, No. 2 (Summer 1981), p. 21.

Warheit, George J., Roger Bell, and John J. Schwab. *Planning for Change: Needs Assessment Approaches* (Rockville, Md.: U.S. Department of Health, Education and Welfare; Alcohol, Drug Abuse, and Mental Health Administration, n.d.).

Watson, Frank. *The Charity Organization Movement in the United States* (New York: The Macmillan Company, 1922).

Webber, Melvin M. "A Different Paradigm for Planning," in Robert Burchell and George Sternlieb, eds., *Planning Theory in the 1980s* (New Brunswick, N.J.: Rutgers Center for Urban Policy Research, 1978), pp. 151-162.

Webster's New Universal Dictionary of the English Language, Unabridged (New York: Webster's International Press, 1976).

Weisbrod, Burton. *The Voluntary Nonprofit Sector: An Economic Analysis* (Lexington, Mass.: Lexington Books, 1977).

Weisel, Elie. *The Gates of the Forest*, translated by Frances Frenaye (New York: Holt, Rinehart and Winston, Inc., 1966; originally published as *Les Portes de la Forêt*, Paris: Editions du Seuil, 1964).

Welniak, Edward J., and Carol Fendler. *Money Income and Poverty Status of Families and Persons in the United States: 1980*, Series P-60, No. 140 (Washington, D.C.: Bureau of the Census, U.S. Department of Commerce; issued July 1983).

Wendel, Kenneth R., Arthur J. Katz, and Ann Weick, eds. *Social Services by Government Contracts: A Policy Analysis* (New York: Praeger Publishers, 1979).

Wenocur, Stanley. "The Structure and Politics of Local United Way Organizations," *The Grantsmanship Center News* (September-December 1978), pp. 24-43.

Whitacker, Ben. *The Foundations: An Anatomy of Philanthropy and Society* (London: Eyre Methuen Press, 1974).

Wildavsky, Aaron. *Speaking Truth to Power* (Boston: Little, Brown and Co., 1979).

_____. *The Politics of the Budgetary Process* (New York: Little, Brown and Co., 1964).

Wilson, Marlene. "Reversing the Resistance of Staff to Volunteers," *Voluntary Action Leadership* 14, No. 1 (Spring 1981), p. 21.

Wolch, Jennifer. "Philanthropy and Economic Development of the Metropolitan Region," Working Paper of the Planning Institute, University of Southern California (Los Angeles, 1982).

Wolch, Jennifer, and Robert Geiger. "The Distribution of Urban Voluntary Resources: An Exploratory Analysis," *Environment and Planning A* 15 (August 1983), pp. 1067-1082.

Wolpert, Julian. "Social Income and the Voluntary Sector," *Papers, Regional Science Association* 39 (1977), pp. 217-229.

Wolpert, Julian, and Thomas Reiner. *The Metropolitan Philadelphia Philanthropy Study* (Philadelphia: School of Public and Urban Policy, University of Pennsylvania, 1980).

_____. "The Nonprofit Sector in the Region's Economy," *Regional Plan News* 111 (1982), pp. 1-22.

Woodroofe, Kathleen. *From Charity to Social Work in England and the United States* (Toronto: University of Toronto Press, 1962).

Woolsey, Suzanne. "Pied Piper Politics and the Child-Care Debate," *Daedalus* 106, No. 2 (Spring 1977), pp. 127-142.

Wyllie, Irvin G. "The Search for an American Law of Charity, 1776-1844," *Mississippi Valley Historical Review* 46 (September 1959), pp. 203-221.

Young, Dennis R., and Stephen J. Finch. *Foster Care and Non-Profit Agencies* (Lexington, Mass.: Lexington Books, 1977).

Zaltman, Gerald, and Robert Duncan. *Strategies for Planned Change* (New York: John Wiley and Sons, 1977).

Zangwill, Bruce. *A Compendium of Laws and Regulations Requiring Needs Assessment*, HEW Publication No. 05-77-006 (Washington, D.C.: U.S. Department of Health, Education and Welfare, May 1977)

Zentner, R. D. "Scenarios, Past, Present and Future," in *Long Range Planning* 15, No. 3 (June 1982), pp. 12-20.

Index

Accountability in human services delivery, 160-61

Accounting, as a planning paradigm, 156

ACTION agency, 227, 228

Active Corps of Executives, 237

Addams, Jane, 16

Advocacy, 57, 60-61, 72-73, 186; constraints on, 66-67. *See also* Lobbying; Reformism

Aid for Dependent Children, 22, 41, 89, 90

Alcoholics Anonymous, 24

American Association of Social Workers, 27

American Civil Liberties Union, 18, 72

Association for Organizing Social Work, 25

Association of Voluntary Action Scholars, 250

Autonomy, of religious groups, 70-72

Baltimore, Maryland, 6; role of city government and voluntary sector, 131-38

Base and contingency plans, and strategic planning, 190, 203-5

Basic needs problems, 109

Benevolent societies, 19th century, 5-11, 48

Benveniste, Guy, 144, 145

Beverly Enterprises, 65

Big Brothers, Big Sisters, 23

Blacks, 24

Boston, 5, 6

Boy Scouts, 23

Brace, Charles Loring, 9

Buber, Martin, 151

Bureau of Jewish Social Research, 26

Business: and human services, 64-66; and metropolitan development, 134-37; and strategic planning, 193

Campfire Girls, 23

Canvassing, and volunteer recruitment, 235

Carter, James Earl, 63, 95
Catholic Charities Review, 21
Catholic Health Corporation, 70
Catholic Youth Organization, 20
Charity, 3-20, 48-50. *See also* Welfare programs
Charity Organization Societies, 14, 50, 52
Child care: American attitudes toward, 83-84; debate over, 75; developmental needs of children and, 79-87; employers' policies toward, 78, 88; feminist theory regarding, 76-79; parental preference for, 77, 87-88; public policy toward, 88-92, utilization patterns of, 87, 88
Child Care Tax Credit, 89, 90
Child Welfare League of America, 25
Children, services to: in the 19th century, 9, 11, 19; in the 20th century, 21-22; and voluntary sector child care, 75-92. *See also* Child care
Children's Defense Fund, 90
Christian stewardship, concept of, 4, 6-7
Church World Service, 57
Civil War, voluntary welfare during, 11-13, 49
Clients of human services, xxvi; participation in human service agencies, 209-24
Coalitions, political, and lobbying, 99-100
Combined Federal Campaign, 66
Community Chest, 26, 52
Community education, and needs assessment, 186
Compromise, and planning, 154
Consumer movement, and needs assessment, 161
Control Data Corporation, 65-66

Corporations. *See* Business
Council of Jewish Federations and Welfare Funds, 51
Courts, and voluntary sector goals, 101-2
Criminal justice services, 115, 123
Cultural/social factors and volunteer motivation, 238-42

The Dangerous Classes of New York, 9
Data collection: and needs assessment process, 179-80, 186; and power, 148; and strategic planning, 192
Delivery systems: design and management of, 69-70; macro- and micro-, 56-57; and needs assessment, 185
Demographic changes, and strategic planning, 193
Direction setting, and strategic planning, 190, 194-203
The Discovery of the Asylum, 6
Domain of voluntary sector vs. public sector, 105-29; population covered, 117, 118 (table), 119; problems covered, 110 (table), 113-16, 125; services rendered, 111 (table), 116-17, 125; theory and hypothesis, 106-8; voluntary domain and public revenue, 120-21, 122 (table), 123-25

Economy, national: and the Great Depression, 20, 51; in the 19th century, 13-14; in the 1980s, 63-64, 193, 231-33
Efficiency of human services, xxvi, xxviii, 141-42, 155, 160-61
Eisenstadt, Stuart, 63
Employee assistance programs, 65-66

Employment, 15, 115, 123

Ethics, and planning for the voluntary sector, 141-58

Evaluation: of needs assessment, 181-82; of strategic plans, 192, 206-7

External environment, and strategic planning, 190, 192

Family income in 1980s, 63-64

Family life, and child care, 77, 78, 90-91

Family Service Association, 25

Family Welfare Association of America, 25

Feminism: and child care, 76-79; and 19th-century benevolent societies, 11; and resistance to volunteerism, 230

Food Stamps, 41

Ford Foundation, 26

Formal volunteers, xii, 233

Foundation for Child Development, 26

4-H, 23

Friedan, Betty, 230

Fund raising, 26, 30-33, 58; and needs assessment, 184-85. *See also* Revenue

The Gates of the Forest, 158

Girl Scouts, 23

Goals, and ethics of planning, 143-45, 147, 154

Goodwill Industries, 22, 23, 50

Government: distrust of, xxvi, xxvii, 15, 95; domain of, vs. voluntary sector, 105-29; effect of federal cutbacks on voluntary sector, xxix, 29, 41-43, 64, 129; and federal funding to voluntary sector, 22, 31, 54, 55, 56-58, 93-94, 120-5, 159-60; fragmentation of, 94-97; individual costs vs. collective benefits of, 95-96, 102-3; massive entry into human services, 51-53; maxims on how to lobby, 96-104; "new federalism", 62-63; relationships to volunteering, 225-28. *See also* Political system, revenue generating ability of, xxv

Government, local, 54; city government of Baltimore and voluntary sector, 131-38

Government, state, 62-63

Great Society programs, xxviii

Grønbjerg, Kirsten A., 106-8

Group identities in urban areas, 34

Head Start, 20, 89

Hebrew Sheltering and Immigrant Aid society, 21

Henry Street Settlement, 16

Hillhaven Corporation, 65

Hoover, Herbert, 3

Horizontal integration of volunteer work settings, xiv, xv

Hospitals, proprietary, 65

Hull House, 16

Human services, xii-xiii; emerging issues in, 67-73; provision of, in urban areas, 33-40; in the 1980s, 62-67; review process (case study), 209-24. *See also* Government; Voluntary sector

The Immigrant Church: New York's Irish and German Catholics, 1815-1865, 8

Immigrants to the United States, 6, 13-14, 23-24, 49

Implementation of strategic plans, 192, 205

INDEPENDENT SECTOR, 250

Influences on voluntary sector, xxv

Information and referral, and needs assessment, 185-86

Information control, and power, 149

Interest groups, and ethics, 153

Internal environment, and strategic planning, 190, 194

Inventory of resources, and needs identification, 176-77

Investor-owned human service groups, 64-66, 69

Issues, strategic, 196-203; implications wheel, 199 (fig.); life cycle of, 198 (fig.); priority matrix, 202-3 (fig.); probability/impact/maturity test, 201 (fig.)

Jewish community and human services, 21, 51

Jewish Family Service, 21, 51

Kagan, Jerome, 80, 81

Kahn, Paul, 63

Knowledge, as power, 148

Language: and actions of planners, 157-58; control of, and power, 149-50

Law vs. regulations, and lobbying, 100-101

Legislation, and needs assessment, 185. *See also* Lobbying government

Legislators: as champions for voluntary sector causes, 97-99; relationship to staff, clients, in review process, 209-24

Life Extension Institute, 66

Lobbying government, 96-104

Lutheran Council in the United States of America, 57

Luthern Immigration and Refugee Services, 57

Lutheran Institute of Human Ecology, 70

Lutheran Social Services, 70

Mailed surveys, and needs identification, 169

Management: and ethical planning, 141-42; by objectives, 205; systems of, and strategic planning, 189-90

Management Information System, and needs identification, 175

March of Dimes, 195-96

Marcuse, Herbert, 143, 151

Maryland Food Bank, 136

Mass society, and voluntary agencies, 106-8

Media: and exposure for voluntary sector, 96-97; and volunteer recruitment, 234-35

Medicare and Medicaid, 41, 65

Metropolitan development, and volunteerism, 36-39, 131-38

Mission statement for voluntary organizations, 194-96

Moral debate in the political arena, 153-56

Mother-child bond, 81-82

Mutual aid societies, 23-24, 49

Nader, Ralph, 161

National Assembly of National Voluntary Health and Social Welfare Organizations, 26

National Association for the Advancement of Colored People, 18, 72, 101

National Association of Social Work, 27

National Benevolent Association of the Christian Church, 53

National Catholic Welfare Conference, 21

National Childcare Consumer Study, 1975, 87

National Conference of Catholic Charities, 20, 51, 57; income sources reported, 55 (table)

National Conference of Charities and Correction, 25
National Conference of Social Work, 25
National Conference on Citizen Involvement, 1980, xiii
National Conference on Social Welfare, 25
National Council of Christian Churches, 57
National Day Care Home Study, 80
National Federation of Settlements, 50
National Forum on Volunteerism (1980), 229, 231
National Foundation, 196
National Foundation for Infantile Paralysis, 195-96
National Foundation for Volunteering, 227-28
National Housing Act of 1934, 51
National Jewish Welfare Board, 21, 51
National Medical Enterprises, 65
National Organization of Women: on child care, 76; on volunteerism, 230
National Social Work Council, 26
Need, xxvii; definition of, 163-65
Needs assessment: definition of, 165-66; federal requirements for, 159-60; five-phase process of, 177-82; level and scope of, 167; limitation of, 162-63; research methods for, 167-82; supported by consumer movement, 161; uses of, 182-87; within the planning context, 161-62
Needs Assessment Week, 172-74
Needs identification, and planning, 159-88; research methods for, 167-82
New Deal, xxvii

New York Children's Aid Society, 9
New York City, 5, 6
New York City Infant Day-Care Study, 80, 81
Nominal group technique to formulate strategies, 204
Nursing homes, 65

Organizational variables, and volunteer motivation, 244-43

Particularism of voluntary sector, xxiv, 107, 117-19, 124
Pepper, Claude, 97
Personal interviews, and needs identification, 168-69
Philadelphia, 5, 6
Philanthropy, 5, 106-8
Planning, xxiii; definition of, 161-62; differentiated from political activity, 145-47; as an ethical activity, 143-45; language and actions of, 156-58; professionalism and, 150-52; using political skills for, 147-50
Planning in the voluntary sector, xxiii-xxiv, 105; ethics of, 141-58; needs identification and, 159-88; strategic, 189-207; structure of, (case study), 209-24; for volunteer recruitment and staffing, 225-51
Planning-Programming-Budgeting Systems, 161
Political system: constraints on advocacy within, 66-67; current climate in, and volunteering, 225-28; differentiated from planning, 145-47; maxims for lobbying, 96-104; planning, using skills from, 147-50; problems of, 94-96. *See also* Government
The Politics of Expertise, 144

Poor Laws, British, 4

Poverty in the 1980s, 63-64

Power, and planning, 146, 147-50

Priorities ranking, and needs assessment, 182-834

Private sector, 26, 52, 54. *See also* United Way

Professionals in human services delivery, xxvii, 19, 56, 107, 117, 123; role of, and ethics of planning, 150-52; relationship to volunteer leaders, and the review process, 209-24; resistance to volunteers, 229, 242

Program planning and development: and needs assessment, 183-84; and revenue, 56-59

Project reviews (case study), 209-24

Proprietary human service groups, 64-66, 69

Protestant churches and human services, 21-23, 48, 52

Psychological variables, and volunteer motivation, 244-46

Public assistance, 9, 50. *See also* Welfare programs

Public institutions, 6, 48

Public meetings, and needs identification, 171

Public sector, *See* Government

Quality-of-life problems, 107, 109, 114, 115, 121

QUBE interactive television, 172

Race, and particularistic human services, 124

Rates-under-treatment, and needs identification, 175

Reagan, Ronald, 3, 95

Reagan administration economic policies, xxvi, xxvii-xxviii, 41-43, 62, 90, 231-33

Recruitment of volunteers, xiv; definition of, 233-34; modes of, 234-37; key factors in, 237-48

Red Cross, 13

Reformism, 11, 60-61, 72. *See also* Advocacy

Regulations vs. law, and lobbying, 100-101

Religious institutions, and human services, 47-73, 124; historically, in the United States, 4-5, 6-7, 20-23, 48-50; impact of partnership with private and government sectors on, 53-62; in the 1980s, 62-67; new issues for, 67-73. *See also* Jewish community; Protestant churches; Roman Catholic Church

Research: methods for needs identification, 167-77; and needs assessment, 179, 186-87; required for lobbying, 98-99; on volunteerism, 250-51

Resource allocation, and needs assessment, 183

Revenue: allocation, and review process (case study), 209-24; allocation of, in the future, 69; contributed by voluntary sector to cities, 36-37; effect of government cutbacks on voluntary sector, xxix, 29, 41-43, 64, 129; flow of voluntary sector's, 31 (fig.); from government to voluntary sector, 22, 31, 54, 55, 56-58, 93, 120-25, 159-60; lobbying for, 102; multibased, in voluntary sector, 54, 55 (table); program development and, 58-

59; public vs. voluntary sector's ability to generate, xxv; *See also* Fund raising

Rockefeller Foundation, 26

Roman Catholic Church, 8, 20-21, 49, 51

Roosevelt, Franklin D., 195

Rossi, Alice, 77-78

Russell Sage Foundation, 26

Salvation Army, 22, 23, 50

Schattschneider, E. E., 95, 222-23

Second Great Awakening, Protestant, 7, 48

The Semisovereign People, 95

Senior Corps of Retired Executives, 237

Service statistics, and needs identification, 175-76

Settlement house movement, 16-20, 50, 72

Sheltering Arms homes, 21-22

Skillsbank of volunteers, 237

Social action for justice, 60-61, 72-73

Social background and volunteer motivation, 244

Social control services, 115

Social Darwinism, 15

Social democracy, and settlement houses, 17-20

Social interaction and structure, and urban volunteerism, 34-35

Social ministry, inclusiveness of in the future, 68-69

Social order, concern for, 6, 14

Social Security, xxvii, 41, 51. *See also* Title XX

Society of St. Vincent de Paul, 8, 53

Sociopolitical stability, and urban volunteerism, 35-36

South, the American, welfare in, 9, 12

South End House, 16

The Southern Lady, 12

Staffing, human services: and voluntary sector, xxvii; and lobbying, 100; relationship of, to volunteer leaders, 209, 211-12; shrinkage of, 231-33. *See also* Professionalism

Stand-alone volunteer organizations, xvi

Strategic planning in the voluntary sector: management systems and environmental conditions, 189-90; process of, 190-207

Structure of the voluntary sector, xxii-xxiii; and children's services, 75-92; domain of, 105-29; historical, 3-28; planning structure, (case study), 209-24; political nature of, 93-104; and religious organizations, 47-73; and role of city government, 131-38; in urban areas, 29-45; and volunteer utilization, 230

Suransky, Valerie, on child care, 84-86

Surveys, needs identification: donors, 174-75; general population and sub-population, 168-70; of key informants, 170; of service providers, 170-71

Synectics, and strategy formulation, 204

Technology, and strategic planning, 193

Teledemocracy, and needs identification, 171-72

Telephone surveys, and needs identification, 169

Title XX, Social Security Act, 41,
89, 90, 160

Unemployment services, 115, 123
Unionized labor, 17; resistance to
volunteers of, 229-30
U.S. Catholic Conference, 57
U.S. Office of Budget and Manage-
ment, 66
U.S. Office of Personnel Manage-
ment, 66
United States Sanitary
Commission, 12
United Way, xxiii, 3, 26, 52, 64, 166,
196
Universalism, trend toward in
human services, 106, 107, 117-19
Urban centers: growth of, and
voluntarism, 5-7, 13, 48
Urban League, 18, 72
Urban voluntary sector: contribu-
40; definition and structure of,
30-33; effect of public policy
shifts on, 41-43; and
redistribution of resources, 39-40;
social costs of, 44-45
Utopias, and planning, 147

Values, and ethics of planning, 143-
45, 152, 192
Vertical integration of volunteer
work settings, xiv-xv
Voluntary sector, xxi-xxx; coordination of, 13-16, 25-28; developmental role of, 36-39; differences
in, xxiv-xxv; myths about, xxv-
xxviii; role of funding on structure and delivery systems of, 56-
58. See also Domain of the voluntary sector; Planning in the voluntary sector; Revenue; Structure
of the voluntary sector

VOLUNTEER: The National
Center for Citizen Involvement,
150, 237
Volunteer(s): definition of, xi-xii;
fairs, 235-36; government
relationships to, 255-28;
motivations of, 238-48; recruitment of, xiv, 233-48; registers of,
236-37; relationship to professional staff, and review process,
209-24; resistance to, 229-30, 242
retention of, 248-50; training of,
248-49; utilization of, 228-31. See
also Volunteerism
Volunteer Action Centers, xv, 237
Volunteer Bureaus, xv, 236, 237
Volunteerism: scope of, xiii-xiv; in
U.S., xv, 59-60; and current political climate, 225-28; research
on, 250-51. See also Volunteer(s)
Volunteer service delivery, xi-xiv;
structural work settings of, xiv-
xvii
Volunteers in Technical Assistance,
237
Volunteers of America, 22, 50

Wald, Lillian, 16
War Chests, 13, 26, 52
Welfare programs, xxvi, 223; in
19th century, 10; during Civil
War, 11-13; in 20th century, 20-
25. See also Charity, Public assis-
tance
Wiesel, Elie, 158
Wilson, Bill, 24
Women: in the labor force, 75, 83-
84; role in 19th-century welfare,
10-11, 12
Women's International League for
Peace and Freedom, 18

Women's Trade Union League, 18
Woods, Robert A., 16
Word-of-mouth volunteer recruit-
    ment, 234
Work settings, and volunteer moti-
    vation, 238-42

Young Men's, Young Women's
    Christian Association, 23
Young Men's, Young Women's
    Hebrew Associations, 21

Zero-Base Budgeting, 161

About the Contributors

CLARKE A. CHAMBERS has been a Professor of History and American Studies at the University of Minnesota, Twin Cities Campus, since 1951; as an Adjunct Professor of Social Work, he also offers courses in welfare history. In 1964 he founded, and still directs, the Social Welfare History Archives, a center that holds the records of national voluntary agencies and associations in diverse human service fields. He is the author of several books and many articles in social history, including an influential study of social service and social action in the interwar era of the 1920s and 1930s, *Seedtime of Reform*, a biography of Paul U. Kellogg. He is also the editor of the *Survey* journal and a recently published extensive analysis of welfare programs and policies on Minnesota's Iron Range.

JOHN FORESTER is an Associate Professor in the Department of City and Regional Planning at Cornell University. Interested in the daily work of the members of "the helping profession," he writes about issues of power, organizational dynamics, policy analysis, the politics of information, and the applicability of critical social theory to contemporary social problems. He is the co-editor of *Urban and Regional Planning in an Age of Austerity* and has recently edited the forthcoming *Critical Theory and Public Life*. Recent articles include "Bounded Rationality and the Politics of Muddling Through," *Public Administration Review*, January-February, 1984.

FRANCES L. HOFFMANN is Dean of Student Affairs and Assistant Professor of Sociology at Skidmore College. She is a feminist theorist with particular interests in women and work, family and social policy, and women in higher education.

E. TERRENCE JONES is Dean of the College of Arts and Sciences and Professor of Political Science and Public Policy Administration at the University of Missouri, St. Louis. He is the author of *Conducting Political Research* and more than thirty professional articles.

WILLIAM DONALD SCHAEFER, Mayor of the city of Baltimore, is esteemed and respected for his meritorious civic leadership and his outstanding commitment to improving the quality of life for others.

First elected mayor in 1971, he has been thrice reelected (1975, 1979, and 1983) with overwhelming margins of support. Selected by *Quest Magazine* as the "Best Big-City Mayor in America," he has been the driving force behind the transformation of an aging, port city into a sparkling showcase for tourism, cultural activities, and urban rejuvenation.

Unique among big city mayors in making himself available to the average citizen, he does a live, weekly call-in radio program now in its seventh year. His playtime consists of "walking the city," where he gives his undivided attention to anyone who asks him a question.

Born and raised in Baltimore, he has been a dedicated public servant involved in city government for nearly three decades. After service in the U.S. Army in World War II and practicing law for a number of years, he was elected to the Baltimore City Council where he served for the next sixteen years, holding such key leadership positions as committee chairman, vice president, and president.

His untiring efforts on behalf of his city have earned Mayor Schaefer numerous awards and honors including: the Jefferson Award for Public Service; the Distinguished Mayor Award, the National Urban Coalition; the Michael A. diNunzio Award, the United States Conference of Mayors; the Distinguished Service Award, the National Council for Urban Development; the Distinguished Public Service Award, Brandeis University; Man of the Decade Civic Award, the Advertising Club of Baltimore; numerous honorary doctoral degrees; and the acclaim of *Time* magazine as "one of the most effective urban executives in the United States today."

DAVID HORTON SMITH is a Professor of Sociology at Boston College. He has done research on volunteerism for twenty years, publishing several books and numerous articles and book chapters. *International Perspectives on Voluntary Action Research* is the latest volume he has edited. He founded and served as first president of the Association of Voluntary Action Scholars.

MICHAEL SOSIN is Associate Professor, School of Social Work, and Affiliate, Institute for Research on Poverty, at the University of Wisconsin at Madison. His research primarily concerns the organization of social welfare programs, particularly those involving services to children and the provision of material needs. He has published a number of articles and two books, the latest of which, *Private Benefits: Material Assistance in the Private Sector*, examines the role of voluntary agencies in meeting the financial needs of the poor. He is currently engaged in research concerning social movements and social change in welfare policy.

RUSSY D. SUMARIWALLA is Senior Vice President of United Way of America and Senior Fellow of United Way Institute. He has a B.A., M.A., and LL.B. from the University of Bombay, India, an LL.M. from the University School of Law, Charlottesville, Virginia, and an M.A. in Government from the University of Massachusetts, Amherst. Prior to joining United Way of America in 1971, he was senior planner with the San Francisco Bay Area Social Planning Council, a five-county non-profit health and welfare planning organization. Mr. Sumariwalla is the author of several books, articles, studies, and papers related to accounting, budgeting, planning, and other aspects of the voluntary non-profit sector.

GARY TOBIN is currently an Associate Professor of Jewish Community Research and Planning at the Center for Modern Jewish Studies at Brandeis University. He holds a Ph.D. in Social Policy and Planning from the University of California at Berkeley, Department of City and Regional Planning. Dr. Tobin has published extensively in the areas of housing policy, planning, human service delivery, and Jewish community planning. He is the editor of *The Changing Structure of the City: What Happened to the Urban Crisis?* and is currently writing a book on human service delivery in the Jewish community.

ORVAL WESTBY is a graduate of Luther-Northwestern Theological Seminary and earned his Ph.D. in sociology at the Univesity of Minnesota. He has served most recently as executive director of Lutheran Social Service System, an inter-Lutheran national office that provides support services to over 300 Lutheran social ministry organizations affiliated with the Lutheran church. These organizations provide health, housing, and social services throughout the nation.

In 1973 he established a new Department of Social Services as part of state executive reorganization in South Dakota and served as its Secretary until October 1978.

For twenty-five years he was Professor and Chair of the Department of

Sociology, Social Work, and Criminal Justice at Augustana College in Sioux Falls, South Dakota. During that time his professional and civic service included membership (and sometimes chair) of the boards of Lutheran Social Services of South Dakota, the Southeast Mental Health Center, the National Council of Social Work Education, the South Dakota Board of Charities and Corrections, and the South Dakota Public Welfare Commission.

GEORGE WILKINSON is Vice President of Strategic Planning, United Way of America, Alexandria, Virginia. At the nation's largest charitable organization, he is responsible for corporate strategic planning and the development of consultation and technical assistance programs for the organization's 2,200 local and autonomous United Way organizations.

Dr. Wilkinson began his United Way career in 1972 at the United Way in Bridgeport, Connecticut. Here he developed and directed numerous public/private partnership efforts in the fields of criminal justice, home health care, day-care, and refugee settlement. His work in pioneering long-range planning in the United Way system led to his joining United Way of America in 1980. He is the author of several articles and publications on environmental scanning and strategic planning.

He holds three college degrees, including a doctorate in educational administration.

JENNIFER R. WOLCH received her doctorate in urban planning from Princeton University. She is currently Assistant Professor of Urban and Regional Planning at the University of Southern California, where she teaches courses on urban theory, social policy, political economy, and the voluntary sector. She is co-author (with Michael J. Dear) of *Back Wards to Back Streets, Deinstitutionalization and the North American City* (forthcoming).

DATE DUE